Get the eBooks FREE!

(PDF, ePub, Kindle, and liveBook all included)

We believe that once you buy a book from us, you should be able to read it in any format we have available. To get electronic versions of this book at no additional cost to you, purchase and then register this book at the Manning website.

Go to https://www.manning.com/freebook and follow the instructions to complete your pBook registration.

That's it!
Thanks from Manning!

Unit Testing: Principles, Practices, and Patterns

VLADIMIR KHORIKOV

MANNING

SHELTER ISLAND

For online information and ordering of this and other Manning books, please visit
www.manning.com. The publisher offers discounts on this book when ordered in quantity.
For more information, please contact

  Special Sales Department
  Manning Publications Co.
  20 Baldwin Road
  PO Box 761
  Shelter Island, NY 11964
  Email: orders@manning.com

Manning Publications Co.   Acquisitions editor: Mike Stephens
20 Baldwin Road   Development editor: Marina Michaels
PO Box 761   Technical development editor: Sam Zaydel
Shelter Island, NY 11964   Review editor: Aleksandar Dragosavljević
                                   Production editor: Anthony Calcara
                                          Copy editor: Tiffany Taylor
                                     ESL copyeditor: Frances Buran
                                        Proofreader: Keri Hales
                             Technical proofreader: Alessandro Campeis
                                          Typesetter: Dennis Dalinnik
                                     Cover designer: Marija Tudor

ISBN: 9781617296277
Printed in the United States of America

To my wife, Nina

brief contents

contents

preface

I remember my first project where I tried out unit testing. It went relatively well; but after it was finished, I looked at the tests and thought that a lot of them were a pure waste of time. Most of my unit tests spent a great deal of time setting up expectations and wiring up a complicated web of dependencies—all that, just to check that the three lines of code in my controller were correct. I couldn't pinpoint what exactly was wrong with the tests, but my sense of proportion sent me unambiguous signals that something was off.

Luckily, I didn't abandon unit testing and continued applying it in subsequent projects. However, disagreement with common (at that time) unit testing practices has been growing in me ever since. Throughout the years, I've written a lot about unit testing. In those writings, I finally managed to crystallize what exactly was wrong with my first tests and generalized this knowledge to broader areas of unit testing. This book is a culmination of all my research, trial, and error during that period—compiled, refined, and distilled.

I come from a mathematical background and strongly believe that guidelines in programming, like theorems in math, should be derived from first principles. I've tried to structure this book in a similar way: start with a blank slate by not jumping to conclusions or throwing around unsubstantiated claims, and gradually build my case from the ground up. Interestingly enough, once you establish such first principles, guidelines and best practices often flow naturally as mere implications.

I believe that unit testing is becoming a de facto requirement for software projects, and this book will give you everything you need to create valuable, highly maintainable tests.

acknowledgments

This book was a lot of work. Even though I was prepared mentally, it was still much more work than I could ever have imagined.

A big "thank you" to Sam Zaydel, Alessandro Campeis, Frances Buran, Tiffany Taylor, and especially Marina Michaels, whose invaluable feedback helped shape the book and made me a better writer along the way. Thanks also to everyone else at Manning who worked on this book in production and behind the scenes.

I'd also like to thank the reviewers who took the time to read my manuscript at various stages during its development and who provided valuable feedback: Aaron Barton, Alessandro Campeis, Conor Redmond, Dror Helper, Greg Wright, Hemant Koneru, Jeremy Lange, Jorge Ezequiel Bo, Jort Rodenburg, Mark Nenadov, Marko Umek, Markus Matzker, Srihari Sridharan, Stephen John Warnett, Sumant Tambe, Tim van Deurzen, and Vladimir Kuptsov.

Above all, I would like to thank my wife Nina, who supported me during the whole process.

about this book

Unit Testing: Principles, Practices, and Patterns provides insights into the best practices and common anti-patterns that surround the topic of unit testing. After reading this book, armed with your newfound skills, you'll have the knowledge needed to become an expert at delivering successful projects that are easy to maintain and extend, thanks to the tests you build along the way.

Who should read this book

Most online and print resources have one drawback: they focus on the basics of unit testing but don't go much beyond that. There's a lot of value in such resources, but the learning doesn't end there. There's a next level: not just writing tests, but doing it in a way that gives you the best return on your efforts. When you reach this point on the learning curve, you're pretty much left to your own devices to figure out how to get to the next level.

This book takes you to that next level. It teaches a scientific, precise definition of the ideal unit test. That definition provides a universal frame of reference, which will help you look at many of your tests in a new light and see which of them contribute to the project and which must be refactored or removed.

If you don't have much experience with unit testing, you'll learn a lot from this book. If you're an experienced programmer, you most likely already understand some of the ideas taught in this book. The book will help you articulate why the techniques and best practices you've been using all along are so helpful. And don't underestimate this skill: the ability to clearly communicate your ideas to colleagues is priceless.

How this book is organized: A roadmap

The book's 11 chapters are divided into 4 parts. Part 1 introduces unit testing and gives a refresher on some of the more generic unit testing principles:

- Chapter 1 defines the goal of unit testing and gives an overview of how to differentiate a good test from a bad one.
- Chapter 2 explores the definition of *unit test* and discusses the two schools of unit testing.
- Chapter 3 provides a refresher on some basic topics, such as structuring of unit tests, reusing test fixtures, and test parameterization.

Part 2 gets to the heart of the subject—it shows what makes a good unit test and provides details about how to refactor your tests toward being more valuable:

- Chapter 4 defines the four pillars that form a good unit test and provide a common frame of reference that is used throughout the book.
- Chapter 5 builds a case for mocks and explores their relation to test fragility.
- Chapter 6 examines the three styles of unit testing, along with which of those styles produces tests of the best quality and why.
- Chapter 7 teaches you how to refactor away from bloated, overcomplicated tests and achieve tests that provide maximum value with minimum maintenance costs.

Part 3 explores the topic of integration testing:

- Chapter 8 looks at integration testing in general along with its benefits and trade-offs.
- Chapter 9 discusses mocks and how to use them in a way that benefits your tests the most.
- Chapter 10 explores working with relational databases in tests.

Part 4's chapter 11 covers common unit testing anti-patterns, some of which you've possibly encountered before.

About the Code

The code samples are written in C#, but the topics they illustrate are applicable to any object-oriented language, such as Java or C++. C# is just the language that I happen to work with the most.

I tried not to use any C#-specific language features, and I made the sample code as simple as possible, so you shouldn't have any trouble understanding it. You can download all of the code samples online at www.manning.com/books/unit-testing.

liveBook discussion forum

Purchase of *Unit Testing: Principles, Practices, and Patterns* includes free access to a private web forum run by Manning Publications where you can make comments about the book, ask technical questions, and receive help from the author and from other users. To access the forum, go to https://livebook.manning.com/#!/book/unit-testing/discussion. You can also learn more about Manning's forums and the rules of conduct at https://livebook.manning.com/#!/discussion.

Manning's commitment to our readers is to provide a venue where a meaningful dialogue between individual readers and between readers and the author can take place. It is not a commitment to any specific amount of participation on the part of the author, whose contribution to the forum remains voluntary (and unpaid). We suggest you try asking the author some challenging questions lest his interest stray! The forum and the archives of previous discussions will be accessible from the publisher's website as long as the book is in print.

Other online resources

- My blog is at EnterpriseCraftsmanship.com.
- I also have an online course about unit testing (in the works, as of this writing), which you can enroll in at UnitTestingCourse.com.

about the author

VLADIMIR KHORIKOV is a software engineer, Microsoft MVP, and Pluralsight author. He has been professionally involved in software development for over 15 years, including mentoring teams on the ins and outs of unit testing. During the past several years, Vladimir has written several popular blog post series and an online training course on the topic of unit testing. The biggest advantage of his teaching style, and the one students often praise, is his tendency to have a strong theoretic background, which he then applies to practical examples.

about the cover illustration

The figure on the cover of *Unit Testing: Principles, Practices, and Patterns* is captioned "Esthinienne." The illustration is taken from a collection of dress costumes from various countries by Jacques Grasset de Saint-Sauveur (1757–1810), titled *Costumes Civils Actuels de Tous les Peuples Connus,* published in France in 1788. Each illustration is finely drawn and colored by hand. The rich variety of Grasset de Saint-Sauveur's collection reminds us vividly of how culturally apart the world's towns and regions were just 200 years ago. Isolated from each other, people spoke different dialects and languages. In the streets or in the countryside, it was easy to identify where they lived and what their trade or station in life was just by their dress.

The way we dress has changed since then and the diversity by region, so rich at the time, has faded away. It is now hard to tell apart the inhabitants of different continents, let alone different towns, regions, or countries. Perhaps we have traded cultural diversity for a more varied personal life—certainly for a more varied and fast-paced technological life.

At a time when it is hard to tell one computer book from another, Manning celebrates the inventiveness and initiative of the computer business with book covers based on the rich diversity of regional life of two centuries ago, brought back to life by Grasset de Saint-Sauveur's pictures.

Part 1

The bigger picture

This part of the book will get you up to speed with the current state of unit testing. In chapter 1, I'll define the goal of unit testing and give an overview of how to differentiate a good test from a bad one. We'll talk about coverage metrics and discuss properties of a good unit test in general.

In chapter 2, we'll look at the definition of *unit test*. A seemingly minor disagreement over this definition has led to the formation of two schools of unit testing, which we'll also dive into. Chapter 3 provides a refresher on some basic topics, such as structuring of unit tests, reusing test fixtures, and test parametrization.

Part

The bigger picture

The goal of unit testing

Learning unit testing doesn't stop at mastering the technical bits of it, such as your favorite test framework, mocking library, and so on. There's much more to unit testing than the act of writing tests. You always have to strive to achieve the best return on the time you invest in unit testing, minimizing the effort you put into tests and maximizing the benefits they provide. Achieving both things isn't an easy task.

It's fascinating to watch projects that have achieved this balance: they grow effortlessly, don't require much maintenance, and can quickly adapt to their customers' ever-changing needs. It's equally frustrating to see projects that failed to do so. Despite all the effort and an impressive number of unit tests, such projects drag on slowly, with lots of bugs and upkeep costs.

That's the difference between various unit testing techniques. Some yield great outcomes and help maintain software quality. Others don't: they result in tests that don't contribute much, break often, and require a lot of maintenance in general.

What you learn in this book will help you differentiate between good and bad unit testing techniques. You'll learn how to do a cost-benefit analysis of your tests and apply proper testing techniques in your particular situation. You'll also learn how to avoid common anti-patterns—patterns that may make sense at first but lead to trouble down the road.

But let's start with the basics. This chapter gives a quick overview of the state of unit testing in the software industry, describes the goal behind writing and maintaining tests, and provides you with the idea of what makes a test suite successful.

1.1   *The current state of unit testing*

For the past two decades, there's been a push toward adopting unit testing. The push has been so successful that unit testing is now considered mandatory in most companies. Most programmers practice unit testing and understand its importance. There's no longer any dispute as to whether you should do it. Unless you're working on a throwaway project, the answer is, yes, you do.

When it comes to enterprise application development, almost every project includes at least some unit tests. A significant percentage of such projects go far beyond that: they achieve good code coverage with lots and lots of unit and integration tests. The ratio between the production code and the test code could be anywhere between 1:1 and 1:3 (for each line of production code, there are one to three lines of test code). Sometimes, this ratio goes much higher than that, to a whopping 1:10.

But as with all new technologies, unit testing continues to evolve. The discussion has shifted from "Should we *write* unit tests?" to "What does it mean to write *good* unit tests?" This is where the main confusion still lies.

You can see the results of this confusion in software projects. Many projects have automated tests; they may even have a lot of them. But the existence of those tests often doesn't provide the results the developers hope for. It can still take programmers a lot of effort to make progress in such projects. New features take forever to implement, new bugs constantly appear in the already implemented and accepted functionality, and the unit tests that are supposed to help don't seem to mitigate this situation at all. They can even make it worse.

It's a horrible situation for anyone to be in—and it's the result of having unit tests that don't do their job properly. The difference between good and bad tests is not merely a matter of taste or personal preference, it's a matter of succeeding or failing at this critical project you're working on.

It's hard to overestimate the importance of the discussion of what makes a good unit test. Still, this discussion isn't occurring much in the software development industry today. You'll find a few articles and conference talks online, but I've yet to see any comprehensive material on this topic.

The situation in books isn't any better; most of them focus on the basics of unit testing but don't go much beyond that. Don't get me wrong. There's a lot of value in such books, especially when you are just starting out with unit testing. However, the learning doesn't end with the basics. There's a next level: not just writing tests, but doing unit testing in a way that provides you with the best return on your efforts. When you reach this point, most books pretty much leave you to your own devices to figure out how to get to that next level.

This book takes you there. It teaches a precise, scientific definition of the ideal unit test. You'll see how this definition can be applied to practical, real-world examples. My hope is that this book will help you understand why your particular project may have gone sideways despite having a good number of tests, and how to correct its course for the better.

You'll get the most value out of this book if you work in enterprise application development, but the core ideas are applicable to any software project.

What is an enterprise application?

An *enterprise application* is an application that aims at automating or assisting an organization's inner processes. It can take many forms, but usually the characteristics of an enterprise software are

- High business logic complexity
- Long project lifespan
- Moderate amounts of data
- Low or moderate performance requirements

1.2 *The goal of unit testing*

Before taking a deep dive into the topic of unit testing, let's step back and consider the goal that unit testing helps you to achieve. It's often said that unit testing practices lead to a better design. And it's true: the necessity to write unit tests for a code base normally leads to a better design. But that's not the main goal of unit testing; it's merely a pleasant side effect.

The relationship between unit testing and code design

The ability to unit test a piece of code is a nice litmus test, but it only works in one direction. It's a good negative indicator—it points out poor-quality code with relatively high accuracy. If you find that code is hard to unit test, it's a strong sign that the code needs improvement. The poor quality usually manifests itself in *tight coupling*, which means different pieces of production code are not decoupled from each other enough, and it's hard to test them separately.

> **(continued)**
> Unfortunately, the ability to unit test a piece of code is a bad positive indicator. The fact that you can easily unit test your code base doesn't necessarily mean it's of good quality. The project can be a disaster even when it exhibits a high degree of decoupling.

What is the goal of unit testing, then? The goal is to enable sustainable growth of the software project. The term *sustainable* is key. It's quite easy to grow a project, especially when you start from scratch. It's much harder to sustain this growth over time.

Figure 1.1 shows the growth dynamic of a typical project without tests. You start off quickly because there's nothing dragging you down. No bad architectural decisions have been made yet, and there isn't any existing code to worry about. As time goes by, however, you have to put in more and more hours to make the same amount of progress you showed at the beginning. Eventually, the development speed slows down significantly, sometimes even to the point where you can't make any progress whatsoever.

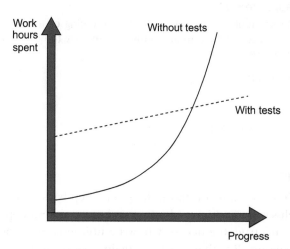

Figure 1.1   **The difference in growth dynamics between projects with and without tests. A project without tests has a head start but quickly slows down to the point that it's hard to make any progress.**

This phenomenon of quickly decreasing development speed is also known as *software entropy*. Entropy (the amount of disorder in a system) is a mathematical and scientific concept that can also apply to software systems. (If you're interested in the math and science of entropy, look up the second law of thermodynamics.)

In software, entropy manifests in the form of code that tends to deteriorate. Each time you change something in a code base, the amount of disorder in it, or entropy, increases. If left without proper care, such as constant cleaning and refactoring, the system becomes increasingly complex and disorganized. Fixing one bug introduces more bugs, and modifying one part of the software breaks several others—it's like a domino effect. Eventually, the code base becomes unreliable. And worst of all, it's hard to bring it back to stability.

Tests help overturn this tendency. They act as a safety net—a tool that provides insurance against a vast majority of regressions. Tests help make sure the existing functionality works, even after you introduce new features or refactor the code to better fit new requirements.

> **DEFINITION** A *regression* is when a feature stops working as intended after a certain event (usually, a code modification). The terms *regression* and *software bug* are synonyms and can be used interchangeably.

The downside here is that tests require initial—sometimes significant—effort. But they pay for themselves in the long run by helping the project to grow in the later stages. Software development without the help of tests that constantly verify the code base simply doesn't scale.

Sustainability and scalability are the keys. They allow you to maintain development speed in the long run.

1.2.1 What makes a good or bad test?

Although unit testing helps maintain project growth, it's not enough to just write tests. Badly written tests still result in the same picture.

As shown in figure 1.2, bad tests do help to slow down code deterioration at the beginning: the decline in development speed is less prominent compared to the situation with no tests at all. But nothing really changes in the grand scheme of things. It might take longer for such a project to enter the stagnation phase, but stagnation is still inevitable.

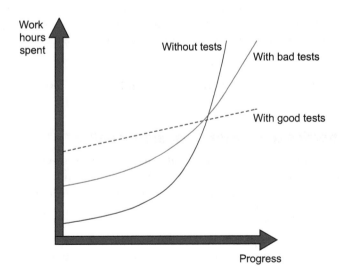

Figure 1.2 The difference in growth dynamics between projects with good and bad tests. A project with badly written tests exhibits the properties of a project with good tests at the beginning, but it eventually falls into the stagnation phase.

Remember, *not all tests are created equal.* Some of them are valuable and contribute a lot to overall software quality. Others don't. They raise false alarms, don't help you catch regression errors, and are slow and difficult to maintain. It's easy to fall into the trap of writing unit tests for the sake of unit testing without a clear picture of whether it helps the project.

You can't achieve the goal of unit testing by just throwing more tests at the project. You need to consider both the test's value and its upkeep cost. The cost component is determined by the amount of time spent on various activities:

- Refactoring the test when you refactor the underlying code
- Running the test on each code change
- Dealing with false alarms raised by the test
- Spending time reading the test when you're trying to understand how the underlying code behaves

It's easy to create tests whose net value is close to zero or even is negative due to high maintenance costs. To enable sustainable project growth, you have to exclusively focus on high-quality tests—those are the only type of tests that are worth keeping in the test suite.

Production code vs. test code

People often think production code and test code are different. Tests are assumed to be an addition to production code and have no cost of ownership. By extension, people often believe that the more tests, the better. This isn't the case. *Code is a liability, not an asset.* The more code you introduce, the more you extend the surface area for potential bugs in your software, and the higher the project's upkeep cost. It's always better to solve problems with the minimum amount of code.

Tests are code, too. You should view them as the part of your code base that aims at solving a particular problem: ensuring the application's correctness. Unit tests, just like any other code, are also vulnerable to bugs and require maintenance.

It's crucial to learn how to differentiate between good and bad unit tests. I cover this topic in chapter 4.

1.3   *Using coverage metrics to measure test suite quality*

In this section, I talk about the two most popular coverage metrics—code coverage and branch coverage—how to calculate them, how they're used, and problems with them. I'll show why it's detrimental for programmers to aim at a particular coverage number and why you can't just rely on coverage metrics to determine the quality of your test suite.

DEFINITION   A *coverage metric* shows how much source code a test suite executes, from none to 100%.

There are different types of coverage metrics, and they're often used to assess the quality of a test suite. The common belief is that the higher the coverage number, the better.

Unfortunately, it's not that simple, and coverage metrics, while providing valuable feedback, can't be used to effectively measure the *quality* of a test suite. It's the same situation as with the ability to unit test the code: coverage metrics are a good negative indicator but a bad positive one.

If a metric shows that there's too little coverage in your code base—say, only 10%—that's a good indication that you are not testing enough. But the reverse isn't true: even 100% coverage isn't a guarantee that you have a good-quality test suite. A test suite that provides high coverage can still be of poor quality.

I already touched on why this is so—you can't just throw random tests at your project with the hope those tests will improve the situation. But let's discuss this problem in detail with respect to the code coverage metric.

1.3.1 Understanding the code coverage metric

The first and most-used coverage metric is *code coverage*, also known as *test coverage*; see figure 1.3. This metric shows the ratio of the number of code lines executed by at least one test and the total number of lines in the production code base.

$$\text{Code coverage (test coverage)} = \frac{\text{Lines of code executed}}{\text{Total number of lines}}$$

Figure 1.3 The code coverage (test coverage) metric is calculated as the ratio between the number of code lines executed by the test suite and the total number of lines in the production code base.

Let's see an example to better understand how this works. Listing 1.1 shows an IsStringLong method and a test that covers it. The method determines whether a string provided to it as an input parameter is long (here, the definition of *long* is any string with the length greater than five characters). The test exercises the method using "abc" and checks that this string is not considered long.

Listing 1.1 A sample method partially covered by a test

```
public static bool IsStringLong(string input)
{
    if (input.Length > 5)
        return true;

    return false;
}
```

Not covered by the test

Covered by the test

```
public void Test()
{
    bool result = IsStringLong("abc");
    Assert.Equal(false, result);
}
```

It's easy to calculate the code coverage here. The total number of lines in the method is five (curly braces count, too). The number of lines executed by the test is four—the test goes through all the code lines except for the return true; statement. This gives us $4/5 = 0.8 = 80\%$ code coverage.

Now, what if I refactor the method and inline the unnecessary if statement, like this?

```
public static bool IsStringLong(string input)
{
    return input.Length > 5 ? true : false;
}

public void Test()
{
    bool result = IsStringLong("abc");
    Assert.Equal(false, result);
}
```

Does the code coverage number change? Yes, it does. Because the test now exercises all three lines of code (the return statement plus two curly braces), the code coverage increases to 100%.

But did I improve the test suite with this refactoring? Of course not. I just shuffled the code inside the method. The test still verifies the same number of possible outcomes.

This simple example shows how easy it is to game the coverage numbers. The more compact your code is, the better the test coverage metric becomes, because it only accounts for the raw line numbers. At the same time, squashing more code into less space doesn't (and shouldn't) change the value of the test suite or the maintainability of the underlying code base.

1.3.2   *Understanding the branch coverage metric*

Another coverage metric is called *branch coverage*. Branch coverage provides more precise results than code coverage because it helps cope with code coverage's shortcomings. Instead of using the raw number of code lines, this metric focuses on control structures, such as if and switch statements. It shows how many of such control structures are traversed by at least one test in the suite, as shown in figure 1.4.

$$\text{Branch coverage} = \frac{\text{Branches traversed}}{\text{Total number of branches}}$$

Figure 1.4   The branch metric is calculated as the ratio of the number of code branches exercised by the test suite and the total number of branches in the production code base.

To calculate the branch coverage metric, you need to sum up all possible branches in your code base and see how many of them are visited by tests. Let's take our previous example again:

```
public static bool IsStringLong(string input)
{
    return input.Length > 5 ? true : false;
}

public void Test()
{
    bool result = IsStringLong("abc");
    Assert.Equal(false, result);
}
```

There are two branches in the `IsStringLong` method: one for the situation when the length of the string argument is greater than five characters, and the other one when it's not. The test covers only one of these branches, so the branch coverage metric is $1/2 = 0.5 = 50\%$. And it doesn't matter how we represent the code under test—whether we use an `if` statement as before or use the shorter notation. The branch coverage metric only accounts for the number of branches; it doesn't take into consideration how many lines of code it took to implement those branches.

Figure 1.5 shows a helpful way to visualize this metric. You can represent all possible paths the code under test can take as a graph and see how many of them have been traversed. `IsStringLong` has two such paths, and the test exercises only one of them.

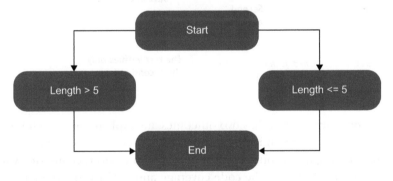

Figure 1.5 The method `IsStringLong` represented as a graph of possible code paths. `Test` covers only one of the two code paths, thus providing 50% branch coverage.

1.3.3   *Problems with coverage metrics*

Although the branch coverage metric yields better results than code coverage, you still can't rely on either of them to determine the quality of your test suite, for two reasons:

- You can't guarantee that the test verifies all the possible outcomes of the system under test.
- No coverage metric can take into account code paths in external libraries.

Let's look more closely at each of these reasons.

YOU CAN'T GUARANTEE THAT THE TEST VERIFIES ALL THE POSSIBLE OUTCOMES

For the code paths to be actually tested and not just exercised, your unit tests must have appropriate assertions. In other words, you need to check that the outcome the system under test produces is the exact outcome you expect it to produce. Moreover, this outcome may have several components; and for the coverage metrics to be meaningful, you need to verify all of them.

The next listing shows another version of the IsStringLong method. It records the last result into a public WasLastStringLong property.

Listing 1.2   Version of IsStringLong that records the last result

```
public static bool WasLastStringLong { get; private set; }

public static bool IsStringLong(string input)
{
    bool result = input.Length > 5 ? true : false;
    WasLastStringLong = result;          ◁──┐  First
    return result;       ◁──┐               │  outcome
}                           │ Second
                            │ outcome
public void Test()
{
    bool result = IsStringLong("abc");    │ The test verifies only
    Assert.Equal(false, result);    ◁──┘  │ the second outcome.
}
```

The IsStringLong method now has two outcomes: an explicit one, which is encoded by the return value; and an implicit one, which is the new value of the property. And in spite of not verifying the second, implicit outcome, the coverage metrics would still show the same results: 100% for the code coverage and 50% for the branch coverage. As you can see, the coverage metrics don't guarantee that the underlying code is tested, only that it has been executed at some point.

An extreme version of this situation with partially tested outcomes is *assertion-free testing*, which is when you write tests that don't have any assertion statements in them whatsoever. Here's an example of assertion-free testing.

Listing 1.3   A test with no assertions always passes.

```
public void Test()
{                                                    Returns true
    bool result1 = IsStringLong("abc");      ←┘
    bool result2 = IsStringLong("abcdef");   ←┐ Returns false
}
```

This test has both code and branch coverage metrics showing 100%. But at the same time, it is completely useless because it doesn't verify anything.

A story from the trenches

The concept of assertion-free testing might look like a dumb idea, but it does happen in the wild.

Years ago, I worked on a project where management imposed a strict requirement of having 100% code coverage for every project under development. This initiative had noble intentions. It was during the time when unit testing wasn't as prevalent as it is today. Few people in the organization practiced it, and even fewer did unit testing consistently.

A group of developers had gone to a conference where many talks were devoted to unit testing. After returning, they decided to put their new knowledge into practice. Upper management supported them, and the great conversion to better programming techniques began. Internal presentations were given. New tools were installed. And, more importantly, a new company-wide rule was imposed: all development teams had to focus on writing tests exclusively until they reached the 100% code coverage mark. After they reached this goal, any code check-in that lowered the metric had to be rejected by the build systems.

As you might guess, this didn't play out well. Crushed by this severe limitation, developers started to seek ways to game the system. Naturally, many of them came to the same realization: if you wrap all tests with `try/catch` blocks and don't introduce any assertions in them, those tests are guaranteed to pass. People started to mindlessly create tests for the sake of meeting the mandatory 100% coverage requirement. Needless to say, those tests didn't add any value to the projects. Moreover, they damaged the projects because of all the effort and time they steered away from productive activities, and because of the upkeep costs required to maintain the tests moving forward.

Eventually, the requirement was lowered to 90% and then to 80%; after some period of time, it was retracted altogether (for the better!).

But let's say that you thoroughly verify each outcome of the code under test. Does this, in combination with the branch coverage metric, provide a reliable mechanism, which you can use to determine the quality of your test suite? Unfortunately, no.

NO COVERAGE METRIC CAN TAKE INTO ACCOUNT CODE PATHS IN EXTERNAL LIBRARIES

The second problem with all coverage metrics is that they don't take into account code paths that external libraries go through when the system under test calls methods on them. Let's take the following example:

```
public static int Parse(string input)
{
    return int.Parse(input);
}

public void Test()
{
    int result = Parse("5");
    Assert.Equal(5, result);
}
```

The branch coverage metric shows 100%, and the test verifies all components of the method's outcome. It has a single such component anyway—the return value. At the same time, this test is nowhere near being exhaustive. It doesn't take into account the code paths the .NET Framework's `int.Parse` method may go through. And there are quite a number of code paths, even in this simple method, as you can see in figure 1.6.

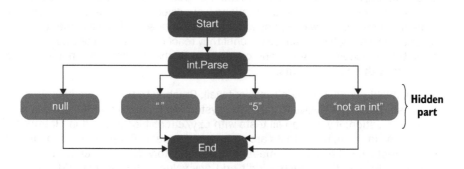

Figure 1.6   Hidden code paths of external libraries. Coverage metrics have no way to see how many of them there are and how many of them your tests exercise.

The built-in `integer` type has plenty of branches that are hidden from the test and that might lead to different results, should you change the method's input parameter. Here are just a few possible arguments that can't be transformed into an integer:

- Null value
- An empty string
- "Not an int"
- A string that's too large

You can fall into numerous edge cases, and there's no way to see if your tests account for all of them.

This is not to say that coverage metrics *should* take into account code paths in external libraries (they shouldn't), but rather to show you that you can't rely on those metrics to see how good or bad your unit tests are. Coverage metrics can't possibly tell whether your tests are exhaustive; nor can they say if you have enough tests.

1.3.4 *Aiming at a particular coverage number*

At this point, I hope you can see that relying on coverage metrics to determine the quality of your test suite is not enough. It can also lead to dangerous territory if you start making a specific coverage number a target, be it 100%, 90%, or even a moderate 70%. The best way to view a coverage metric is as an indicator, not a goal in and of itself.

Think of a patient in a hospital. Their high temperature might indicate a fever and is a helpful observation. But the hospital shouldn't make the proper temperature of this patient a goal to target by any means necessary. Otherwise, the hospital might end up with the quick and "efficient" solution of installing an air conditioner next to the patient and regulating their temperature by adjusting the amount of cold air flowing onto their skin. Of course, this approach doesn't make any sense.

Likewise, targeting a specific coverage number creates a perverse incentive that goes against the goal of unit testing. Instead of focusing on testing the things that matter, people start to seek ways to attain this artificial target. Proper unit testing is difficult enough already. Imposing a mandatory coverage number only distracts developers from being mindful about what they test, and makes proper unit testing even harder to achieve.

> **TIP** It's good to have a high level of coverage in core parts of your system. It's bad to make this high level a requirement. The difference is subtle but critical.

Let me repeat myself: coverage metrics are a good negative indicator, but a bad positive one. Low coverage numbers—say, below 60%—are a certain sign of trouble. They mean there's a lot of untested code in your code base. But high numbers don't mean anything. Thus, measuring the code coverage should be only a first step on the way to a quality test suite.

1.4 *What makes a successful test suite?*

I've spent most of this chapter discussing improper ways to measure the quality of a test suite: using coverage metrics. What about a proper way? How should you measure your test suite's quality? The only reliable way is to evaluate each test in the suite individually, one by one. Of course, you don't have to evaluate all of them at once; that could be quite a large undertaking and require significant upfront effort. You can perform this evaluation gradually. The point is that there's no automated way to see how good your test suite is. You have to apply your personal judgment.

Let's look at a broader picture of what makes a test suite successful as a whole. (We'll dive into the specifics of differentiating between good and bad tests in chapter 4.) A successful test suite has the following properties:

- It's integrated into the development cycle.
- It targets only the most important parts of your code base.
- It provides maximum value with minimum maintenance costs.

1.4.1   It's integrated into the development cycle

The only point in having automated tests is if you constantly use them. All tests should be integrated into the development cycle. Ideally, you should execute them on every code change, even the smallest one.

1.4.2   It targets only the most important parts of your code base

Just as all tests are not created equal, not all parts of your code base are worth the same attention in terms of unit testing. The value the tests provide is not only in how those tests themselves are structured, but also in the code they verify.

It's important to direct your unit testing efforts to the most critical parts of the system and verify the others only briefly or indirectly. In most applications, the most important part is the part that contains business logic—the *domain model*.[1] Testing business logic gives you the best return on your time investment.

All other parts can be divided into three categories:

- Infrastructure code
- External services and dependencies, such as the database and third-party systems
- Code that glues everything together

Some of these other parts may still need thorough unit testing, though. For example, the infrastructure code may contain complex and important algorithms, so it would make sense to cover them with a lot of tests, too. But in general, most of your attention should be spent on the domain model.

Some of your tests, such as integration tests, can go beyond the domain model and verify how the system works as a whole, including the noncritical parts of the code base. And that's fine. But the focus should remain on the domain model.

Note that in order to follow this guideline, you should isolate the domain model from the non-essential parts of the code base. You have to keep the domain model separated from all other application concerns so you can focus your unit testing

---

[1] See *Domain-Driven Design: Tackling Complexity in the Heart of Software* by Eric Evans (Addison-Wesley, 2003).

efforts on that domain model exclusively. We talk about all this in detail in part 2 of the book.

1.4.3 *It provides maximum value with minimum maintenance costs*

The most difficult part of unit testing is achieving maximum value with minimum maintenance costs. That's the main focus of this book.

It's not enough to incorporate tests into a build system, and it's not enough to maintain high test coverage of the domain model. It's also crucial to keep in the suite only the tests whose value exceeds their upkeep costs by a good margin.

This last attribute can be divided in two:

- Recognizing a valuable test (and, by extension, a test of low value)
- Writing a valuable test

Although these skills may seem similar, they're different by nature. To recognize a test of high value, you need a frame of reference. On the other hand, *writing* a valuable test requires you to also know code design techniques. Unit tests and the underlying code are highly intertwined, and it's impossible to create valuable tests without putting significant effort into the code base they cover.

You can view it as the difference between recognizing a good song and being able to compose one. The amount of effort required to become a composer is asymmetrically larger than the effort required to differentiate between good and bad music. The same is true for unit tests. Writing a new test requires more effort than examining an existing one, mostly because you don't write tests in a vacuum: you have to take into account the underlying code. And so although I focus on unit tests, I also devote a significant portion of this book to discussing code design.

1.5 *What you will learn in this book*

This book teaches a frame of reference that you can use to analyze any test in your test suite. This frame of reference is foundational. After learning it, you'll be able to look at many of your tests in a new light and see which of them contribute to the project and which must be refactored or gotten rid of altogether.

After setting this stage (chapter 4), the book analyzes the existing unit testing techniques and practices (chapters 4–6, and part of 7). It doesn't matter whether you're familiar with those techniques and practices. If you are familiar with them, you'll see them from a new angle. Most likely, you already *get* them at the intuitive level. This book can help you articulate *why* the techniques and best practices you've been using all along are so helpful.

Don't underestimate this skill. The ability to clearly communicate your ideas to colleagues is priceless. A software developer—even a great one—rarely gets full credit for a design decision if they can't explain why, exactly, that decision was made. This book can help you transform your knowledge from the realm of the unconscious to something you are able to talk about with anyone.

If you don't have much experience with unit testing techniques and best practices, you'll learn a lot. In addition to the frame of reference that you can use to analyze any test in a test suite, the book teaches

- How to refactor the test suite along with the production code it covers
- How to apply different styles of unit testing
- Using integration tests to verify the behavior of the system as a whole
- Identifying and avoiding anti-patterns in unit tests

In addition to unit tests, this book covers the entire topic of automated testing, so you'll also learn about integration and end-to-end tests.

I use C# and .NET in my code samples, but you don't have to be a C# professional to read this book; C# is just the language that I happen to work with the most. All the concepts I talk about are non-language-specific and can be applied to any other object-oriented language, such as Java or C++.

Summary

- Code tends to deteriorate. Each time you change something in a code base, the amount of disorder in it, or entropy, increases. Without proper care, such as constant cleaning and refactoring, the system becomes increasingly complex and disorganized. Tests help overturn this tendency. They act as a safety net— a tool that provides insurance against the vast majority of regressions.
- It's important to write unit tests. It's equally important to write *good* unit tests. The end result for projects with bad tests or no tests is the same: either stagnation or a lot of regressions with every new release.
- The goal of unit testing is to enable sustainable growth of the software project. A good unit test suite helps avoid the stagnation phase and maintain the development pace over time. With such a suite, you're confident that your changes won't lead to regressions. This, in turn, makes it easier to refactor the code or add new features.
- All tests are not created equal. Each test has a cost and a benefit component, and you need to carefully weigh one against the other. Keep only tests of positive net value in the suite, and get rid of all others. Both the application code and the test code are liabilities, not assets.
- The ability to unit test code is a good litmus test, but it only works in one direction. It's a good negative indicator (if you can't unit test the code, it's of poor quality) but a bad positive one (the ability to unit test the code doesn't guarantee its quality).
- Likewise, coverage metrics are a good negative indicator but a bad positive one. Low coverage numbers are a certain sign of trouble, but a high coverage number doesn't automatically mean your test suite is of high quality.
- Branch coverage provides better insight into the completeness of the test suite than code coverage, but still can't indicate whether the suite is good enough. It

doesn't take into account the presence of assertions, and it can't account for code paths in third-party libraries that your code base uses.

- Imposing a particular coverage number creates a perverse incentive. It's good to have a high level of coverage in core parts of your system, but it's bad to make this high level a requirement.
- A successful test suite exhibits the following attributes:
  - It is integrated into the development cycle.
  - It targets only the most important parts of your code base.
  - It provides maximum value with minimum maintenance costs.
- The only way to achieve the goal of unit testing (that is, enabling sustainable project growth) is to
  - Learn how to differentiate between a good and a bad test.
  - Be able to refactor a test to make it more valuable.

What is a unit test?

As mentioned in chapter 1, there are a surprising number of nuances in the definition of a unit test. Those nuances are more important than you might think—so much so that the differences in interpreting them have led to two distinct views on how to approach unit testing.

These views are known as the *classical* and the *London* schools of unit testing. The classical school is called "classical" because it's how everyone originally approached unit testing and test-driven development. The London school takes root in the programming community in London. The discussion in this chapter about the differences between the classical and London styles lays the foundation for chapter 5, where I cover the topic of mocks and test fragility in detail.

Let's start by defining a unit test, with all due caveats and subtleties. This definition is the key to the difference between the classical and London schools.

2.1 The definition of "unit test"

There are a lot of definitions of a unit test. Stripped of their non-essential bits, the definitions all have the following three most important attributes. A unit test is an automated test that

- Verifies a small piece of code (also known as a *unit*),
- Does it quickly,
- And does it in an isolated manner.

The first two attributes here are pretty non-controversial. There might be some dispute as to what exactly constitutes a fast unit test because it's a highly subjective measure. But overall, it's not that important. If your test suite's execution time is good enough for you, it means your tests are quick enough.

What people have vastly different opinions about is the third attribute. The isolation issue is the root of the differences between the classical and London schools of unit testing. As you will see in the next section, all other differences between the two schools flow naturally from this single disagreement on what exactly *isolation* means. I prefer the classical style for the reasons I describe in section 2.3.

The classical and London schools of unit testing

The classical approach is also referred to as the *Detroit* and, sometimes, the *classicist* approach to unit testing. Probably the most canonical book on the classical school is the one by Kent Beck: *Test-Driven Development: By Example* (Addison-Wesley Professional, 2002).

The London style is sometimes referred to as *mockist*. Although the term *mockist* is widespread, people who adhere to this style of unit testing generally don't like it, so I call it the London style throughout this book. The most prominent proponents of this approach are Steve Freeman and Nat Pryce. I recommend their book, *Growing Object-Oriented Software, Guided by Tests* (Addison-Wesley Professional, 2009), as a good source on this subject.

2.1.1 The isolation issue: The London take

What does it mean to verify a piece of code—a unit—in an isolated manner? The London school describes it as isolating the system under test from its collaborators. It means if a class has a dependency on another class, or several classes, you need to replace all such dependencies with test doubles. This way, you can focus on the class under test exclusively by separating its behavior from any external influence.

DEFINITION   A *test double* is an object that looks and behaves like its release-intended counterpart but is actually a simplified version that reduces the complexity and facilitates testing. This term was introduced by Gerard Meszaros in his book, *xUnit Test Patterns: Refactoring Test Code* (Addison-Wesley, 2007). The name itself comes from the notion of a stunt double in movies.

Figure 2.1 shows how the isolation is usually achieved. A unit test that would otherwise verify the system under test along with all its dependencies now can do that separately from those dependencies.

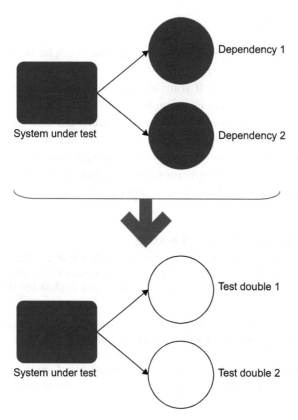

Figure 2.1 Replacing the dependencies of the system under test with test doubles allows you to focus on verifying the system under test exclusively, as well as split the otherwise large interconnected object graph.

One benefit of this approach is that if the test fails, you know for sure which part of the code base is broken: it's the system under test. There could be no other suspects, because all of the class's neighbors are replaced with the test doubles.

Another benefit is the ability to split the *object graph*—the web of communicating classes solving the same problem. This web may become quite complicated: every class in it may have several immediate dependencies, each of which relies on dependencies of their own, and so on. Classes may even introduce circular dependencies, where the chain of dependency eventually comes back to where it started.

Trying to test such an interconnected code base is hard without test doubles. Pretty much the only choice you are left with is re-creating the full object graph in the test, which might not be a feasible task if the number of classes in it is too high.

With test doubles, you can put a stop to this. You can substitute the immediate dependencies of a class; and, by extension, you don't have to deal with the dependencies of those dependencies, and so on down the recursion path. You are effectively breaking up the graph—and that can significantly reduce the amount of preparations you have to do in a unit test.

And let's not forget another small but pleasant side benefit of this approach to unit test isolation: it allows you to introduce a project-wide guideline of testing only one class at a time, which establishes a simple structure in the whole unit test suite. You no longer have to think much about how to cover your code base with tests. Have a class? Create a corresponding class with unit tests! Figure 2.2 shows how it usually looks.

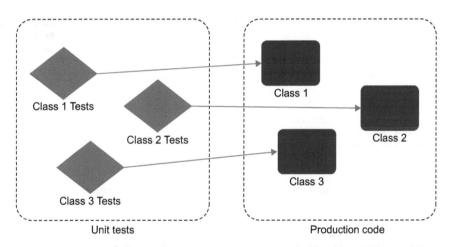

Figure 2.2   Isolating the class under test from its dependencies helps establish a simple test suite structure: one class with tests for each class in the production code.

Let's now look at some examples. Since the classical style probably looks more familiar to most people, I'll show sample tests written in that style first and then rewrite them using the London approach.

Let's say that we operate an online store. There's just one simple use case in our sample application: a customer can purchase a product. When there's enough inventory in the store, the purchase is deemed to be successful, and the amount of the product in the store is reduced by the purchase's amount. If there's not enough product, the purchase is not successful, and nothing happens in the store.

Listing 2.1 shows two tests verifying that a purchase succeeds only when there's enough inventory in the store. The tests are written in the classical style and use the typical three-phase sequence: arrange, act, and assert (AAA for short—I talk more about this sequence in chapter 3).

Listing 2.1   Tests written using the classical style of unit testing

```
[Fact]
public void Purchase_succeeds_when_enough_inventory()
{
    // Arrange
    var store = new Store();
    store.AddInventory(Product.Shampoo, 10);
    var customer = new Customer();

    // Act
    bool success = customer.Purchase(store, Product.Shampoo, 5);

    // Assert
    Assert.True(success);
    Assert.Equal(5, store.GetInventory(Product.Shampoo));   ⟵─┐ Reduces the
}                                                              │ product amount in
                                                               │ the store by five

[Fact]
public void Purchase_fails_when_not_enough_inventory()
{
    // Arrange
    var store = new Store();
    store.AddInventory(Product.Shampoo, 10);
    var customer = new Customer();

    // Act
    bool success = customer.Purchase(store, Product.Shampoo, 15);

    // Assert
    Assert.False(success);
    Assert.Equal(10, store.GetInventory(Product.Shampoo));   ⟵─┐ The product
}                                                               │ amount in the
                                                                │ store remains
public enum Product                                             │ unchanged.
{
    Shampoo,
    Book
}
```

As you can see, the arrange part is where the tests make ready all dependencies and the system under test. The call to customer.Purchase() is the act phase, where you exercise the behavior you want to verify. The assert statements are the verification stage, where you check to see if the behavior led to the expected results.

During the arrange phase, the tests put together two kinds of objects: the system under test (SUT) and one collaborator. In this case, Customer is the SUT and Store is the collaborator. We need the collaborator for two reasons:

- To get the method under test to compile, because `customer.Purchase()` requires a `Store` instance as an argument
- For the assertion phase, since one of the results of `customer.Purchase()` is a potential decrease in the product amount in the store

`Product.Shampoo` and the numbers 5 and 15 are constants.

> **DEFINITION** A *method under test* (*MUT*) is a method in the SUT called by the test. The terms *MUT* and *SUT* are often used as synonyms, but normally, *MUT* refers to a method while *SUT* refers to the whole class.

This code is an example of the classical style of unit testing: the test doesn't replace the collaborator (the `Store` class) but rather uses a production-ready instance of it. One of the natural outcomes of this style is that the test now effectively verifies both `Customer` and `Store`, not just `Customer`. Any bug in the inner workings of `Store` that affects `Customer` will lead to failing these unit tests, even if `Customer` still works correctly. The two classes are not isolated from each other in the tests.

Let's now modify the example toward the London style. I'll take the same tests and replace the `Store` instances with test doubles—specifically, mocks.

I use Moq (https://github.com/moq/moq4) as the mocking framework, but you can find several equally good alternatives, such as NSubstitute (https://github.com/nsubstitute/NSubstitute). All object-oriented languages have analogous frameworks. For instance, in the Java world, you can use Mockito, JMock, or EasyMock.

> **DEFINITION** A *mock* is a special kind of test double that allows you to examine interactions between the system under test and its collaborators.

We'll get back to the topic of mocks, stubs, and the differences between them in later chapters. For now, the main thing to remember is that mocks are a subset of test doubles. People often use the terms *test double* and *mock* as synonyms, but technically, they are not (more on this in chapter 5):

- *Test double* is an overarching term that describes all kinds of non-production-ready, fake dependencies in a test.
- *Mock* is just one kind of such dependencies.

The next listing shows how the tests look after isolating `Customer` from its collaborator, `Store`.

Listing 2.2 Tests written using the London style of unit testing

```
[Fact]
public void Purchase_succeeds_when_enough_inventory()
{
    // Arrange
    var storeMock = new Mock<IStore>();
    storeMock
```

```
        .Setup(x => x.HasEnoughInventory(Product.Shampoo, 5))
        .Returns(true);
    var customer = new Customer();

    // Act
    bool success = customer.Purchase(
        storeMock.Object, Product.Shampoo, 5);

    // Assert
    Assert.True(success);
    storeMock.Verify(
        x => x.RemoveInventory(Product.Shampoo, 5),
        Times.Once);
}

[Fact]
public void Purchase_fails_when_not_enough_inventory()
{
    // Arrange
    var storeMock = new Mock<IStore>();
    storeMock
        .Setup(x => x.HasEnoughInventory(Product.Shampoo, 5))
        .Returns(false);
    var customer = new Customer();

    // Act
    bool success = customer.Purchase(
        storeMock.Object, Product.Shampoo, 5);

    // Assert
    Assert.False(success);
    storeMock.Verify(
        x => x.RemoveInventory(Product.Shampoo, 5),
        Times.Never);
}
```

Note how different these tests are from those written in the classical style. In the arrange phase, the tests no longer instantiate a production-ready instance of Store but instead create a substitution for it, using Moq's built-in class Mock<T>.

Furthermore, instead of modifying the state of Store by adding a shampoo inventory to it, we directly tell the mock how to respond to calls to HasEnoughInventory(). The mock reacts to this request the way the tests need, regardless of the actual state of Store. In fact, the tests no longer use Store—we have introduced an IStore interface and are mocking that interface instead of the Store class.

In chapter 8, I write in detail about working with interfaces. For now, just make a note that interfaces are required for isolating the system under test from its collaborators. (You can also mock a concrete class, but that's an anti-pattern; I cover this topic in chapter 11.)

The assertion phase has changed too, and that's where the key difference lies. We still check the output from customer.Purchase as before, but the way we verify that the customer did the right thing to the store is different. Previously, we did that by asserting against the store's state. Now, we examine the interactions between Customer and Store: the tests check to see if the customer made the correct call on the store. We do this by passing the method the customer should call on the store (x.Remove-Inventory) as well as the number of times it should do that. If the purchases succeeds, the customer should call this method once (Times.Once). If the purchases fails, the customer shouldn't call it at all (Times.Never).

2.1.2 *The isolation issue: The classical take*

To reiterate, the London style approaches the isolation requirement by segregating the piece of code under test from its collaborators with the help of test doubles: specifically, mocks. Interestingly enough, this point of view also affects your standpoint on what constitutes a small piece of code (a unit). Here are all the attributes of a unit test once again:

- A unit test verifies a small piece of code (a unit),
- Does it quickly,
- And does it in an isolated manner.

In addition to the third attribute leaving room for interpretation, there's some room in the possible interpretations of the first attribute as well. How small should a small piece of code be? As you saw from the previous section, if you adopt the position of isolating every individual class, then it's natural to accept that the piece of code under test should also be a single class, or a method inside that class. It can't be more than that due to the way you approach the isolation issue. In some cases, you might test a couple of classes at once; but in general, you'll always strive to maintain this guideline of unit testing one class at a time.

As I mentioned earlier, there's another way to interpret the isolation attribute—the classical way. In the classical approach, it's not the code that needs to be tested in an isolated manner. Instead, unit tests themselves should be run in isolation from each other. That way, you can run the tests in parallel, sequentially, and in any order, whatever fits you best, and they still won't affect each other's outcome.

Isolating tests from each other means it's fine to exercise several classes at once as long as they all reside in the memory and don't reach out to a shared state, through which the tests can communicate and affect each other's execution context. Typical examples of such a shared state are out-of-process dependencies—the database, the file system, and so on.

For instance, one test could create a customer in the database as part of its arrange phase, and another test would delete it as part of its own arrange phase, before the first test completes executing. If you run these two tests in parallel, the first test will fail, not because the production code is broken, but rather because of the interference from the second test.

Shared, private, and out-of-process dependencies

A *shared dependency* is a dependency that is shared between tests and provides means for those tests to affect each other's outcome. A typical example of *shared dependencies* is a static mutable field. A change to such a field is visible across all unit tests running within the same process. A database is another typical example of a *shared dependency*.

A *private dependency* is a dependency that is not shared.

An *out-of-process dependency* is a dependency that runs outside the application's execution process; it's a proxy to data that is not yet in the memory. An *out-of-process dependency* corresponds to a shared dependency in the vast majority of cases, but not always. For example, a database is both out-of-process and shared. But if you launch that database in a Docker container before each test run, that would make this dependency out-of-process but not shared, since tests no longer work with the same instance of it. Similarly, a read-only database is also out-of-process but not shared, even if it's reused by tests. Tests can't mutate data in such a database and thus can't affect each other's outcome.

This take on the isolation issue entails a much more modest view on the use of mocks and other test doubles. You can still use them, but you normally do that for only those dependencies that introduce a shared state between tests. Figure 2.3 shows how it looks.

Note that shared dependencies are shared *between unit tests*, not between classes under test (units). In that sense, a singleton dependency is not shared as long as you are able to create a new instance of it in each test. While there's only one instance of a

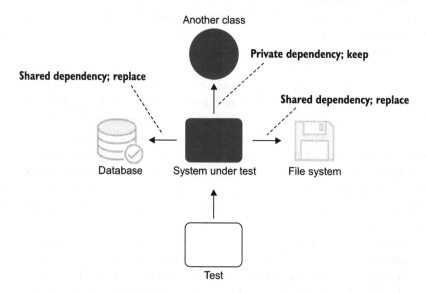

Figure 2.3 Isolating unit tests from each other entails isolating the class under test from shared dependencies only. Private dependencies can be kept intact.

singleton in the production code, tests may very well not follow this pattern and not reuse that singleton. Thus, such a dependency would be private.

For example, there's normally only one instance of a configuration class, which is reused across all production code. But if it's injected into the SUT the way all other dependencies are, say, via a constructor, you can create a new instance of it in each test; you don't have to maintain a single instance throughout the test suite. You can't create a new file system or a database, however; they must be either shared between tests or substituted away with test doubles.

Shared vs. volatile dependencies

Another term has a similar, yet not identical, meaning: *volatile dependency*. I recommend *Dependency Injection: Principles, Practices, Patterns* by Steven van Deursen and Mark Seemann (Manning Publications, 2018) as a go-to book on the topic of dependency management.

A *volatile dependency* is a dependency that exhibits one of the following properties:

- *It introduces a requirement to set up and configure a runtime environment in addition to what is installed on a developer's machine by default.* Databases and API services are good examples here. They require additional setup and are not installed on machines in your organization by default.
- *It contains nondeterministic behavior.* An example would be a random number generator or a class returning the current date and time. These dependencies are non-deterministic because they provide different results on each invocation.

As you can see, there's an overlap between the notions of *shared* and *volatile* dependencies. For example, a dependency on the database is both shared and volatile. But that's not the case for the file system. The file system is not volatile because it is installed on every developer's machine and it behaves deterministically in the vast majority of cases. Still, the file system introduces a means by which the unit tests can interfere with each other's execution context; hence it is shared. Likewise, a random number generator is volatile, but because you can supply a separate instance of it to each test, it isn't shared.

Another reason for substituting shared dependencies is to increase the test execution speed. Shared dependencies almost always reside outside the execution process, while private dependencies usually don't cross that boundary. Because of that, calls to shared dependencies, such as a database or the file system, take more time than calls to private dependencies. And since the necessity to run quickly is the second attribute of the unit test definition, such calls push the tests with shared dependencies out of the realm of unit testing and into the area of integration testing. I talk more about integration testing later in this chapter.

This alternative view of isolation also leads to a different take on what constitutes a unit (a small piece of code). A unit doesn't necessarily have to be limited to a class.

You can just as well unit test a group of classes, as long as none of them is a shared dependency.

2.2   *The classical and London schools of unit testing*

As you can see, the root of the differences between the London and classical schools is the isolation attribute. The London school views it as isolation of the system under test from its collaborators, whereas the classical school views it as isolation of unit tests themselves from each other.

This seemingly minor difference has led to a vast disagreement about how to approach unit testing, which, as you already know, produced the two schools of thought. Overall, the disagreement between the schools spans three major topics:

- The isolation requirement
- What constitutes a piece of code under test (a unit)
- Handling dependencies

Table 2.1 sums it all up.

Table 2.1   The differences between the London and classical schools of unit testing, summed up by the approach to isolation, the size of a unit, and the use of test doubles

	Isolation of	A *unit* is	Uses test doubles for
London school	Units	A class	All but immutable dependencies
Classical school	Unit tests	A class or a set of classes	Shared dependencies

2.2.1   *How the classical and London schools handle dependencies*

Note that despite the ubiquitous use of test doubles, the London school still allows for using some dependencies in tests as-is. The litmus test here is whether a dependency is mutable. It's fine not to substitute objects that don't ever change—*immutable* objects.

And you saw in the earlier examples that, when I refactored the tests toward the London style, I didn't replace the `Product` instances with mocks but rather used the real objects, as shown in the following code (repeated from listing 2.2 for your convenience):

```
[Fact]
public void Purchase_fails_when_not_enough_inventory()
{
    // Arrange
    var storeMock = new Mock<IStore>();
    storeMock
        .Setup(x => x.HasEnoughInventory(Product.Shampoo, 5))
        .Returns(false);
    var customer = new Customer();
```

```
    // Act
    bool success = customer.Purchase(storeMock.Object, Product.Shampoo, 5);

    // Assert
    Assert.False(success);
    storeMock.Verify(
        x => x.RemoveInventory(Product.Shampoo, 5),
        Times.Never);
}
```

Of the two dependencies of Customer, only Store contains an internal state that can change over time. The Product instances are immutable (Product itself is a C# enum). Hence I substituted the Store instance only.

It makes sense, if you think about it. You wouldn't use a test double for the 5 number in the previous test either, would you? That's because it is also immutable—you can't possibly modify this number. Note that I'm not talking about a variable containing the number, but rather the number itself. In the statement Remove-Inventory(Product.Shampoo, 5), we don't even use a variable; 5 is declared right away. The same is true for Product.Shampoo.

Such immutable objects are called *value objects* or *values*. Their main trait is that they have no individual identity; they are identified solely by their content. As a corollary, if two such objects have the same content, it doesn't matter which of them you're working with: these instances are interchangeable. For example, if you've got two 5 integers, you can use them in place of one another. The same is true for the products in our case: you can reuse a single Product.Shampoo instance or declare several of them—it won't make any difference. These instances will have the same content and thus can be used interchangeably.

Note that the concept of a *value object* is language-agnostic and doesn't require a particular programming language or framework. You can read more about value objects in my article "Entity vs. Value Object: The ultimate list of differences" at http://mng.bz/KE9O.

Figure 2.4 shows the categorization of dependencies and how both schools of unit testing treat them. A *dependency* can be either *shared* or *private*. A *private* dependency, in turn, can be either *mutable* or *immutable*. In the latter case, it is called a *value object*. For example, a database is a shared dependency—its internal state is shared across all automated tests (that don't replace it with a test double). A Store instance is a private dependency that is mutable. And a Product instance (or an instance of a number 5, for that matter) is an example of a private dependency that is immutable—a value object. All shared dependencies are mutable, but for a mutable dependency to be shared, it has to be reused by tests.

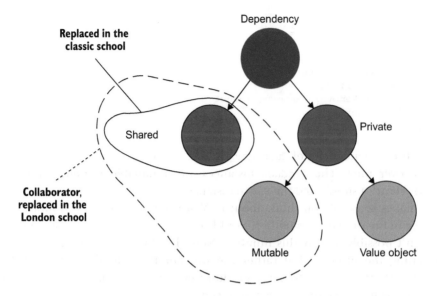

Replaced in the
classic school

Dependency

Shared

Private

Collaborator,
replaced in the
London school

Mutable

Value object

Figure 2.4   The hierarchy of dependencies. The classical school advocates for replacing shared dependencies with test doubles. The London school advocates for the replacement of private dependencies as well, as long as they are mutable.

I'm repeating table 2.1 with the differences between the schools for your convenience.

	Isolation of	A *unit* is	Uses test doubles for
London school	Units	A class	All but immutable dependencies
Classical school	Unit tests	A class or a set of classes	Shared dependencies

Collaborator vs. dependency

A *collaborator* is a dependency that is either shared or mutable. For example, a class providing access to the database is a collaborator since the database is a shared dependency. Store is a collaborator too, because its state can change over time.

Product and number 5 are also dependencies, but they're not collaborators. They're *values* or *value objects*.

A typical class may work with dependencies of both types: *collaborators* and *values*. Look at this method call:

```
customer.Purchase(store, Product.Shampoo, 5)
```

Here we have three dependencies. One of them (store) is a collaborator, and the other two (Product.Shampoo, 5) are not.

And let me reiterate one point about the types of dependencies. Not all out-of-process dependencies fall into the category of shared dependencies. A shared dependency almost always resides outside the application's process, but the opposite isn't true (see figure 2.5). In order for an out-of-process dependency to be shared, it has to provide means for unit tests to communicate with each other. The communication is done through modifications of the dependency's internal state. In that sense, an immutable out-of-process dependency doesn't provide such a means. The tests simply can't modify anything in it and thus can't interfere with each other's execution context.

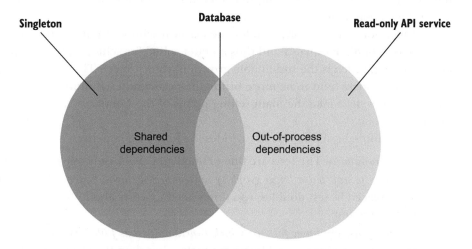

Figure 2.5   The relation between shared and out-of-process dependencies. An example of a dependency that is shared but not out-of-process is a singleton (an instance that is reused by all tests) or a static field in a class. A database is shared and out-of-process—it resides outside the main process and is mutable. A read-only API is out-of-process but not shared, since tests can't modify it and thus can't affect each other's execution flow.

For example, if there's an API somewhere that returns a catalog of all products the organization sells, this isn't a shared dependency as long as the API doesn't expose the functionality to change the catalog. It's true that such a dependency is volatile and sits outside the application's boundary, but since the tests can't affect the data it returns, it isn't shared. This doesn't mean you have to include such a dependency in the testing scope. In most cases, you still need to replace it with a test double to keep the test fast. But if the out-of-process dependency is quick enough and the connection to it is stable, you can make a good case for using it as-is in the tests.

Having that said, in this book, I use the terms *shared dependency* and *out-of-process dependency* interchangeably unless I explicitly state otherwise. In real-world projects, you rarely have a shared dependency that isn't out-of-process. If a dependency is in-process, you can easily supply a separate instance of it to each test; there's no need to share it between tests. Similarly, you normally don't encounter an out-of-process dependency that's not shared. Most such dependencies are mutable and thus can be modified by tests.

With this foundation of definitions, let's contrast the two schools on their merits.

2.3   Contrasting the classical and London schools of unit testing

To reiterate, the main difference between the classical and London schools is in how they treat the isolation issue in the definition of a unit test. This, in turn, spills over to the treatment of a *unit*—the thing that should be put under test—and the approach to handling dependencies.

As I mentioned previously, I prefer the classical school of unit testing. It tends to produce tests of higher quality and thus is better suited for achieving the ultimate goal of unit testing, which is the sustainable growth of your project. The reason is fragility: tests that use mocks tend to be more brittle than classical tests (more on this in chapter 5). For now, let's take the main selling points of the London school and evaluate them one by one.

The London school's approach provides the following benefits:

- *Better granularity*. The tests are fine-grained and check only one class at a time.
- *It's easier to unit test a larger graph of interconnected classes*. Since all collaborators are replaced by test doubles, you don't need to worry about them at the time of writing the test.
- *If a test fails, you know for sure which functionality has failed*. Without the class's collaborators, there could be no suspects other than the class under test itself. Of course, there may still be situations where the system under test uses a value object and it's the change in this value object that makes the test fail. But these cases aren't that frequent because all other dependencies are eliminated in tests.

2.3.1   Unit testing one class at a time

The point about better granularity relates to the discussion about what constitutes a *unit* in unit testing. The London school considers a class as such a unit. Coming from an object-oriented programming background, developers usually regard classes as the atomic building blocks that lie at the foundation of every code base. This naturally leads to treating classes as the atomic units to be verified in tests, too. This tendency is understandable but misleading.

> **TIP**   Tests shouldn't verify *units of code*. Rather, they should verify *units of behavior:* something that is meaningful for the problem domain and, ideally, something that a business person can recognize as useful. The number of classes it takes to implement such a unit of behavior is irrelevant. The unit could span across multiple classes or only one class, or even take up just a tiny method.

And so, aiming at better code granularity isn't helpful. As long as the test checks a single unit of behavior, it's a good test. Targeting something less than that can in fact damage your unit tests, as it becomes harder to understand exactly what these tests verify. *A test should tell a story about the problem your code helps to solve, and this story should be cohesive and meaningful to a non-programmer.*

For instance, this is an example of a cohesive story:

```
When I call my dog, he comes right to me.
```

Now compare it to the following:

```
When I call my dog, he moves his front left leg first, then the front right
leg, his head turns, the tail start wagging...
```

The second story makes much less sense. What's the purpose of all those movements? Is the dog coming to me? Or is he running away? You can't tell. This is what your tests start to look like when you target individual classes (the dog's legs, head, and tail) instead of the actual behavior (the dog coming to his master). I talk more about this topic of observable behavior and how to differentiate it from internal implementation details in chapter 5.

2.3.2 *Unit testing a large graph of interconnected classes*

The use of mocks in place of real collaborators can make it easier to test a class—especially when there's a complicated dependency graph, where the class under test has dependencies, each of which relies on dependencies of its own, and so on, several layers deep. With test doubles, you can substitute the class's immediate dependencies and thus break up the graph, which can significantly reduce the amount of preparation you have to do in a unit test. If you follow the classical school, you have to re-create the full object graph (with the exception of shared dependencies) just for the sake of setting up the system under test, which can be a lot of work.

Although this is all true, this line of reasoning focuses on the wrong problem. Instead of finding ways to test a large, complicated graph of interconnected classes, you should focus on not having such a graph of classes in the first place. More often than not, a large class graph is a result of a code design problem.

It's actually a good thing that the tests point out this problem. As we discussed in chapter 1, the ability to unit test a piece of code is a good negative indicator—it predicts poor code quality with a relatively high precision. If you see that to unit test a class, you need to extend the test's arrange phase beyond all reasonable limits, it's a certain sign of trouble. The use of mocks only hides this problem; it doesn't tackle the root cause. I talk about how to fix the underlying code design problem in part 2.

2.3.3   *Revealing the precise bug location*

If you introduce a bug to a system with London-style tests, it normally causes only tests whose SUT contains the bug to fail. However, with the classical approach, tests that target the clients of the malfunctioning class can also fail. This leads to a ripple effect where a single bug can cause test failures across the whole system. As a result, it becomes harder to find the root of the issue. You might need to spend some time debugging the tests to figure it out.

It's a valid concern, but I don't see it as a big problem. If you run your tests regularly (ideally, after each source code change), then you know what caused the bug—it's what you edited last, so it's not that difficult to find the issue. Also, you don't have to look at all the failing tests. Fixing one automatically fixes all the others.

Furthermore, there's some value in failures cascading all over the test suite. If a bug leads to a fault in not only one test but a whole lot of them, it shows that the piece of code you have just broken is of great value—the entire system depends on it. That's useful information to keep in mind when working with the code.

2.3.4   *Other differences between the classical and London schools*

Two remaining differences between the classical and London schools are

- Their approach to system design with test-driven development (TDD)
- The issue of over-specification

Test-driven development

Test-driven development is a software development process that relies on tests to drive the project development. The process consists of three (some authors specify four) stages, which you repeat for every test case:

1 Write a failing test to indicate which functionality needs to be added and how it should behave.
2 Write just enough code to make the test pass. At this stage, the code doesn't have to be elegant or clean.
3 Refactor the code. Under the protection of the passing test, you can safely clean up the code to make it more readable and maintainable.

Good sources on this topic are the two books I recommended earlier: Kent Beck's *Test-Driven Development: By Example*, and *Growing Object-Oriented Software, Guided by Tests* by Steve Freeman and Nat Pryce.

The London style of unit testing leads to outside-in TDD, where you start from the higher-level tests that set expectations for the whole system. By using mocks, you specify which collaborators the system should communicate with to achieve the expected result. You then work your way through the graph of classes until you implement every one of them. Mocks make this design process possible because you can focus on one class at a time. You can cut off all of the SUT's collaborators when testing it and thus postpone implementing those collaborators to a later time.

The classical school doesn't provide quite the same guidance since you have to deal with the real objects in tests. Instead, you normally use the inside-out approach. In this style, you start from the domain model and then put additional layers on top of it until the software becomes usable by the end user.

But the most crucial distinction between the schools is the issue of over-specification: that is, coupling the tests to the SUT's implementation details. The London style tends to produce tests that couple to the implementation more often than the classical style. And this is the main objection against the ubiquitous use of mocks and the London style in general.

There's much more to the topic of mocking. Starting with chapter 4, I gradually cover everything related to it.

2.4 *Integration tests in the two schools*

The London and classical schools also diverge in their definition of an *integration test*. This disagreement flows naturally from the difference in their views on the isolation issue.

The London school considers any test that uses a real collaborator object an integration test. Most of the tests written in the classical style would be deemed integration tests by the London school proponents. For an example, see listing 1.4, in which I first introduced the two tests covering the customer purchase functionality. That code is a typical unit test from the classical perspective, but it's an integration test for a follower of the London school.

In this book, I use the classical definitions of both unit and integration testing. Again, a unit test is an automated test that has the following characteristics:

- It verifies a small piece of code,
- Does it quickly,
- And does it in an isolated manner.

Now that I've clarified what the first and third attributes mean, I'll redefine them from the point of view of the classical school. A unit test is a test that

- Verifies a *single unit of behavior,*
- Does it quickly,
- And does it in isolation *from other tests.*

An integration test, then, is a test that doesn't meet one of these criteria. For example, a test that reaches out to a shared dependency—say, a database—can't run in isolation from other tests. A change in the database's state introduced by one test would alter the outcome of all other tests that rely on the same database if run in parallel. You'd have to take additional steps to avoid this interference. In particular, you would have to run such tests sequentially, so that each test would wait its turn to work with the shared dependency.

Similarly, an outreach to an out-of-process dependency makes the test slow. A call to a database adds hundreds of milliseconds, potentially up to a second, of additional execution time. Milliseconds might not seem like a big deal at first, but when your test suite grows large enough, every second counts.

In theory, you could write a slow test that works with in-memory objects only, but it's not that easy to do. Communication between objects inside the same memory space is much less expensive than between separate processes. Even if the test works with hundreds of in-memory objects, the communication with them will still execute faster than a call to a database.

Finally, a test is an integration test when it verifies two or more units of behavior. This is often a result of trying to optimize the test suite's execution speed. When you have two slow tests that follow similar steps but verify different units of behavior, it might make sense to merge them into one: one test checking two similar things runs faster than two more-granular tests. But then again, the two original tests would have been integration tests already (due to them being slow), so this characteristic usually isn't decisive.

An integration test can also verify how two or more modules developed by separate teams work together. This also falls into the third bucket of tests that verify multiple units of behavior at once. But again, because such an integration normally requires an out-of-process dependency, the test will fail to meet all three criteria, not just one.

Integration testing plays a significant part in contributing to software quality by verifying the system as a whole. I write about integration testing in detail in part 3.

2.4.1   *End-to-end tests are a subset of integration tests*

In short, an *integration test* is a test that verifies that your code works in integration with shared dependencies, out-of-process dependencies, or code developed by other teams in the organization. There's also a separate notion of an *end-to-end test*. End-to-end tests are a subset of integration tests. They, too, check to see how your code works with out-of-process dependencies. The difference between an end-to-end test and an integration test is that end-to-end tests usually include more of such dependencies.

The line is blurred at times, but in general, an integration test works with only one or two out-of-process dependencies. On the other hand, an end-to-end test works with all out-of-process dependencies, or with the vast majority of them. Hence the name *end-to-end*, which means the test verifies the system from the end user's point of view, including all the external applications this system integrates with (see figure 2.6).

People also use such terms as *UI tests* (UI stands for *user interface*), *GUI tests* (GUI is *graphical user interface*), and *functional tests*. The terminology is ill-defined, but in general, these terms are all synonyms.

Let's say your application works with three out-of-process dependencies: a database, the file system, and a payment gateway. A typical integration test would include only the database and file system in scope and use a test double to replace the payment gateway. That's because you have full control over the database and file system,

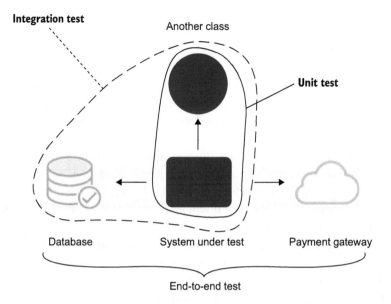

Figure 2.6   End-to-end tests normally include all or almost all out-of-process dependencies in the scope. Integration tests check only one or two such dependencies—those that are easier to set up automatically, such as the database or the file system.

and thus can easily bring them to the required state in tests, whereas you don't have the same degree of control over the payment gateway. With the payment gateway, you may need to contact the payment processor organization to set up a special test account. You might also need to check that account from time to time to manually clean up all the payment charges left over from the past test executions.

Since end-to-end tests are the most expensive in terms of maintenance, it's better to run them late in the build process, after all the unit and integration tests have passed. You may possibly even run them only on the build server, not on individual developers' machines.

Keep in mind that even with end-to-end tests, you might not be able to tackle all of the out-of-process dependencies. There may be no test version of some dependencies, or it may be impossible to bring those dependencies to the required state automatically. So you may still need to use a test double, reinforcing the fact that there isn't a distinct line between integration and end-to-end tests.

Summary

- Throughout this chapter, I've refined the definition of a unit test:
  - A unit test verifies a single unit of behavior,
  - Does it quickly,
  - And does it in isolation from other tests.

- The isolation issue is disputed the most. The dispute led to the formation of two schools of unit testing: the classical (Detroit) school, and the London (mockist) school. This difference of opinion affects the view of what constitutes a unit and the treatment of the system under test's (SUT's) dependencies.
  - The London school states that the units under test should be isolated from each other. A unit under test is a *unit of code*, usually a class. All of its dependencies, except immutable dependencies, should be replaced with test doubles in tests.
  - The classical school states that the *unit tests* need to be isolated from each other, not units. Also, a unit under test is a *unit of behavior*, not a unit of code. Thus, only shared dependencies should be replaced with test doubles. Shared dependencies are dependencies that provide means for tests to affect each other's execution flow.
- The London school provides the benefits of better granularity, the ease of testing large graphs of interconnected classes, and the ease of finding which functionality contains a bug after a test failure.
- The benefits of the London school look appealing at first. However, they introduce several issues. First, the focus on classes under test is misplaced: tests should verify units of behavior, not units of code. Furthermore, the inability to unit test a piece of code is a strong sign of a problem with the code design. The use of test doubles doesn't fix this problem, but rather only hides it. And finally, while the ease of determining which functionality contains a bug after a test failure is helpful, it's not that big a deal because you often know what caused the bug anyway—it's what you edited last.
- The biggest issue with the London school of unit testing is the problem of over-specification—coupling tests to the SUT's implementation details.
- An integration test is a test that doesn't meet at least one of the criteria for a unit test. End-to-end tests are a subset of integration tests; they verify the system from the end user's point of view. End-to-end tests reach out directly to all or almost all out-of-process dependencies your application works with.
- For a canonical book about the classical style, I recommend Kent Beck's *Test-Driven Development: By Example*. For more on the London style, see *Growing Object-Oriented Software, Guided by Tests*, by Steve Freeman and Nat Pryce. For further reading about working with dependencies, I recommend *Dependency Injection: Principles, Practices, Patterns* by Steven van Deursen and Mark Seemann.

The anatomy of a unit test

This chapter covers

- The structure of a unit test
- Unit test naming best practices
- Working with parameterized tests
- Working with fluent assertions

In this remaining chapter of part 1, I'll give you a refresher on some basic topics. I'll go over the structure of a typical unit test, which is usually represented by the *arrange, act, and assert* (AAA) pattern. I'll also show the unit testing framework of my choice—xUnit—and explain why I'm using it and not one of its competitors.

Along the way, we'll talk about naming unit tests. There are quite a few competing pieces of advice on this topic, and unfortunately, most of them don't do a good enough job improving your unit tests. In this chapter, I describe those less-useful naming practices and show why they usually aren't the best choice. Instead of those practices, I give you an alternative—a simple, easy-to-follow guideline for naming tests in a way that makes them readable not only to the programmer who wrote them, but also to any other person familiar with the problem domain.

Finally, I'll talk about some features of the framework that help streamline the process of unit testing. Don't worry about this information being too specific to C#

and .NET; most unit testing frameworks exhibit similar functionality, regardless of the programming language. If you learn one of them, you won't have problems working with another.

3.1 How to structure a unit test

This section shows how to structure unit tests using the arrange, act, and assert pattern, what pitfalls to avoid, and how to make your tests as readable as possible.

3.1.1 Using the AAA pattern

The AAA pattern advocates for splitting each test into three parts: *arrange*, *act*, and *assert*. (This pattern is sometimes also called the *3A pattern*.) Let's take a `Calculator` class with a single method that calculates a sum of two numbers:

```
public class Calculator
{
    public double Sum(double first, double second)
    {
        return first + second;
    }
}
```

The following listing shows a test that verifies the class's behavior. This test follows the AAA pattern.

Listing 3.1 A test covering the `Sum` method in `calculator`

```
public class CalculatorTests          ⟵──────┐  Class-container for a
{                                               cohesive set of tests
    [Fact]                            ⟵──────┐
    public void Sum_of_two_numbers()          │  xUnit's attribute
    {                                            indicating a test
        // Arrange
        double first = 10;
        double second = 20;                      Arrange
        var calculator = new Calculator();       section

        // Act
        double result = calculator.Sum(first, second);  ⟵──── Act section

        // Assert
        Assert.Equal(30, result);  ⟵─┐  Assert section
    }
}
```

Name of the unit test

The AAA pattern provides a simple, uniform structure for all tests in the suite. This uniformity is one of the biggest advantages of this pattern: once you get used to it, you can easily read and understand any test. That, in turn, reduces maintenance costs for your entire test suite. The structure is as follows:

- In the *arrange section*, you bring the system under test (SUT) and its dependencies to a desired state.
- In the *act section*, you call methods on the SUT, pass the prepared dependencies, and capture the output value (if any).
- In the *assert section*, you verify the outcome. The outcome may be represented by the return value, the final state of the SUT and its collaborators, or the methods the SUT called on those collaborators.

Given-When-Then pattern

You might have heard of the *Given-When-Then* pattern, which is similar to AAA. This pattern also advocates for breaking the test down into three parts:

- *Given*—Corresponds to the arrange section
- *When*—Corresponds to the act section
- *Then*—Corresponds to the assert section

There's no difference between the two patterns in terms of the test composition. The only distinction is that the Given-When-Then structure is more readable to non-programmers. Thus, Given-When-Then is more suitable for tests that are shared with non-technical people.

The natural inclination is to start writing a test with the *arrange* section. After all, it comes before the other two. This approach works well in the vast majority of cases, but starting with the *assert* section is a viable option too. When you practice Test-Driven Development (TDD)—that is, when you create a failing test before developing a feature—you don't know enough about the feature's behavior yet. So, it becomes advantageous to first outline what you expect from the behavior and then figure out how to develop the system to meet this expectation.

Such a technique may look counterintuitive, but it's how we approach problem solving. We start by thinking about the objective: what a particular behavior should to do for us. The actual solving of the problem comes after that. Writing down the assertions before everything else is merely a formalization of this thinking process. But again, this guideline is only applicable when you follow TDD—when you write a test before the production code. If you write the production code before the test, by the time you move on to the test, you already know what to expect from the behavior, so starting with the *arrange* section is a better option.

3.1.2 Avoid multiple arrange, act, and assert sections

Occasionally, you may encounter a test with multiple *arrange*, *act*, or *assert* sections. It usually works as shown in figure 3.1.

When you see multiple *act* sections separated by *assert* and, possibly, *arrange* sections, it means the test verifies multiple units of behavior. And, as we discussed in chapter 2, such a test is no longer a unit test but rather is an integration test. It's best

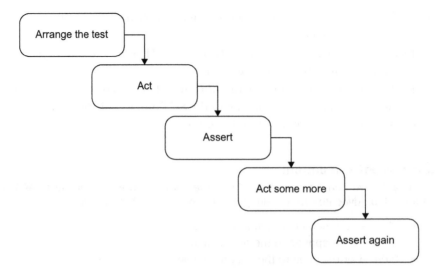

Figure 3.1   Multiple arrange, act, and assert sections are a hint that the test verifies too many things at once. Such a test needs to be split into several tests to fix the problem.

to avoid such a test structure. A single action ensures that your tests remain within the realm of unit testing, which means they are simple, fast, and easy to understand. If you see a test containing a sequence of actions and assertions, refactor it. Extract each act into a test of its own.

It's sometimes fine to have multiple *act* sections in integration tests. As you may remember from the previous chapter, integration tests can be slow. One way to speed them up is to group several integration tests together into a single test with multiple *acts* and *assertions*. It's especially helpful when system states naturally flow from one another: that is, when an *act* simultaneously serves as an *arrange* for the subsequent *act*.

But again, this optimization technique is only applicable to integration tests—and not all of them, but rather those that are already slow and that you don't want to become even slower. There's no need for such an optimization in unit tests or integration tests that are fast enough. It's always better to split a multistep unit test into several tests.

3.1.3   *Avoid if statements in tests*

Similar to multiple occurrences of the *arrange, act,* and *assert* sections, you may sometimes encounter a unit test with an `if` statement. This is also an anti-pattern. A test—whether a unit test or an integration test—should be a simple sequence of steps with no branching.

An `if` statement indicates that the test verifies too many things at once. Such a test, therefore, should be split into several tests. But unlike the situation with multiple AAA sections, there's no exception for integration tests. There are no benefits in branching within a test. You only gain additional maintenance costs: `if` statements make the tests harder to read and understand.

3.1.4 *How large should each section be?*

A common question people ask when starting out with the AAA pattern is, how large should each section be? And what about the teardown section—the section that cleans up after the test? There are different guidelines regarding the size for each of the test sections.

THE ARRANGE SECTION IS THE LARGEST

The *arrange* section is usually the largest of the three. It can be as large as the *act* and *assert* sections combined. But if it becomes significantly larger than that, it's better to extract the arrangements either into private methods within the same test class or to a separate factory class. Two popular patterns can help you reuse the code in the *arrange* sections: *Object Mother* and *Test Data Builder*.

WATCH OUT FOR ACT SECTIONS THAT ARE LARGER THAN A SINGLE LINE

The *act* section is normally just a single line of code. If the *act* consists of two or more lines, it could indicate a problem with the SUT's public API.

It's best to express this point with an example, so let's take one from chapter 2, which I repeat in the following listing. In this example, the customer makes a purchase from a store.

Listing 3.2 A single-line *act* section

```
[Fact]
public void Purchase_succeeds_when_enough_inventory()
{
    // Arrange
    var store = new Store();
    store.AddInventory(Product.Shampoo, 10);
    var customer = new Customer();

    // Act
    bool success = customer.Purchase(store, Product.Shampoo, 5);

    // Assert
    Assert.True(success);
    Assert.Equal(5, store.GetInventory(Product.Shampoo));
}
```

Notice that the *act* section in this test is a single method call, which is a sign of a well-designed class's API. Now compare it to the version in listing 3.3: this *act* section contains two lines. And that's a sign of a problem with the SUT: it requires the client to remember to make the second method call to finish the purchase and thus lacks encapsulation.

```
Listing 3.3  A two-line act section

[Fact]
public void Purchase_succeeds_when_enough_inventory()
{
    // Arrange
    var store = new Store();
    store.AddInventory(Product.Shampoo, 10);
    var customer = new Customer();

    // Act
    bool success = customer.Purchase(store, Product.Shampoo, 5);
    store.RemoveInventory(success, Product.Shampoo, 5);

    // Assert
    Assert.True(success);
    Assert.Equal(5, store.GetInventory(Product.Shampoo));
}
```

Here's what you can read from listing 3.3's *act* section:

- In the first line, the customer tries to acquire five units of shampoo from the store.
- In the second line, the inventory is removed from the store. The removal takes place only if the preceding call to `Purchase()` returns a success.

The issue with the new version is that it requires two method calls to perform a single operation. Note that this is not an issue with the test itself. The test still verifies the same unit of behavior: the process of making a purchase. The issue lies in the API surface of the `Customer` class. It shouldn't require the client to make an additional method call.

From a business perspective, a successful purchase has two outcomes: the acquisition of a product by the customer and the reduction of the inventory in the store. Both of these outcomes must be achieved together, which means there should be a single public method that does both things. Otherwise, there's a room for inconsistency if the client code calls the first method but not the second, in which case the customer will acquire the product but its available amount won't be reduced in the store.

Such an inconsistency is called an *invariant violation*. The act of protecting your code against potential inconsistencies is called *encapsulation*. When an inconsistency penetrates into the database, it becomes a big problem: now it's impossible to reset the state of your application by simply restarting it. You'll have to deal with the corrupted data in the database and, potentially, contact customers and handle the situation on a case-by-case basis. Just imagine what would happen if the application generated confirmation receipts without actually reserving the inventory. It might issue claims to, and even charge for, more inventory than you could feasibly acquire in the near future.

The remedy is to maintain code encapsulation at all times. In the previous example, the customer should remove the acquired inventory from the store as part of its

Purchase method and not rely on the client code to do so. When it comes to maintaining invariants, you should eliminate any potential course of action that could lead to an invariant violation.

This guideline of keeping the *act* section down to a single line holds true for the vast majority of code that contains business logic, but less so for utility or infrastructure code. Thus, I won't say "never do it." Be sure to examine each such case for a potential breach in encapsulation, though.

3.1.5   *How many assertions should the assert section hold?*

Finally, there's the *assert* section. You may have heard about the guideline of having one assertion per test. It takes root in the premise discussed in the previous chapter: the premise of targeting the smallest piece of code possible.

As you already know, this premise is incorrect. A *unit* in unit testing is a unit of *behavior, not* a unit of *code.* A single unit of behavior can exhibit multiple outcomes, and it's fine to evaluate them all in one test.

Having that said, you need to watch out for assertion sections that grow too large: it could be a sign of a missing abstraction in the production code. For example, instead of asserting all properties inside an object returned by the SUT, it may be better to define proper equality members in the object's class. You can then compare the object to an expected value using a single assertion.

3.1.6   *What about the teardown phase?*

Some people also distinguish a fourth section, *teardown,* which comes after *arrange, act,* and *assert.* For example, you can use this section to remove any files created by the test, close a database connection, and so on. The teardown is usually represented by a separate method, which is reused across all tests in the class. Thus, I don't include this phase in the AAA pattern.

Note that most unit tests don't need teardown. Unit tests don't talk to out-of-process dependencies and thus don't leave side effects that need to be disposed of. That's a realm of integration testing. We'll talk more about how to properly clean up after integration tests in part 3.

3.1.7   *Differentiating the system under test*

The SUT plays a significant role in tests. It provides an entry point for the behavior you want to invoke in the application. As we discussed in the previous chapter, this behavior can span across as many as several classes or as little as a single method. But there can be only one entry point: one class that triggers that behavior.

Thus it's important to differentiate the SUT from its dependencies, especially when there are quite a few of them, so that you don't need to spend too much time figuring out who is who in the test. To do that, always name the SUT in tests sut. The following listing shows how CalculatorTests would look after renaming the Calculator instance.

Listing 3.4   **Differentiating the SUT from its dependencies**

```
public class CalculatorTests
{
    [Fact]
    public void Sum_of_two_numbers()
    {
        // Arrange
        double first = 10;
        double second = 20;                    The calculator is
        var sut = new Calculator();    <——┘   now called sut.

        // Act
        double result = sut.Sum(first, second);

        // Assert
        Assert.Equal(30, result);
    }
}
```

3.1.8   *Dropping the arrange, act, and assert comments from tests*

Just as it's important to set the SUT apart from its dependencies, it's also important to differentiate the three sections from each other, so that you don't spend too much time figuring out what section a particular line in the test belongs to. One way to do that is to put // Arrange, // Act, and // Assert comments before the beginning of each section. Another way is to separate the sections with empty lines, as shown next.

Listing 3.5   **Calculator with sections separated by empty lines**

```
public class CalculatorTests
{
    [Fact]
    public void Sum_of_two_numbers()
    {
        double first = 10;
        double second = 20;                    Arrange
        var sut = new Calculator();

        double result = sut.Sum(first, second);   <——— Act

        Assert.Equal(30, result);   <——— Assert
    }
}
```

Separating sections with empty lines works great in most unit tests. It allows you to keep a balance between brevity and readability. It doesn't work as well in large tests, though, where you may want to put additional empty lines inside the *arrange* section to differentiate between configuration stages. This is often the case in integration tests—they frequently contain complicated setup logic. Therefore,

- Drop the section comments in tests that follow the AAA pattern and where you can avoid additional empty lines inside the *arrange* and *assert* sections.
- Keep the section comments otherwise.

3.2 *Exploring the xUnit testing framework*

In this section, I give a brief overview of unit testing tools available in .NET, and their features. I'm using xUnit (https://github.com/xunit/xunit) as the unit testing framework (note that you need to install the `xunit.runner.visualstudio` NuGet package in order to run xUnit tests from Visual Studio). Although this framework works in .NET only, every object-oriented language (Java, C++, JavaScript, and so on) has unit testing frameworks, and all those frameworks look quite similar to each other. If you've worked with one of them, you won't have any issues working with another.

In .NET alone, there are several alternatives to choose from, such as NUnit (https://github.com/nunit/nunit) and the built-in Microsoft MSTest. I personally prefer xUnit for the reasons I'll describe shortly, but you can also use NUnit; these two frameworks are pretty much on par in terms of functionality. I don't recommend MSTest, though; it doesn't provide the same level of flexibility as xUnit and NUnit. And don't take my word for it—even people inside Microsoft refrain from using MSTest. For example, the ASP.NET Core team uses xUnit.

I prefer xUnit because it's a cleaner, more concise version of NUnit. For example, you may have noticed that in the tests I've brought up so far, there are no framework-related attributes other than `[Fact]`, which marks the method as a unit test so the unit testing framework knows to run it. There are no `[TestFixture]` attributes; any public class can contain a unit test. There's also no `[SetUp]` or `[TearDown]`. If you need to share configuration logic between tests, you can put it inside the constructor. And if you need to clean something up, you can implement the `IDisposable` interface, as shown in this listing.

Listing 3.6 Arrangement and teardown logic, shared by all tests

```
public class CalculatorTests : IDisposable
{
    private readonly Calculator _sut;

    public CalculatorTests()
    {                                      Called before
        _sut = new Calculator();           each test in
    }                                      the class

    [Fact]
    public void Sum_of_two_numbers()
    {
        /* ... */
    }
```

```
public void Dispose()               Called after
{                                   each test in
    _sut.CleanUp();                 the class
}
}
```

As you can see, the xUnit authors took significant steps toward simplifying the framework. A lot of notions that previously required additional configuration (like [TestFixture] or [SetUp] attributes) now rely on conventions or built-in language constructs.

I particularly like the [Fact] attribute, specifically because it's called Fact and not Test. It emphasizes the rule of thumb I mentioned in the previous chapter: *each test should tell a story*. This story is an individual, atomic scenario or fact about the problem domain, and the passing test is a proof that this scenario or fact holds true. If the test fails, it means either the story is no longer valid and you need to rewrite it, or the system itself has to be fixed.

I encourage you to adopt this way of thinking when you write unit tests. Your tests shouldn't be a dull enumeration of what the production code does. Rather, they should provide a higher-level description of the application's behavior. Ideally, this description should be meaningful not just to programmers but also to business people.

3.3   *Reusing test fixtures between tests*

It's important to know how and when to reuse code between tests. Reusing code between *arrange* sections is a good way to shorten and simplify your tests, and this section shows how to do that properly.

I mentioned earlier that often, fixture arrangements take up too much space. It makes sense to extract these arrangements into separate methods or classes that you then reuse between tests. There are two ways you can perform such reuse, but only one of them is beneficial; the other leads to increased maintenance costs.

Test fixture

The term *test fixture* has two common meanings:

1   A *test fixture* is an object the test runs against. This object can be a regular dependency—an argument that is passed to the SUT. It can also be data in the database or a file on the hard disk. Such an object needs to remain in a known, *fixed* state before each test run, so it produces the same result. Hence the word *fixture*.

2   The other definition comes from the NUnit testing framework. In NUnit, Test-Fixture is an attribute that marks a class containing tests.

I use the first definition throughout this book.

The first—incorrect—way to reuse test fixtures is to initialize them in the test's constructor (or the method marked with a [SetUp] attribute if you are using NUnit), as shown next.

Listing 3.7   Extracting the initialization code into the test constructor

```
public class CustomerTests
{                                                    Common test
    private readonly Store _store;          ◁——┘     fixture
    private readonly Customer _sut;

    public CustomerTests()
    {
        _store = new Store();                        Runs before
        _store.AddInventory(Product.Shampoo, 10);    each test in
        _sut = new Customer();                        the class
    }

    [Fact]
    public void Purchase_succeeds_when_enough_inventory()
    {
        bool success = _sut.Purchase(_store, Product.Shampoo, 5);

        Assert.True(success);
        Assert.Equal(5, _store.GetInventory(Product.Shampoo));
    }

    [Fact]
    public void Purchase_fails_when_not_enough_inventory()
    {
        bool success = _sut.Purchase(_store, Product.Shampoo, 15);

        Assert.False(success);
        Assert.Equal(10, _store.GetInventory(Product.Shampoo));
    }
}
```

The two tests in listing 3.7 have common configuration logic. In fact, their *arrange* sections are the same and thus can be fully extracted into CustomerTests's constructor—which is precisely what I did here. The tests themselves no longer contain arrangements.

With this approach, you can significantly reduce the amount of test code—you can get rid of most or even all test fixture configurations in tests. But this technique has two significant drawbacks:

- It introduces high coupling between tests.
- It diminishes test readability.

Let's discuss these drawbacks in more detail.

3.3.1   *High coupling between tests is an anti-pattern*

In the new version, shown in listing 3.7, all tests are coupled to each other: a modification of one test's arrangement logic will affect all tests in the class. For example, changing this line

```
_store.AddInventory(Product.Shampoo, 10);
```

to this

```
_store.AddInventory(Product.Shampoo, 15);
```

would invalidate the assumption the tests make about the store's initial state and therefore would lead to unnecessary test failures.

That's a violation of an important guideline: *a modification of one test should not affect other tests*. This guideline is similar to what we discussed in chapter 2—that tests should run in isolation from each other. It's not the same, though. Here, we are talking about independent modification of tests, not independent execution. Both are important attributes of a well-designed test.

To follow this guideline, you need to avoid introducing shared state in test classes. These two private fields are examples of such a shared state:

```
private readonly Store _store;
private readonly Customer _sut;
```

3.3.2   *The use of constructors in tests diminishes test readability*

The other drawback to extracting the arrangement code into the constructor is diminished test readability. You no longer see the full picture just by looking at the test itself. You have to examine different places in the class to understand what the test method does.

Even if there's not much arrangement logic—say, only instantiation of the fixtures—you are still better off moving it directly to the test method. Otherwise, you'll wonder if it's really just instantiation or something else being configured there, too. A self-contained test doesn't leave you with such uncertainties.

3.3.3   *A better way to reuse test fixtures*

The use of the constructor is not the best approach when it comes to reusing test fixtures. The second way—the beneficial one—is to introduce private factory methods in the test class, as shown in the following listing.

> **Listing 3.8   Extracting the common initialization code into private factory methods**

```
public class CustomerTests
{
    [Fact]
    public void Purchase_succeeds_when_enough_inventory()
    {
```

```
        Store store = CreateStoreWithInventory(Product.Shampoo, 10);
        Customer sut = CreateCustomer();

        bool success = sut.Purchase(store, Product.Shampoo, 5);

        Assert.True(success);
        Assert.Equal(5, store.GetInventory(Product.Shampoo));
    }

    [Fact]
    public void Purchase_fails_when_not_enough_inventory()
    {
        Store store = CreateStoreWithInventory(Product.Shampoo, 10);
        Customer sut = CreateCustomer();

        bool success = sut.Purchase(store, Product.Shampoo, 15);

        Assert.False(success);
        Assert.Equal(10, store.GetInventory(Product.Shampoo));
    }

    private Store CreateStoreWithInventory(
        Product product, int quantity)
    {
        Store store = new Store();
        store.AddInventory(product, quantity);
        return store;
    }

    private static Customer CreateCustomer()
    {
        return new Customer();
    }
}
```

By extracting the common initialization code into private factory methods, you can also shorten the test code, but at the same time keep the full context of what's going on in the tests. Moreover, the private methods don't couple tests to each other as long as you make them generic enough. That is, allow the tests to specify how they want the fixtures to be created.

Look at this line, for example:

```
Store store = CreateStoreWithInventory(Product.Shampoo, 10);
```

The test explicitly states that it wants the factory method to add 10 units of shampoo to the store. This is both highly readable and reusable. It's *readable* because you don't need to examine the internals of the factory method to understand the attributes of the created store. It's *reusable* because you can use this method in other tests, too.

Note that in this particular example, there's no need to introduce factory methods, as the arrangement logic is quite simple. View it merely as a demonstration.

There's one exception to this rule of reusing test fixtures. You can instantiate a fixture in the constructor if it's used by all or almost all tests. This is often the case for integration tests that work with a database. All such tests require a database connection, which you can initialize once and then reuse everywhere. But even then, it would make more sense to introduce a base class and initialize the database connection in that class's constructor, not in individual test classes. See the following listing for an example of common initialization code in a base class.

Listing 3.9   Common initialization code in a base class

```
public class CustomerTests : IntegrationTests
{
    [Fact]
    public void Purchase_succeeds_when_enough_inventory()
    {
        /* use _database here */
    }
}

public abstract class IntegrationTests : IDisposable
{
    protected readonly Database _database;

    protected IntegrationTests()
    {
        _database = new Database();
    }

    public void Dispose()
    {
        _database.Dispose();
    }
}
```

Notice how `CustomerTests` remains constructor-less. It gets access to the _database instance by inheriting from the `IntegrationTests` base class.

3.4   Naming a unit test

It's important to give expressive names to your tests. Proper naming helps you understand what the test verifies and how the underlying system behaves.

So, how should you name a unit test? I've seen and tried a lot of naming conventions over the past decade. One of the most prominent, and probably least helpful, is the following convention:

```
[MethodUnderTest]_[Scenario]_[ExpectedResult]
```

where

- `MethodUnderTest` is the name of the method you are testing.
- `Scenario` is the condition under which you test the method.

- ExpectedResult is what you expect the method under test to do in the current scenario.

It's unhelpful specifically because it encourages you to focus on implementation details instead of the behavior.

Simple phrases in plain English do a much better job: they are more expressive and don't box you in a rigid naming structure. With simple phrases, you can describe the system behavior in a way that's meaningful to a customer or a domain expert. To give you an example of a test titled in plain English, here's the test from listing 3.5 once again:

```
public class CalculatorTests
{
    [Fact]
    public void Sum_of_two_numbers()
    {
        double first = 10;
        double second = 20;
        var sut = new Calculator();

        double result = sut.Sum(first, second);

        Assert.Equal(30, result);
    }
}
```

How could the test's name (Sum_of_two_numbers) be rewritten using the [MethodUnder-Test]_[Scenario]_[ExpectedResult] convention? Probably something like this:

```
public void Sum_TwoNumbers_ReturnsSum()
```

The method under test is Sum, the scenario includes two numbers, and the expected result is a sum of those two numbers. The new name looks logical to a programmer's eye, but does it really help with test readability? Not at all. It's Greek to an uninformed person. Think about it: Why does Sum appear twice in the name of the test? And what is this Returns phrasing all about? Where is the sum returned to? You can't know.

Some might argue that it doesn't really matter what a non-programmer would think of this name. After all, unit tests are written by programmers for programmers, not domain experts. And programmers are good at deciphering cryptic names—it's their job!

This is true, but only to a degree. Cryptic names impose a cognitive tax on everyone, programmers or not. They require additional brain capacity to figure out what exactly the test verifies and how it relates to business requirements. This may not seem like much, but the mental burden adds up over time. It slowly but surely increases the maintenance cost for the entire test suite. It's especially noticeable if you return to the test after you've forgotten about the feature's specifics, or try to understand a test written by a colleague. Reading someone else's code is already difficult enough—any help understanding it is of considerable use.

Here are the two versions again:

```
public void Sum_of_two_numbers()
public void Sum_TwoNumbers_ReturnsSum()
```

The initial name written in plain English is much simpler to read. It is a down-to-earth description of the behavior under test.

3.4.1   Unit test naming guidelines

Adhere to the following guidelines to write expressive, easily readable test names:

- *Don't follow a rigid naming policy.* You simply can't fit a high-level description of a complex behavior into the narrow box of such a policy. Allow freedom of expression.
- *Name the test as if you were describing the scenario to a non-programmer who is familiar with the problem domain.* A domain expert or a business analyst is a good example.
- *Separate words with underscores.* Doing so helps improve readability, especially in long names.

Notice that I didn't use underscores when naming the test class, `CalculatorTests`. Normally, the names of classes are not as long, so they read fine without underscores.

Also notice that although I use the pattern `[ClassName]Tests` when naming test classes, it doesn't mean the tests are limited to verifying only that class. Remember, the *unit* in unit testing is a *unit of behavior*, not a class. This unit can span across one or several classes; the actual size is irrelevant. Still, you have to start somewhere. View the class in `[ClassName]Tests` as just that: an entry point, an API, using which you can verify a unit of behavior.

3.4.2   Example: Renaming a test toward the guidelines

Let's take a test as an example and try to gradually improve its name using the guidelines I just outlined. In the following listing, you can see a test verifying that a delivery with a past date is invalid. The test's name is written using the rigid naming policy that doesn't help with the test readability.

Listing 3.10   A test named using the rigid naming policy

```
[Fact]
public void IsDeliveryValid_InvalidDate_ReturnsFalse()
{
    DeliveryService sut = new DeliveryService();
    DateTime pastDate = DateTime.Now.AddDays(-1);
    Delivery delivery = new Delivery
    {
        Date = pastDate
    };
```

```
    bool isValid = sut.IsDeliveryValid(delivery);

    Assert.False(isValid);
}
```

This test checks that `DeliveryService` properly identifies a delivery with an incorrect date as invalid. How would you rewrite the test's name in plain English? The following would be a good first try:

```
public void Delivery_with_invalid_date_should_be_considered_invalid()
```

Notice two things in the new version:

- The name now makes sense to a non-programmer, which means programmers will have an easier time understanding it, too.
- The name of the SUT's method—`IsDeliveryValid`—is no longer part of the test's name.

The second point is a natural consequence of rewriting the test's name in plain English and thus can be easily overlooked. However, this consequence is important and can be elevated into a guideline of its own.

Method under test in the test's name

Don't include the name of the SUT's method in the test's name.

Remember, you don't test *code*, you test *application behavior*. Therefore, it doesn't matter what the name of the method under test is. As I mentioned previously, the SUT is just an entry point: a means to invoke a behavior. You can decide to rename the method under test to, say, `IsDeliveryCorrect`, and it will have no effect on the SUT's behavior. On the other hand, if you follow the original naming convention, you'll have to rename the test. This once again shows that targeting *code* instead of *behavior* couples tests to that code's implementation details, which negatively affects the test suite's maintainability. More on this issue in chapter 5.

The only exception to this guideline is when you work on utility code. Such code doesn't contain business logic—its behavior doesn't go much beyond simple auxiliary functionality and thus doesn't mean anything to business people. It's fine to use the SUT's method names there.

But let's get back to the example. The new version of the test's name is a good start, but it can be improved further. What does it mean for a delivery date to be invalid, exactly? From the test in listing 3.10, we can see that an invalid date is any date in the past. This makes sense—you should only be allowed to choose a delivery date in the future.

So let's be specific and reflect this knowledge in the test's name:

```
public void Delivery_with_past_date_should_be_considered_invalid()
```

This is better but still not ideal. It's too verbose. We can get rid of the word considered without any loss of meaning:

```
public void Delivery_with_past_date_should_be_invalid()
```

The wording *should be* is another common anti-pattern. Earlier in this chapter, I mentioned that a test is a single, atomic fact about a unit of behavior. There's no place for a wish or a desire when stating a fact. Name the test accordingly—replace *should be* with *is*:

```
public void Delivery_with_past_date_is_invalid()
```

And finally, there's no need to avoid basic English grammar. Articles help the test read flawlessly. Add the article *a* to the test's name:

```
public void Delivery_with_a_past_date_is_invalid()
```

There you go. This final version is a straight-to-the-point statement of a fact, which itself describes one of the aspects of the application behavior under test: in this particular case, the aspect of determining whether a delivery can be done.

3.5 *Refactoring to parameterized tests*

One test usually is not enough to fully describe a unit of behavior. Such a unit normally consists of multiple components, each of which should be captured with its own test. If the behavior is complex enough, the number of tests describing it can grow dramatically and may become unmanageable. Luckily, most unit testing frameworks provide functionality that allows you to group similar tests using parameterized tests (see figure 3.2).

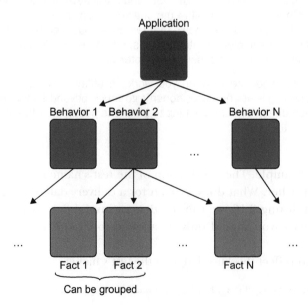

Figure 3.2 **A typical application exhibits multiple behaviors. The greater the complexity of the behavior, the more facts are required to fully describe it. Each fact is represented by a test. Similar facts can be grouped into a single test method using parameterized tests.**

In this section, I'll first show each such behavior component described by a separate test and then demonstrate how these tests can be grouped together.

Let's say that our delivery functionality works in such a way that the soonest allowed delivery date is two days from now. Clearly, the one test we have isn't enough. In addition to the test that checks for a past delivery date, we'll also need tests that check for today's date, tomorrow's date, and the date after that.

The existing test is called `Delivery_with_a_past_date_is_invalid`. We could add three more:

```
public void Delivery_for_today_is_invalid()
public void Delivery_for_tomorrow_is_invalid()
public void The_soonest_delivery_date_is_two_days_from_now()
```

But that would result in four test methods, with the only difference between them being the delivery date.

A better approach is to group these tests into one in order to reduce the amount of test code. xUnit (like most other test frameworks) has a feature called *parameterized tests* that allows you to do exactly that. The next listing shows how such grouping looks. Each `InlineData` attribute represents a separate fact about the system; it's a test case in its own right.

Listing 3.11 A test that encompasses several facts

```
public class DeliveryServiceTests
{
    [InlineData(-1, false)]        The InlineData attribute sends a
    [InlineData(0, false)]         set of input values to the test
    [InlineData(1, false)]         method. Each line represents a
    [InlineData(2, true)]          separate fact about the behavior.
    [Theory]
    public void Can_detect_an_invalid_delivery_date(
        int daysFromNow,
        bool expected)             Parameters to which the attributes
    {                              attach the input values

        DeliveryService sut = new DeliveryService();
        DateTime deliveryDate = DateTime.Now
            .AddDays(daysFromNow);
        Delivery delivery = new Delivery
        {
            Date = deliveryDate
        };                                          Uses the
                                                    parameters
        bool isValid = sut.IsDeliveryValid(delivery);

        Assert.Equal(expected, isValid);
    }
}
```

TIP Notice the use of the `[Theory]` attribute instead of `[Fact]`. A theory is a bunch of facts about the behavior.

Each fact is now represented by an [InlineData] line rather than a separate test. I also renamed the test method something more generic: it no longer mentions what constitutes a valid or invalid date.

Using parameterized tests, you can significantly reduce the amount of test code, but this benefit comes at a cost. It's now hard to figure out what facts the test method represents. And the more parameters there are, the harder it becomes. As a compromise, you can extract the positive test case into its own test and benefit from the descriptive naming where it matters the most—in determining what differentiates valid and invalid delivery dates, as shown in the following listing.

Listing 3.12 Two tests verifying the positive and negative scenarios

```
public class DeliveryServiceTests
{
    [InlineData(-1)]
    [InlineData(0)]
    [InlineData(1)]
    [Theory]
    public void Detects_an_invalid_delivery_date(int daysFromNow)
    {
        /* ... */
    }

    [Fact]
    public void The_soonest_delivery_date_is_two_days_from_now()
    {
        /* ... */
    }
}
```

This approach also simplifies the negative test cases, since you can remove the expected Boolean parameter from the test method. And, of course, you can transform the positive test method into a parameterized test as well, to test multiple dates.

As you can see, there's a trade-off between the amount of test code and the readability of that code. As a rule of thumb, keep both positive and negative test cases together in a single method only when it's self-evident from the input parameters which case stands for what. Otherwise, extract the positive test cases. And if the behavior is too complicated, don't use the parameterized tests at all. Represent each negative and positive test case with its own test method.

3.5.1 *Generating data for parameterized tests*

There are some caveats in using parameterized tests (at least, in .NET) that you need to be aware of. Notice that in listing 3.11, I used the daysFromNow parameter as an input to the test method. Why not the actual date and time, you might ask? Unfortunately, the following code won't work:

```
[InlineData(DateTime.Now.AddDays(-1), false)]
[InlineData(DateTime.Now, false)]
```

```
[InlineData(DateTime.Now.AddDays(1), false)]
[InlineData(DateTime.Now.AddDays(2), true)]
[Theory]
public void Can_detect_an_invalid_delivery_date(
    DateTime deliveryDate,
    bool expected)
{
    DeliveryService sut = new DeliveryService();
    Delivery delivery = new Delivery
    {
        Date = deliveryDate
    };

    bool isValid = sut.IsDeliveryValid(delivery);

    Assert.Equal(expected, isValid);
}
```

In C#, the content of all attributes is evaluated at compile time. You have to use only those values that the compiler can understand, which are as follows:

- Constants
- Literals
- typeof() expressions

The call to DateTime.Now relies on the .NET runtime and thus is not allowed.

There is a way to overcome this problem. xUnit has another feature that you can use to generate custom data to feed into the test method: [MemberData]. The next listing shows how we can rewrite the previous test using this feature.

Listing 3.13 Generating complex data for the parameterized test

```
[Theory]
[MemberData(nameof(Data))]
public void Can_detect_an_invalid_delivery_date(
    DateTime deliveryDate,
    bool expected)
{
    /* ... */
}


public static List<object[]> Data()
{
    return new List<object[]>
    {
        new object[] { DateTime.Now.AddDays(-1), false },
        new object[] { DateTime.Now, false },
        new object[] { DateTime.Now.AddDays(1), false },
        new object[] { DateTime.Now.AddDays(2), true }
    };
}
```

`MemberData` accepts the name of a static method that generates a collection of input data (the compiler translates `nameof(Data)` into a `"Data"` literal). Each element of the collection is itself a collection that is mapped into the two input parameters: `deliveryDate` and `expected`. With this feature, you can overcome the compiler's restrictions and use parameters of any type in the parameterized tests.

3.6   *Using an assertion library to further improve test readability*

One more thing you can do to improve test readability is to use an assertion library. I personally prefer Fluent Assertions (https://fluentassertions.com), but .NET has several competing libraries in this area.

The main benefit of using an assertion library is how you can restructure the assertions so that they are more readable. Here's one of our earlier tests:

```
[Fact]
public void Sum_of_two_numbers()
{
    var sut = new Calculator();

    double result = sut.Sum(10, 20);

    Assert.Equal(30, result);
}
```

Now compare it to the following, which uses a fluent assertion:

```
[Fact]
public void Sum_of_two_numbers()
{
    var sut = new Calculator();

    double result = sut.Sum(10, 20);

    result.Should().Be(30);
}
```

The assertion from the second test reads as plain English, which is exactly how you want all your code to read. We as humans prefer to absorb information in the form of stories. All stories adhere to this specific pattern:

```
[Subject] [action] [object].
```

For example,

```
Bob opened the door.
```

Here, `Bob` is a subject, `opened` is an action, and `the door` is an object. The same rule applies to code. `result.Should().Be(30)` reads better than `Assert.Equal(30,` result) precisely because it follows the story pattern. It's a simple story in which result is a subject, should be is an action, and 30 is an object.

> **NOTE** The paradigm of object-oriented programming (OOP) has become a success partly because of this readability benefit. With OOP, you, too, can structure the code in a way that reads like a story.

The Fluent Assertions library also provides numerous helper methods to assert against numbers, strings, collections, dates and times, and much more. The only drawback is that such a library is an additional dependency you may not want to introduce to your project (although it's for development only and won't be shipped to production).

Summary

- All unit tests should follow the AAA pattern: *arrange, act, assert.* If a test has multiple *arrange, act,* or *assert* sections, that's a sign that the test verifies multiple units of behavior at once. If this test is meant to be a unit test, split it into several tests—one per each action.
- More than one line in the *act* section is a sign of a problem with the SUT's API. It requires the client to remember to always perform these actions together, which can potentially lead to inconsistencies. Such inconsistencies are called *invariant violations.* The act of protecting your code against potential invariant violations is called *encapsulation.*
- Distinguish the SUT in tests by naming it sut. Differentiate the three test sections either by putting Arrange, Act, and Assert comments before them or by introducing empty lines between these sections.
- Reuse test fixture initialization code by introducing factory methods, not by putting this initialization code to the constructor. Such reuse helps maintain a high degree of decoupling between tests and also provides better readability.
- Don't use a rigid test naming policy. Name each test as if you were describing the scenario in it to a non-programmer who is familiar with the problem domain. Separate words in the test name by underscores, and don't include the name of the method under test in the test name.
- Parameterized tests help reduce the amount of code needed for similar tests. The drawback is that the test names become less readable as you make them more generic.
- Assertion libraries help you further improve test readability by restructuring the word order in assertions so that they read like plain English.

Part 2

Making your tests work for you

N ow that you're armed with the knowledge of what unit testing is for, you're ready to dive into the very crux of what makes a good test and learn how to refactor your tests toward being more valuable. In chapter 4, you'll learn about the four pillars that make up a good unit test. These four pillars set a foundation, a common frame of reference, which we'll use to analyze unit tests and testing approaches moving forward.

Chapter 5 takes the frame of reference established in chapter 4 and builds the case for mocks and their relation to test fragility.

Chapter 6 uses the same the frame of reference to examine the three styles of unit testing. It shows which of those styles tends to produce tests of the best quality, and why.

Chapter 7 puts the knowledge from chapters 4 to 6 into practice and teaches you how to refactor away from bloated, overcomplicated tests to tests that provide as much value with as little maintenance cost as possible.

*The four pillars
of a good unit test*

4

This chapter covers

- Exploring dichotomies between aspects of a good unit test
- Defining an ideal test
- Understanding the Test Pyramid
- Using black-box and white-box testing

Now we are getting to the heart of the matter. In chapter 1, you saw the properties of a good unit test suite:

- *It is integrated into the development cycle.* You only get value from tests that you actively use; there's no point in writing them otherwise.
- *It targets only the most important parts of your code base.* Not all production code deserves equal attention. It's important to differentiate the heart of the application (its *domain model*) from everything else. This topic is tackled in chapter 7.
- *It provides maximum value with minimum maintenance costs.* To achieve this last attribute, you need to be able to
  - Recognize a valuable test (and, by extension, a test of low value)
  - Write a valuable test

As we discussed in chapter 1, *recognizing a valuable test* and *writing a valuable test* are two separate skills. The latter skill requires the former one, though; so, in this chapter, I'll show how to recognize a valuable test. You'll see a universal frame of reference with which you can analyze any test in the suite. We'll then use this frame of reference to go over some popular unit testing concepts: the Test Pyramid and black-box versus white-box testing.

Buckle up: we are starting out.

4.1 Diving into the four pillars of a good unit test

A good unit test has the following four attributes:

- Protection against regressions
- Resistance to refactoring
- Fast feedback
- Maintainability

These four attributes are foundational. You can use them to analyze any automated test, be it unit, integration, or end-to-end. Every such test exhibits some degree of each attribute. In this section, I define the first two attributes; and in section 4.2, I describe the intrinsic connection between them.

4.1.1 The first pillar: Protection against regressions

Let's start with the first attribute of a good unit test: *protection against regressions*. As you know from chapter 1, a *regression* is a software bug. It's when a feature stops working as intended after some code modification, usually after you roll out new functionality.

Such regressions are annoying (to say the least), but that's not the worst part about them. The worst part is that the more features you develop, the more chances there are that you'll break one of those features with a new release. An unfortunate fact of programming life is that *code is not an asset, it's a liability*. The larger the code base, the more exposure it has to potential bugs. That's why it's crucial to develop a good protection against regressions. Without such protection, you won't be able to sustain the project growth in a long run—you'll be buried under an ever-increasing number of bugs.

To evaluate how well a test scores on the metric of protecting against regressions, you need to take into account the following:

- The amount of code that is executed during the test
- The complexity of that code
- The code's domain significance

Generally, the larger the amount of code that gets executed, the higher the chance that the test will reveal a regression. Of course, assuming that this test has a relevant set of assertions, you don't want to merely execute the code. While it helps to know that this code runs without throwing exceptions, you also need to validate the outcome it produces.

Note that it's not only the amount of code that matters, but also its complexity and domain significance. Code that represents complex business logic is more important than boilerplate code—bugs in business-critical functionality are the most damaging.

On the other hand, it's rarely worthwhile to test trivial code. Such code is short and doesn't contain a substantial amount of business logic. Tests that cover trivial code don't have much of a chance of finding a regression error, because there's not a lot of room for a mistake. An example of trivial code is a single-line property like this:

```
public class User
{
    public string Name { get; set; }
}
```

Furthermore, in addition to your code, the code you didn't write also counts: for example, libraries, frameworks, and any external systems used in the project. That code influences the working of your software almost as much as your own code. For the best protection, the test must include those libraries, frameworks, and external systems in the testing scope, in order to check that the assumptions your software makes about these dependencies are correct.

> **TIP** To maximize the metric of protection against regressions, the test needs to aim at exercising as much code as possible.

4.1.2 *The second pillar: Resistance to refactoring*

The second attribute of a good unit test is *resistance to refactoring* (or *resilience to refactoring*)—the degree to which a test can sustain a refactoring of the underlying application code without turning red (failing).

> **DEFINITION** *Refactoring* means changing existing code without modifying its observable behavior. The intention is usually to improve the code's nonfunctional characteristics: increase readability and reduce complexity. Some examples of refactoring are renaming a method and extracting a piece of code into a new class.

Picture this situation. You developed a new feature, and everything works great. The feature itself is doing its job, and all the tests are passing. Now you decide to clean up the code. You do some refactoring here, a little bit of modification there, and everything looks even better than before. Except one thing—the tests are failing. You look more closely to see exactly what you broke with the refactoring, but it turns out that you didn't break anything. The feature works perfectly, just as before. The problem is that the tests are written in such a way that they turn red with any modification of the underlying code. And they do that regardless of whether you actually break the functionality itself.

This situation is called a *false positive*. A false positive is a false alarm. It's a result indicating that the test fails, although in reality, the functionality it covers works as intended. Such false positives usually take place when you refactor the code—when you modify the implementation but keep the observable behavior intact. Hence the name for this attribute of a good unit test: *resistance to refactoring.*

To evaluate how well a test scores on the metric of resisting to refactoring, you need to look at how many false positives the test generates. The fewer, the better.

Why so much attention on false positives? Because they can have a devastating effect on your entire test suite. As you may recall from chapter 1, the goal of unit testing is to enable sustainable project growth. The mechanism by which the tests enable sustainable growth is that they allow you to add new features and conduct regular refactorings without introducing regressions. There are two specific benefits here:

- *Tests provide an early warning when you break existing functionality.* Thanks to such early warnings, you can fix an issue long before the faulty code is deployed to production, where dealing with it would require a significantly larger amount of effort.
- *You become confident that your code changes won't lead to regressions.* Without such confidence, you will be much more hesitant to refactor and much more likely to leave the code base to deteriorate.

False positives interfere with both of these benefits:

- If tests fail with no good reason, they dilute your ability and willingness to react to problems in code. Over time, you get accustomed to such failures and stop paying as much attention. After a while, you start ignoring legitimate failures, too, allowing them to slip into production.
- On the other hand, when false positives are frequent, you slowly lose trust in the test suite. You no longer perceive it as a reliable safety net—the perception is diminished by false alarms. This lack of trust leads to fewer refactorings, because you try to reduce code changes to a minimum in order to avoid regressions.

A story from the trenches

I once worked on a project with a rich history. The project wasn't too old, maybe two or three years; but during that period of time, management significantly shifted the direction they wanted to go with the project, and development changed direction accordingly. During this change, a problem emerged: the code base accumulated large chunks of leftover code that no one dared to delete or refactor. The company no longer needed the features that code provided, but some parts of it were used in new functionality, so it was impossible to get rid of the old code completely.

The project had good test coverage. But every time someone tried to refactor the old features and separate the bits that were still in use from everything else, the tests failed. And not just the old tests—they had been disabled long ago—but the new tests, too. Some of the failures were legitimate, but most were not—they were false positives.

At first, the developers tried to deal with the test failures. However, since the vast majority of them were false alarms, the situation got to the point where the developers ignored such failures and disabled the failing tests. The prevailing attitude was, "If it's because of that old chunk of code, just disable the test; we'll look at it later."

Everything worked fine for a while—until a major bug slipped into production. One of the tests correctly identified the bug, but no one listened; the test was disabled along with all the others. After that accident, the developers stopped touching the old code entirely.

This story is typical of most projects with brittle tests. First, developers take test failures at face value and deal with them accordingly. After a while, people get tired of tests crying "wolf" all the time and start to ignore them more and more. Eventually, there comes a moment when a bunch of real bugs are released to production because developers ignored the failures along with all the false positives.

You don't want to react to such a situation by ceasing all refactorings, though. The correct response is to re-evaluate the test suite and start reducing its brittleness. I cover this topic in chapter 7.

4.1.3　*What causes false positives?*

So, what causes false positives? And how can you avoid them?

The number of false positives a test produces is directly related to the way the test is structured. The more the test is coupled to the implementation details of the system under test (SUT), the more false alarms it generates. The only way to reduce the chance of getting a false positive is to decouple the test from those implementation details. You need to make sure the test verifies the end result the SUT delivers: its observable behavior, not the steps it takes to do that. Tests should approach SUT verification from the end user's point of view and check only the outcome meaningful to that end user. Everything else must be disregarded (more on this topic in chapter 5).

The best way to structure a test is to make it tell a story about the problem domain. Should such a test fail, that failure would mean there's a disconnect between the story and the actual application behavior. It's the only type of test failure that benefits you—such failures are always on point and help you quickly understand what went wrong. All other failures are just noise that steer your attention away from things that matter.

Take a look at the following example. In it, the `MessageRenderer` class generates an HTML representation of a message containing a header, a body, and a footer.

Listing 4.1　Generating an HTML representation of a message

```
public class Message
{
    public string Header { get; set; }
    public string Body { get; set; }
    public string Footer { get; set; }
}
```

```
public interface IRenderer
{
    string Render(Message message);
}


public class MessageRenderer : IRenderer
{
    public IReadOnlyList<IRenderer> SubRenderers { get; }

    public MessageRenderer()
    {
        SubRenderers = new List<IRenderer>
        {
            new HeaderRenderer(),
            new BodyRenderer(),
            new FooterRenderer()
        };
    }

    public string Render(Message message)
    {
        return SubRenderers
            .Select(x => x.Render(message))
            .Aggregate("", (str1, str2) => str1 + str2);
    }
}
```

The `MessageRenderer` class contains several sub-renderers to which it delegates the actual work on parts of the message. It then combines the result into an HTML document. The sub-renderers orchestrate the raw text with HTML tags. For example:

```
public class BodyRenderer : IRenderer
{
    public string Render(Message message)
    {
        return $"<b>{message.Body}</b>";
    }
}
```

How can `MessageRenderer` be tested? One possible approach is to analyze the algorithm this class follows.

Listing 4.2   Verifying that `MessageRenderer` has the correct structure

```
[Fact]
public void MessageRenderer_uses_correct_sub_renderers()
{
    var sut = new MessageRenderer();

    IReadOnlyList<IRenderer> renderers = sut.SubRenderers;
```

```
    Assert.Equal(3, renderers.Count);
    Assert.IsAssignableFrom<HeaderRenderer>(renderers[0]);
    Assert.IsAssignableFrom<BodyRenderer>(renderers[1]);
    Assert.IsAssignableFrom<FooterRenderer>(renderers[2]);
}
```

This test checks to see if the sub-renderers are all of the expected types and appear in the correct order, which presumes that the way `MessageRenderer` processes messages must also be correct. The test might look good at first, but does it really verify `Message-Renderer`'s observable behavior? What if you rearrange the sub-renderers, or replace one of them with a new one? Will that lead to a bug?

Not necessarily. You could change a sub-renderer's composition in such a way that the resulting HTML document remains the same. For example, you could replace `BodyRenderer` with a `BoldRenderer`, which does the same job as `BodyRenderer`. Or you could get rid of all the sub-renderers and implement the rendering directly in `Message-Renderer`.

Still, the test will turn red if you do any of that, even though the end result won't change. That's because the test couples to the SUT's implementation details and not the outcome the SUT produces. This test inspects the algorithm and expects to see one particular implementation, without any consideration for equally applicable alternative implementations (see figure 4.1).

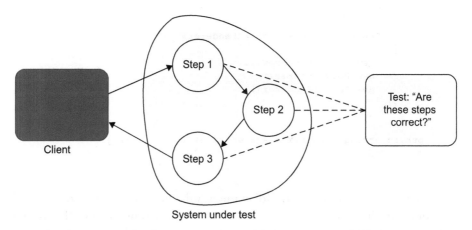

Figure 4.1 A test that couples to the SUT's algorithm. Such a test expects to see one particular implementation (the specific steps the SUT must take to deliver the result) and therefore is brittle. Any refactoring of the SUT's implementation would lead to a test failure.

Any substantial refactoring of the `MessageRenderer` class would lead to a test failure. Mind you, the process of *refactoring* is changing the implementation without affecting the application's observable behavior. And it's precisely because the test is concerned with the implementation details that it turns red every time you change those details.

Therefore, *tests that couple to the SUT's implementation details are not resistant to refactoring.* Such tests exhibit all the shortcomings I described previously:

- They don't provide an early warning in the event of regressions—you simply ignore those warnings due to little relevance.
- They hinder your ability and willingness to refactor. It's no wonder—who would like to refactor, knowing that the tests can't tell which way is up when it comes to finding bugs?

The next listing shows the most egregious example of brittleness in tests that I've ever encountered, in which the test reads the source code of the `MessageRenderer` class and compares it to the "correct" implementation.

Listing 4.3   Verifying the source code of the `MessageRenderer` class

```
[Fact]
public void MessageRenderer_is_implemented_correctly()
{
    string sourceCode = File.ReadAllText(@"[path]\MessageRenderer.cs");

    Assert.Equal(@"
public class MessageRenderer : IRenderer
{
    public IReadOnlyList<<IRenderer> SubRenderers { get; }

    public MessageRenderer()
    {
        SubRenderers = new List<<IRenderer>
        {
            new HeaderRenderer(),
            new BodyRenderer(),
            new FooterRenderer()
        };
    }

    public string Render(Message message) { /* ... */ }
}", sourceCode);
}
```

Of course, this test is just plain ridiculous; it will fail should you modify even the slightest detail in the `MessageRenderer` class. At the same time, it's not that different from the test I brought up earlier. Both insist on a particular implementation without taking into consideration the SUT's observable behavior. And both will turn red each time you change that implementation. Admittedly, though, the test in listing 4.3 will break more often than the one in listing 4.2.

4.1.4   *Aim at the end result instead of implementation details*

As I mentioned earlier, the only way to avoid brittleness in tests and increase their resistance to refactoring is to decouple them from the SUT's implementation details—keep as much distance as possible between the test and the code's inner workings, and instead aim at verifying the end result. Let's do that: let's refactor the test from listing 4.2 into something much less brittle.

To start off, you need to ask yourself the following question: What is the final outcome you get from `MessageRenderer`? Well, it's the HTML representation of a message. And it's the only thing that makes sense to check, since it's the only observable result you get out of the class. As long as this HTML representation stays the same, there's no need to worry about exactly how it's generated. Such implementation details are irrelevant. The following code is the new version of the test.

> **Listing 4.4 Verifying the outcome that `MessageRenderer` produces**

```
[Fact]
public void Rendering_a_message()
{
    var sut = new MessageRenderer();
    var message = new Message
    {
        Header = "h",
        Body = "b",
        Footer = "f"
    };

    string html = sut.Render(message);

    Assert.Equal("<h1>h</h1><b>b</b><i>f</i>", html);
}
```

This test treats `MessageRenderer` as a black box and is only interested in its observable behavior. As a result, the test is much more resistant to refactoring—it doesn't care what changes you make to the SUT as long as the HTML output remains the same (figure 4.2).

Notice the profound improvement in this test over the original version. It aligns itself with the business needs by verifying the only outcome meaningful to end users—

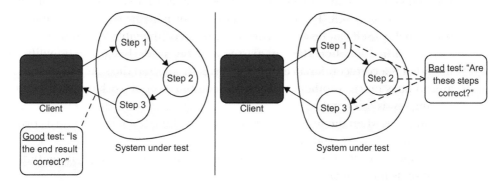

Figure 4.2 The test on the left couples to the SUT's observable behavior as opposed to implementation details. Such a test is resistant to refactoring—it will trigger few, if any, false positives.

how a message is displayed in the browser. Failures of such a test are always on point: they communicate a change in the application behavior that can affect the customer and thus should be brought to the developer's attention. This test will produce few, if any, false positives.

Why *few* and not *none at all?* Because there could still be changes in Message-Renderer that would break the test. For example, you could introduce a new parameter in the Render() method, causing a compilation error. And technically, such an error counts as a false positive, too. After all, the test isn't failing because of a change in the application's behavior.

But this kind of false positive is easy to fix. Just follow the compiler and add a new parameter to all tests that invoke the Render() method. The worse false positives are those that don't lead to compilation errors. Such false positives are the hardest to deal with—they seem as though they point to a legitimate bug and require much more time to investigate.

4.2   The intrinsic connection between the first two attributes

As I mentioned earlier, there's an intrinsic connection between the first two pillars of a good unit test—*protection against regressions* and *resistance to refactoring*. They both contribute to the accuracy of the test suite, though from opposite perspectives. These two attributes also tend to influence the project differently over time: while it's important to have good protection against regressions very soon after the project's initiation, the need for resistance to refactoring is not immediate.

In this section, I talk about

- Maximizing test accuracy
- The importance of false positives and false negatives

4.2.1   Maximizing test accuracy

Let's step back for a second and look at the broader picture with regard to test results. When it comes to code correctness and test results, there are four possible outcomes, as shown in figure 4.3. The test can either pass or fail (the rows of the table). And the functionality itself can be either correct or broken (the table's columns).

The situation when the test passes and the underlying functionality works as intended is a correct inference: the test correctly inferred the state of the system (there are no bugs in it). Another term for this combination of working functionality and a passing test is *true negative.*

Similarly, when the functionality is broken and the test fails, it's also a correct inference. That's because you expect to see the test fail when the functionality is not working properly. That's the whole point of unit testing. The corresponding term for this situation is *true positive.*

But when the test doesn't catch an error, that's a problem. This is the upper-right quadrant, a *false negative.* And this is what the first attribute of a good test—protection

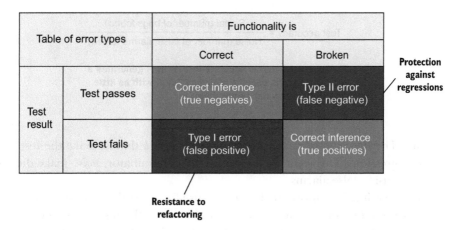

Table of error types		Functionality is	
		Correct	Broken
Test result	Test passes	Correct inference (true negatives)	Type II error (false negative)
	Test fails	Type I error (false positive)	Correct inference (true positives)

Protection against regressions

Resistance to refactoring

Figure 4.3 The relationship between protection against regressions and resistance to refactoring. Protection against regressions guards against false negatives (type II errors). Resistance to refactoring minimizes the number of false positives (type I errors).

against regressions—helps you avoid. Tests with a good protection against regressions help you to minimize the number of *false negatives*—type II errors.

On the other hand, there's a symmetric situation when the functionality is correct but the test still shows a failure. This is a *false positive*, a false alarm. And this is what the second attribute—resistance to refactoring—helps you with.

All these terms (*false positive, type I error* and so on) have roots in statistics, but can also be applied to analyzing a test suite. The best way to wrap your head around them is to think of a flu test. A flu test is positive when the person taking the test has the flu. The term *positive* is a bit confusing because there's nothing positive about having the flu. But the test doesn't evaluate the situation as a whole. In the context of testing, *positive* means that some set of conditions is now true. Those are the conditions the creators of the test have set it to react to. In this particular example, it's the presence of the flu. Conversely, the lack of flu renders the flu test *negative.*

Now, when you evaluate how accurate the flu test is, you bring up terms such as *false positive* or *false negative*. The probability of false positives and false negatives tells you how good the flu test is: the lower that probability, the more accurate the test.

This accuracy is what the first two pillars of a good unit test are all about. *Protection against regressions* and *resistance to refactoring* aim at maximizing the accuracy of the test suite. The accuracy metric itself consists of two components:

- How good the test is at indicating the presence of bugs (lack of false negatives, the sphere of *protection against regressions*)
- How good the test is at indicating the absence of bugs (lack of false positives, the sphere of *resistance to refactoring*)

Another way to think of false positives and false negatives is in terms of signal-to-noise ratio. As you can see from the formula in figure 4.4, there are two ways to improve test

$$\text{Test accuracy} = \frac{\text{Signal (number of bugs found)}}{\text{Noise (number of false alarms raised)}}$$

Figure 4.4   A test is accurate insofar as it generates a strong signal (is capable of finding bugs) with as little noise (false alarms) as possible.

accuracy. The first is to increase the numerator, *signal*: that is, make the test better at finding regressions. The second is to reduce the denominator, *noise*: make the test better at not raising false alarms.

Both are critically important. There's no use for a test that isn't capable of finding any bugs, even if it doesn't raise false alarms. Similarly, the test's accuracy goes to zero when it generates a lot of noise, even if it's capable of finding all the bugs in code. These findings are simply lost in the sea of irrelevant information.

4.2.2   *The importance of false positives and false negatives: The dynamics*

In the short term, false positives are not as bad as false negatives. In the beginning of a project, receiving a wrong warning is not that big a deal as opposed to not being warned at all and running the risk of a bug slipping into production. But as the project grows, false positives start to have an increasingly large effect on the test suite (figure 4.5).

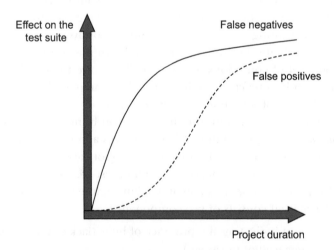

Figure 4.5   False positives (false alarms) don't have as much of a negative effect in the beginning. But they become increasingly important as the project grows—as important as false negatives (unnoticed bugs).

Why are false positives not as important initially? Because the importance of refactoring is also not immediate; it increases gradually over time. You don't need to conduct many code clean-ups in the beginning of the project. Newly written code is often shiny and flawless. It's also still fresh in your memory, so you can easily refactor it even if tests raise false alarms.

But as time goes on, the code base deteriorates. It becomes increasingly complex and disorganized. Thus you have to start conducting regular refactorings in order to mitigate this tendency. Otherwise, the cost of introducing new features eventually becomes prohibitive.

As the need for refactoring increases, the importance of *resistance to refactoring* in tests increases with it. As I explained earlier, you can't refactor when the tests keep crying "wolf" and you keep getting warnings about bugs that don't exist. You quickly lose trust in such tests and stop viewing them as a reliable source of feedback.

Despite the importance of protecting your code against false positives, especially in the later project stages, few developers perceive false positives this way. Most people tend to focus solely on improving the first attribute of a good unit test—protection against regressions, which is not enough to build a valuable, highly accurate test suite that helps sustain project growth.

The reason, of course, is that far fewer projects get to those later stages, mostly because they are small and the development finishes before the project becomes too big. Thus developers face the problem of unnoticed bugs more often than false alarms that swarm the project and hinder all refactoring undertakings. And so, people optimize accordingly. Nevertheless, if you work on a medium to large project, you have to pay equal attention to both false negatives (unnoticed bugs) and false positives (false alarms).

4.3 The third and fourth pillars: Fast feedback and maintainability

In this section, I talk about the two remaining pillars of a good unit test:

- Fast feedback
- Maintainability

As you may remember from chapter 2, fast feedback is an essential property of a unit test. The faster the tests, the more of them you can have in the suite and the more often you can run them.

With tests that run quickly, you can drastically shorten the feedback loop, to the point where the tests begin to warn you about bugs as soon as you break the code, thus reducing the cost of fixing those bugs almost to zero. On the other hand, slow tests delay the feedback and potentially prolong the period during which the bugs remain unnoticed, thus increasing the cost of fixing them. That's because slow tests discourage you from running them often, and therefore lead to wasting more time moving in a wrong direction.

Finally, the fourth pillar of good units tests, the maintainability metric, evaluates maintenance costs. This metric consists of two major components:

- *How hard it is to understand the test*—This component is related to the size of the test. The fewer lines of code in the test, the more readable the test is. It's also easier to change a small test when needed. Of course, that's assuming you don't try to compress the test code artificially just to reduce the line count. The quality of the test code matters as much as the production code. Don't cut corners when writing tests; treat the test code as a first-class citizen.

- *How hard it is to run the test*—If the test works with out-of-process dependencies, you have to spend time keeping those dependencies operational: reboot the database server, resolve network connectivity issues, and so on.

4.4   *In search of an ideal test*

Here are the four attributes of a good unit test once again:

- Protection against regressions
- Resistance to refactoring
- Fast feedback
- Maintainability

These four attributes, when multiplied together, determine the value of a test. And by *multiplied*, I mean in a mathematical sense; that is, if a test gets zero in one of the attributes, its value turns to zero as well:

```
Value estimate = [0..1] * [0..1] * [0..1] * [0..1]
```

> **TIP**   In order to be valuable, the test needs to score at least something in all four categories.

Of course, it's impossible to measure these attributes precisely. There's no code analysis tool you can plug a test into and get the exact numbers. But you can still evaluate the test pretty accurately to see where a test stands with regard to the four attributes. This evaluation, in turn, gives you the test's value estimate, which you can use to decide whether to keep the test in the suite.

Remember, all code, including test code, is a liability. Set a fairly high threshold for the minimum required value, and only allow tests in the suite if they meet this threshold. A small number of highly valuable tests will do a much better job sustaining project growth than a large number of mediocre tests.

I'll show some examples shortly. For now, let's examine whether it's possible to create an ideal test.

4.4.1 Is it possible to create an ideal test?

An ideal test is a test that scores the maximum in all four attributes. If you take the minimum and maximum values as 0 and 1 for each of the attributes, an ideal test must get 1 in all of them.

Unfortunately, it's impossible to create such an ideal test. The reason is that the first three attributes—*protection against regressions, resistance to refactoring,* and *fast feedback*—are mutually exclusive. It's impossible to maximize them all: you have to sacrifice one of the three in order to max out the remaining two.

Moreover, because of the multiplication principle (see the calculation of the value estimate in the previous section), it's even trickier to keep the balance. You can't just forgo one of the attributes in order to focus on the others. As I mentioned previously, a test that scores zero in one of the four categories is worthless. Therefore, you have to maximize these attributes in such a way that none of them is diminished too much. Let's look at some examples of tests that aim at maximizing two out of three attributes at the expense of the third and, as a result, have a value that's close to zero.

4.4.2 Extreme case #1: End-to-end tests

The first example is end-to-end tests. As you may remember from chapter 2, end-to-end tests look at the system from the end user's perspective. They normally go through all of the system's components, including the UI, database, and external applications.

Since end-to-end tests exercise a lot of code, they provide the best protection against regressions. In fact, of all types of tests, end-to-end tests exercise the most code—both your code and the code you didn't write but use in the project, such as external libraries, frameworks, and third-party applications.

End-to-end tests are also immune to false positives and thus have a good resistance to refactoring. A refactoring, if done correctly, doesn't change the system's observable behavior and therefore doesn't affect the end-to-end tests. That's another advantage of such tests: they don't impose any particular implementation. The only thing end-to-end tests look at is how a feature behaves from the end user's point of view. They are as removed from implementation details as tests could possibly be.

However, despite these benefits, end-to-end tests have a major drawback: they are slow. Any system that relies solely on such tests would have a hard time getting rapid feedback. And that is a deal-breaker for many development teams. This is why it's pretty much impossible to cover your code base with only end-to-end tests.

Figure 4.6 shows where end-to-end tests stand with regard to the first three unit testing metrics. Such tests provide great protection against both regression errors and false positives, but lack speed.

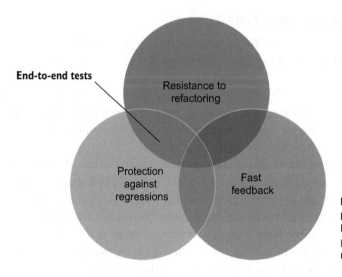

Figure 4.6   End-to-end tests provide great protection against both regression errors and false positives, but they fail at the metric of fast feedback.

4.4.3   *Extreme case #2: Trivial tests*

Another example of maximizing two out of three attributes at the expense of the third is a *trivial test*. Such tests cover a simple piece of code, something that is unlikely to break because it's too trivial, as shown in the following listing.

Listing 4.5   Trivial test covering a simple piece of code

```
public class User
{
    public string Name { get; set; }      ◁⎯  One-liners like
}                                              this are unlikely
                                               to contain bugs.
[Fact]
public void Test()
{
    var sut = new User();

    sut.Name = "John Smith";

    Assert.Equal("John Smith", sut.Name);
}
```

Unlike end-to-end tests, trivial tests do provide fast feedback—they run very quickly. They also have a fairly low chance of producing a false positive, so they have good resistance to refactoring. Trivial tests are unlikely to reveal any regressions, though, because there's not much room for a mistake in the underlying code.

Trivial tests taken to an extreme result in *tautology* tests. They don't test anything because they are set up in such a way that they always pass or contain semantically meaningless assertions.

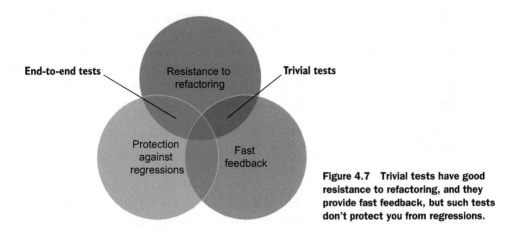

Figure 4.7 Trivial tests have good resistance to refactoring, and they provide fast feedback, but such tests don't protect you from regressions.

Figure 4.7 shows where trivial tests stand. They have good resistance to refactoring and provide fast feedback, but they don't protect you from regressions.

4.4.4 *Extreme case #3: Brittle tests*

Similarly, it's pretty easy to write a test that runs fast and has a good chance of catching a regression but does so with a lot of false positives. Such a test is called a *brittle test*: it can't withstand a refactoring and will turn red regardless of whether the underlying functionality is broken.

You already saw an example of a brittle test in listing 4.2. Here's another one.

Listing 4.6 Test verifying which SQL statement is executed

```
public class UserRepository
{
    public User GetById(int id)
    {
        /* ... */
    }

    public string LastExecutedSqlStatement { get; set; }
}

[Fact]
public void GetById_executes_correct_SQL_code()
{
    var sut = new UserRepository();

    User user = sut.GetById(5);

    Assert.Equal(
        "SELECT * FROM dbo.[User] WHERE UserID = 5",
        sut.LastExecutedSqlStatement);
}
```

This test makes sure the UserRepository class generates a correct SQL statement when fetching a user from the database. Can this test catch a bug? It can. For example, a developer can mess up the SQL code generation and mistakenly use ID instead of UserID, and the test will point that out by raising a failure. But does this test have good resistance to refactoring? Absolutely not. Here are different variations of the SQL statement that lead to the same result:

```
SELECT * FROM dbo.[User] WHERE UserID = 5
SELECT * FROM dbo.User WHERE UserID = 5
SELECT UserID, Name, Email FROM dbo.[User] WHERE UserID = 5
SELECT * FROM dbo.[User] WHERE UserID = @UserID
```

The test in listing 4.6 will turn red if you change the SQL script to any of these variations, even though the functionality itself will remain operational. This is once again an example of coupling the test to the SUT's internal implementation details. The test is focusing on *hows* instead of *whats* and thus ingrains the SUT's implementation details, preventing any further refactoring.

Figure 4.8 shows that brittle tests fall into the third bucket. Such tests run fast and provide good protection against regressions but have little resistance to refactoring.

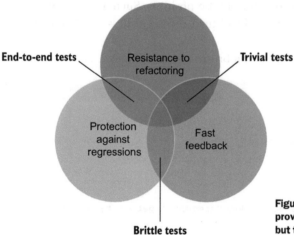

Figure 4.8   Brittle tests run fast and they provide good protection against regressions, but they have little resistance to refactoring.

4.4.5   *In search of an ideal test: The results*

The first three attributes of a good unit test (*protection against regressions, resistance to refactoring,* and *fast feedback*) are mutually exclusive. While it's quite easy to come up with a test that maximizes two out of these three attributes, you can only do that at the expense of the third. Still, such a test would have a close-to-zero value due to the multiplication rule. Unfortunately, it's impossible to create an ideal test that has a perfect score in all three attributes (figure 4.9).

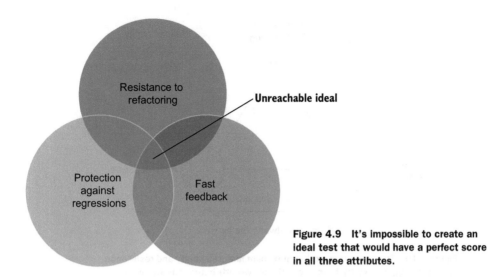

Figure 4.9 It's impossible to create an ideal test that would have a perfect score in all three attributes.

The fourth attribute, *maintainability*, is not correlated to the first three, with the exception of end-to-end tests. End-to-end tests are normally larger in size because of the necessity to set up all the dependencies such tests reach out to. They also require additional effort to keep those dependencies operational. Hence end-to-end tests tend to be more expensive in terms of maintenance costs.

It's hard to keep a balance between the attributes of a good test. A test can't have the maximum score in each of the first three categories, and you also have to keep an eye on the maintainability aspect so the test remains reasonably short and simple. Therefore, you have to make trade-offs. Moreover, you should make those trade-offs in such a way that no particular attribute turns to zero. The sacrifices have to be partial and strategic.

What should those sacrifices look like? Because of the mutual exclusiveness of *protection against regressions*, *resistance to refactoring*, and *fast feedback*, you may think that the best strategy is to concede a little bit of each: just enough to make room for all three attributes.

In reality, though, *resistance to refactoring* is non-negotiable. You should aim at gaining as much of it as you can, provided that your tests remain reasonably quick and you don't resort to the exclusive use of end-to-end tests. The trade-off, then, comes down to the choice between how good your tests are at pointing out bugs and how fast they do that: that is, between *protection against regressions* and *fast feedback*. You can view this choice as a slider that can be freely moved between *protection against regressions* and *fast feedback*. The more you gain in one attribute, the more you lose on the other (see figure 4.10).

The reason *resistance to refactoring* is non-negotiable is that whether a test possesses this attribute is mostly a binary choice: the test either has resistance to refactoring or it doesn't. There are almost no intermediate stages in between. Thus you can't concede

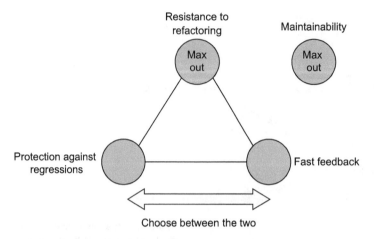

Figure 4.10   The best tests exhibit maximum maintainability and resistance to refactoring; always try to max out these two attributes. The trade-off comes down to the choice between protection against regressions and fast feedback.

just a little *resistance to refactoring*: you'll have to lose it all. On the other hand, the metrics of *protection against regressions* and *fast feedback* are more malleable. You will see in the next section what kind of trade-offs are possible when you choose one over the other.

TIP   Eradicating brittleness (false positives) in tests is the first priority on the path to a robust test suite.

The CAP theorem

The trade-off between the first three attributes of a good unit test is similar to the CAP theorem. The CAP theorem states that it is impossible for a distributed data store to simultaneously provide more than two of the following three guarantees:

- *Consistency*, which means every read receives the most recent write or an error.
- *Availability*, which means every request receives a response (apart from outages that affect all nodes in the system).
- *Partition tolerance*, which means the system continues to operate despite network partitioning (losing connection between network nodes).

The similarity is two-fold:

- First, there is the *two-out-of-three* trade-off.
- Second, the *partition tolerance* component in large-scale distributed systems is also non-negotiable. A large application such as, for example, the Amazon website can't operate on a single machine. The option of preferring *consistency* and *availability* at the expense of *partition tolerance* simply isn't on the table—Amazon has too much data to store on a single server, however big that server is.

The choice, then, also boils down to a trade-off between *consistency* and *availability*. In some parts of the system, it's preferable to concede a little consistency to gain more availability. For example, when displaying a product catalog, it's generally fine if some parts of the catalog are out of date. *Availability* is of higher priority in this scenario. On the other hand, when updating a product description, *consistency* is more important than *availability*: network nodes must have a consensus on what the most recent version of that description is, in order to avoid merge conflicts.

4.5 *Exploring well-known test automation concepts*

The four attributes of a good unit test shown earlier are foundational. All existing, well-known test automation concepts can be traced back to these four attributes. In this section, we'll look at two such concepts: the Test Pyramid and white-box versus black-box testing.

4.5.1 *Breaking down the Test Pyramid*

The *Test Pyramid* is a concept that advocates for a certain ratio of different types of tests in the test suite (figure 4.11):

- Unit tests
- Integration tests
- End-to-end tests

The Test Pyramid is often represented visually as a pyramid with those three types of tests in it. The width of the pyramid layers refers to the prevalence of a particular type

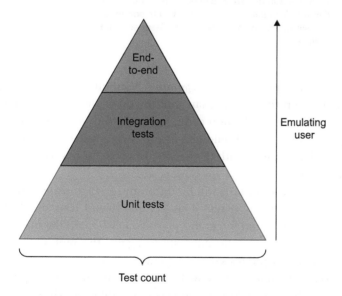

Figure 4.11 The Test Pyramid advocates for a certain ratio of unit, integration, and end-to-end tests.

of test in the suite. The wider the layer, the greater the test count. The height of the layer is a measure of how close these tests are to emulating the end user's behavior. End-to-end tests are at the top—they are the closest to imitating the user experience. Different types of tests in the pyramid make different choices in the trade-off between *fast feedback* and *protection against regressions*. Tests in higher pyramid layers favor *protection against regressions*, while lower layers emphasize execution speed (figure 4.12).

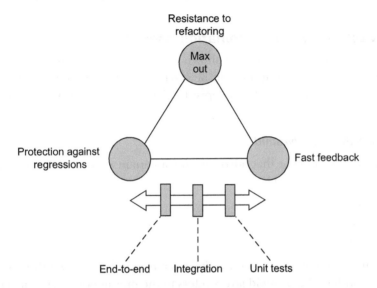

Figure 4.12   Different types of tests in the pyramid make different choices between fast feedback and protection against regressions. End-to-end tests favor protection against regressions, unit tests emphasize fast feedback, and integration tests lie in the middle.

Notice that neither layer gives up *resistance to refactoring*. Naturally, end-to-end and integration tests score higher on this metric than unit tests, but only as a side effect of being more detached from the production code. Still, even unit tests should not concede *resistance to refactoring*. All tests should aim at producing as few false positives as possible, even when working directly with the production code. (How to do that is the topic of the next chapter.)

The exact mix between types of tests will be different for each team and project. But in general, it should retain the pyramid shape: end-to-end tests should be the minority; unit tests, the majority; and integration tests somewhere in the middle.

The reason end-to-end tests are the minority is, again, the multiplication rule described in section 4.4. End-to-end tests score extremely low on the metric of *fast feedback*. They also lack *maintainability*: they tend to be larger in size and require additional effort to maintain the involved out-of-process dependencies. Thus, end-to-end tests only make sense when applied to the most critical functionality—features in which you don't ever want to see any bugs—and only when you can't get the same degree of protection with unit or integration tests. The use of end-to-end tests for anything else shouldn't pass your minimum required value threshold. Unit tests are usually more balanced, and hence you normally have many more of them.

There are exceptions to the Test Pyramid. For example, if all your application does is basic create, read, update, and delete (CRUD) operations with very few business rules or any other complexity, your test "pyramid" will most likely look like a rectangle with an equal number of unit and integration tests and no end-to-end tests.

Unit tests are less useful in a setting without algorithmic or business complexity—they quickly descend into trivial tests. At the same time, integration tests retain their value—it's still important to verify how code, however simple it is, works in integration with other subsystems, such as the database. As a result, you may end up with fewer unit tests and more integration tests. In the most trivial examples, the number of integration tests may even be greater than the number of unit tests.

Another exception to the Test Pyramid is an API that reaches out to a single out-of-process dependency—say, a database. Having more end-to-end tests may be a viable option for such an application. Since there's no user interface, end-to-end tests will run reasonably fast. The maintenance costs won't be too high, either, because you only work with the single external dependency, the database. Basically, end-to-end tests are indistinguishable from integration tests in this environment. The only thing that differs is the entry point: end-to-end tests require the application to be hosted somewhere to fully emulate the end user, while integration tests normally host the application in the same process. We'll get back to the Test Pyramid in chapter 8, when we'll be talking about integration testing.

4.5.2   *Choosing between black-box and white-box testing*

The other well-known test automation concept is black-box versus white-box testing. In this section, I show when to use each of the two approaches:

- *Black-box testing* is a method of software testing that examines the functionality of a system without knowing its internal structure. Such testing is normally built around specifications and requirements: *what* the application is supposed to do, rather than *how* it does it.
- *White-box testing* is the opposite of that. It's a method of testing that verifies the application's inner workings. The tests are derived from the source code, not requirements or specifications.

There are pros and cons to both of these methods. White-box testing tends to be more thorough. By analyzing the source code, you can uncover a lot of errors that you may miss when relying solely on external specifications. On the other hand, tests resulting from white-box testing are often brittle, as they tend to tightly couple to the specific implementation of the code under test. Such tests produce many false positives and thus fall short on the metric of *resistance to refactoring*. They also often can't be traced back to a behavior that is meaningful to a business person, which is a strong sign that these tests are fragile and don't add much value. Black-box testing provides the opposite set of pros and cons (table 4.1).

Table 4.1   The pros and cons of white-box and black-box testing

	Protection against regressions	Resistance to refactoring
White-box testing	Good	Bad
Black-box testing	Bad	Good

As you may remember from section 4.4.5, you can't compromise on *resistance to refactoring*: a test either possesses *resistance to refactoring* or it doesn't. Therefore, *choose black-box testing over white-box testing by default*. Make all tests—be they unit, integration, or end-to-end—view the system as a black box and verify behavior meaningful to the problem domain. If you can't trace a test back to a business requirement, it's an indication of the test's brittleness. Either restructure or delete this test; don't let it into the suite as-is. The only exception is when the test covers utility code with high algorithmic complexity (more on this in chapter 7).

Note that even though black-box testing is preferable when *writing tests*, you can still use the white-box method when *analyzing* the tests. *Use code coverage tools to see which code branches are not exercised, but then turn around and test them as if you know nothing about the code's internal structure.* Such a combination of the white-box and black-box methods works best.

Summary

- A good unit test has four foundational attributes that you can use to analyze any automated test, whether unit, integration, or end-to-end:
  - Protection against regressions
  - Resistance to refactoring
  - Fast feedback
  - Maintainability
- *Protection against regressions* is a measure of how good the test is at indicating the presence of bugs (regressions). The more code the test executes (both your code and the code of libraries and frameworks used in the project), the higher the chance this test will reveal a bug.
- *Resistance to refactoring* is the degree to which a test can sustain application code refactoring without producing a false positive.
- A false positive is a false alarm—a result indicating that the test fails, whereas the functionality it covers works as intended. False positives can have a devastating effect on the test suite:
  - They dilute your ability and willingness to react to problems in code, because you get accustomed to false alarms and stop paying attention to them.

- They diminish your perception of tests as a reliable safety net and lead to losing trust in the test suite.

- False positives are a result of tight coupling between tests and the internal implementation details of the system under test. To avoid such coupling, the test must verify the end result the SUT produces, not the steps it took to do that.

- *Protection against regressions* and *resistance to refactoring* contribute to test accuracy. A test is accurate insofar as it generates a strong signal (is capable of finding bugs, the sphere of *protection against regressions*) with as little noise (false positives) as possible (the sphere of *resistance to refactoring*).

- False positives don't have as much of a negative effect in the beginning of the project, but they become increasingly important as the project grows: as important as false negatives (unnoticed bugs).

- *Fast feedback* is a measure of how quickly the test executes.

- *Maintainability* consists of two components:
  - How hard it is to understand the test. The smaller the test, the more readable it is.
  - How hard it is to run the test. The fewer out-of-process dependencies the test reaches out to, the easier it is to keep them operational.

- A test's value estimate is the product of scores the test gets in each of the four attributes. If the test gets zero in one of the attributes, its value turns to zero as well.

- It's impossible to create a test that gets the maximum score in all four attributes, because the first three—*protection against regressions, resistance to refactoring*, and *fast feedback*—are mutually exclusive. The test can only maximize two out of the three.

- *Resistance to refactoring* is non-negotiable because whether a test possess this attribute is mostly a binary choice: the test either has resistance to refactoring or it doesn't. The trade-off between the attributes comes down to the choice between *protection against regressions* and *fast feedback*.

- The Test Pyramid advocates for a certain ratio of unit, integration, and end-to-end tests: end-to-end tests should be in the minority, unit tests in the majority, and integration tests somewhere in the middle.

- Different types of tests in the pyramid make different choices between *fast feedback* and *protection against regressions*. End-to-end tests favor *protection against regressions*, while unit tests favor *fast feedback*.

- Use the black-box testing method when *writing* tests. Use the white-box method when *analyzing* the tests.

Mocks and test fragility

This chapter covers
- Differentiating mocks from stubs
- Defining observable behavior and implementation details
- Understanding the relationship between mocks and test fragility
- Using mocks without compromising resistance to refactoring

Chapter 4 introduced a frame of reference that you can use to analyze specific tests and unit testing approaches. In this chapter, you'll see that frame of reference in action; we'll use it to dissect the topic of mocks.

The use of mocks in tests is a controversial subject. Some people argue that mocks are a great tool and apply them in most of their tests. Others claim that mocks lead to test fragility and try not to use them at all. As the saying goes, the truth lies somewhere in between. In this chapter, I'll show that, indeed, mocks often result in fragile tests—tests that lack the metric of *resistance to refactoring*. But there are still cases where mocking is applicable and even preferable.

This chapter draws heavily on the discussion about the London versus classical schools of unit testing from chapter 2. In short, the disagreement between the schools stems from their views on the test isolation issue. The London school advocates isolating pieces of code under test from each other and using test doubles for all but immutable dependencies to perform such isolation.

The classical school stands for isolating unit tests themselves so that they can be run in parallel. This school uses test doubles only for dependencies that are shared between tests.

There's a deep and almost inevitable connection between mocks and test fragility. In the next several sections, I will gradually lay down the foundation for you to see why that connection exists. You will also learn how to use mocks so that they don't compromise a test's *resistance to refactoring*.

5.1 Differentiating mocks from stubs

In chapter 2, I briefly mentioned that a *mock* is a test double that allows you to examine interactions between the system under test (SUT) and its collaborators. There's another type of test double: a *stub*. Let's take a closer look at what a mock is and how it is different from a stub.

5.1.1 The types of test doubles

A *test double* is an overarching term that describes all kinds of non-production-ready, fake dependencies in tests. The term comes from the notion of a stunt double in a movie. The major use of test doubles is to facilitate testing; they are passed to the system under test instead of real dependencies, which could be hard to set up or maintain.

According to Gerard Meszaros, there are five variations of test doubles: *dummy, stub, spy, mock,* and *fake.*[1] Such a variety can look intimidating, but in reality, they can all be grouped together into just two types: mocks and stubs (figure 5.1).

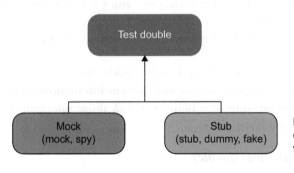

Figure 5.1 All variations of test doubles can be categorized into two types: mocks and stubs.

---

[1] See *xUnit Test Patterns: Refactoring Test Code* (Addison-Wesley, 2007).

The difference between these two types boils down to the following:

- Mocks help to emulate and examine *outcoming* interactions. These interactions are calls the SUT makes to its dependencies to change their state.
- Stubs help to emulate *incoming* interactions. These interactions are calls the SUT makes to its dependencies to get input data (figure 5.2).

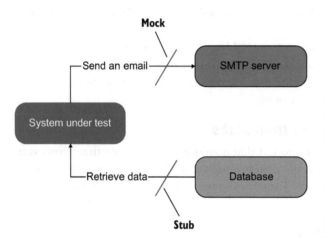

Figure 5.2   Sending an email is an *outcoming* interaction: an interaction that results in a side effect in the SMTP server. A test double emulating such an interaction is a *mock*. Retrieving data from the database is an *incoming* interaction; it doesn't result in a side effect. The corresponding test double is a *stub*.

All other differences between the five variations are insignificant implementation details. For example, *spies* serve the same role as mocks. The distinction is that spies are written manually, whereas mocks are created with the help of a mocking framework. Sometimes people refer to spies as *handwritten mocks*.

On the other hand, the difference between a stub, a dummy, and a fake is in how intelligent they are. A *dummy* is a simple, hardcoded value such as a null value or a made-up string. It's used to satisfy the SUT's method signature and doesn't participate in producing the final outcome. A *stub* is more sophisticated. It's a fully fledged dependency that you configure to return different values for different scenarios. Finally, a *fake* is the same as a stub for most purposes. The difference is in the rationale for its creation: a fake is usually implemented to replace a dependency that doesn't yet exist.

Notice the difference between mocks and stubs (aside from outcoming versus incoming interactions). Mocks help to *emulate and examine* interactions between the SUT and its dependencies, while stubs only help to *emulate* those interactions. This is an important distinction. You will see why shortly.

5.1.2   *Mock (the tool) vs. mock (the test double)*

The term *mock* is overloaded and can mean different things in different circumstances. I mentioned in chapter 2 that people often use this term to mean any test double, whereas mocks are only a subset of test doubles. But there's another meaning for the term *mock*. You can refer to the classes from mocking libraries as mocks, too. These classes help you create actual mocks, but they themselves are not mocks per se. The following listing shows an example.

Listing 5.1 Using the `Mock` class from a mocking library to create a mock

```
[Fact]
public void Sending_a_greetings_email()
{
    var mock = new Mock<IEmailGateway>();
    var sut = new Controller(mock.Object);

    sut.GreetUser("user@email.com");

    mock.Verify(
        x => x.SendGreetingsEmail(
            "user@email.com"),
        Times.Once);
}
```

Uses a mock (the tool) to create a mock (the test double)

Examines the call from the SUT to the test double

The test in listing 5.1 uses the `Mock` class from the mocking library of my choice (Moq). This class is a tool that enables you to create a test double—a mock. In other words, the class `Mock` (or `Mock<IEmailGateway>`) is a *mock (the tool)*, while the instance of that class, `mock`, is a *mock (the test double)*. It's important not to conflate a mock (the tool) with a mock (the test double) because you can use a mock (the tool) to create both types of test doubles: mocks and stubs.

The test in the following listing also uses the `Mock` class, but the instance of that class is not a mock, it's a stub.

Listing 5.2 Using the `Mock` class to create a stub

```
[Fact]
public void Creating_a_report()
{
    var stub = new Mock<IDatabase>();
    stub.Setup(x => x.GetNumberOfUsers())
        .Returns(10);
    var sut = new Controller(stub.Object);

    Report report = sut.CreateReport();

    Assert.Equal(10, report.NumberOfUsers);
}
```

Uses a mock (the tool) to create a stub

Sets up a canned answer

This test double emulates an *incoming* interaction—a call that provides the SUT with input data. On the other hand, in the previous example (listing 5.1), the call to `Send-GreetingsEmail()` is an *outcoming* interaction. Its sole purpose is to incur a side effect—send an email.

5.1.3   *Don't assert interactions with stubs*

As I mentioned in section 5.1.1, mocks help to *emulate and examine* outcoming interactions between the SUT and its dependencies, while stubs only help to *emulate* incoming interactions, not *examine* them. The difference between the two stems from the guideline of *never asserting interactions with stubs*. A call from the SUT to a stub is not part of the end result the SUT produces. Such a call is only a means to produce the end result: a stub provides input from which the SUT then generates the output.

> **NOTE**   Asserting interactions with stubs is a common anti-pattern that leads to fragile tests.

As you might remember from chapter 4, the only way to avoid false positives and thus improve resistance to refactoring in tests is to make those tests verify the end result (which, ideally, should be meaningful to a non-programmer), not implementation details. In listing 5.1, the check

```
mock.Verify(x => x.SendGreetingsEmail("user@email.com"))
```

corresponds to an actual outcome, and that outcome is meaningful to a domain expert: sending a greetings email is something business people would want the system to do. At the same time, the call to `GetNumberOfUsers()` in listing 5.2 is not an outcome at all. It's an internal implementation detail regarding how the SUT gathers data necessary for the report creation. Therefore, asserting this call would lead to test fragility: it shouldn't matter how the SUT generates the end result, as long as that result is correct. The following listing shows an example of such a brittle test.

Listing 5.3   **Asserting an interaction with a stub**

```
[Fact]
public void Creating_a_report()
{
    var stub = new Mock<IDatabase>();
    stub.Setup(x => x.GetNumberOfUsers()).Returns(10);
    var sut = new Controller(stub.Object);

    Report report = sut.CreateReport();

    Assert.Equal(10, report.NumberOfUsers);
    stub.Verify(                              Asserts the
        x => x.GetNumberOfUsers(),            interaction
        Times.Once);                          with the stub
}
```

This practice of verifying things that aren't part of the end result is also called *overspecification*. Most commonly, overspecification takes place when examining interactions. Checking for interactions with stubs is a flaw that's quite easy to spot because tests shouldn't check for *any* interactions with stubs. Mocks are a more complicated subject: not all uses of mocks lead to test fragility, but a lot of them do. You'll see why later in this chapter.

5.1.4 Using mocks and stubs together

Sometimes you need to create a test double that exhibits the properties of both a mock and a stub. For example, here's a test from chapter 2 that I used to illustrate the London style of unit testing.

Listing 5.4 `storeMock`: both a mock and a stub

```
[Fact]
public void Purchase_fails_when_not_enough_inventory()
{
    var storeMock = new Mock<IStore>();
    storeMock
        .Setup(x => x.HasEnoughInventory(        Sets up a
            Product.Shampoo, 5))                 canned
        .Returns(false);                         answer
    var sut = new Customer();

    bool success = sut.Purchase(
        storeMock.Object, Product.Shampoo, 5);

    Assert.False(success);
    storeMock.Verify(
        x => x.RemoveInventory(Product.Shampoo, 5),   Examines a call
        Times.Never);                                 from the SUT
}
```

This test uses `storeMock` for two purposes: it returns a canned answer and verifies a method call made by the SUT. Notice, though, that these are two different methods: the test sets up the answer from `HasEnoughInventory()` but then verifies the call to `RemoveInventory()`. Thus, the rule of not asserting interactions with stubs is not violated here.

When a test double is both a mock and a stub, it's still called a mock, not a stub. That's mostly the case because we need to pick one name, but also because being a mock is a more important fact than being a stub.

5.1.5 How mocks and stubs relate to commands and queries

The notions of mocks and stubs tie to the command query separation (CQS) principle. The CQS principle states that every method should be either a command or a query, but not both. As shown in figure 5.3, *commands* are methods that produce side effects and don't return any value (return void). Examples of side effects include mutating an object's state, changing a file in the file system, and so on. *Queries* are the opposite of that—they are side-effect free and return a value.

To follow this principle, be sure that if a method produces a side effect, that method's return type is void. And if the method returns a value, it must stay side-effect

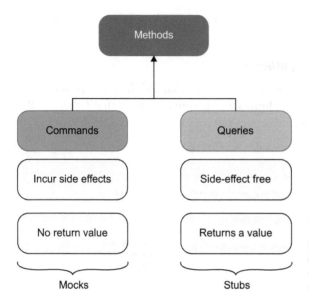

Figure 5.3   In the command query separation (CQS) principle, commands correspond to mocks, while queries are consistent with stubs.

free. In other words, asking a question should not change the answer. Code that maintains such a clear separation becomes easier to read. You can tell what a method does just by looking at its signature, without diving into its implementation details.

Of course, it's not always possible to follow the CQS principle. There are always methods for which it makes sense to both incur a side effect and return a value. A classical example is stack.Pop(). This method both removes a top element from the stack and returns it to the caller. Still, it's a good idea to adhere to the CQS principle whenever you can.

Test doubles that substitute commands become mocks. Similarly, test doubles that substitute queries are stubs. Look at the two tests from listings 5.1 and 5.2 again (I'm showing their relevant parts here):

```
var mock = new Mock<IEmailGateway>();
mock.Verify(x => x.SendGreetingsEmail("user@email.com"));

var stub = new Mock<IDatabase>();
stub.Setup(x => x.GetNumberOfUsers()).Returns(10);
```

SendGreetingsEmail() is a command whose side effect is sending an email. The test double that substitutes this command is a mock. On the other hand, GetNumberOf-Users() is a query that returns a value and doesn't mutate the database state. The corresponding test double is a stub.

5.2   *Observable behavior vs. implementation details*

Section 5.1 showed what a mock is. The next step on the way to explaining the connection between mocks and test fragility is diving into what causes such fragility.

As you might remember from chapter 4, *test fragility* corresponds to the second attribute of a good unit test: resistance to refactoring. (As a reminder, the four attributes are protection against regressions, resistance to refactoring, fast feedback, and maintainability.) The metric of resistance to refactoring is the most important because whether a unit test possesses this metric is mostly a binary choice. Thus, it's good to max out this metric to the extent that the test still remains in the realm of unit testing and doesn't transition to the category of end-to-end testing. The latter, despite being the best at resistance to refactoring, is generally much harder to maintain.

In chapter 4, you also saw that the main reason tests deliver false positives (and thus fail at resistance to refactoring) is because they couple to the code's implementation details. The only way to avoid such coupling is to verify the end result the code produces (its observable behavior) and distance tests from implementation details as much as possible. In other words, tests must focus on the *whats*, not the *hows*. So, what exactly is an implementation detail, and how is it different from an observable behavior?

5.2.1   *Observable behavior is not the same as a public API*

All production code can be categorized along two dimensions:

- Public API vs. private API (where API means *application programming interface*)
- Observable behavior vs. implementation details

The categories in these dimensions don't overlap. A method can't belong to both a public and a private API; it's either one or the other. Similarly, the code is either an internal implementation detail or part of the system's observable behavior, but not both.

Most programming languages provide a simple mechanism to differentiate between the code base's public and private APIs. For example, in C#, you can mark any member in a class with the `private` keyword, and that member will be hidden from the client code, becoming part of the class's private API. The same is true for classes: you can easily make them private by using the `private` or `internal` keyword.

The distinction between observable behavior and internal implementation details is more nuanced. For a piece of code to be part of the system's observable behavior, it has to do one of the following things:

- Expose an operation that helps the client achieve one of its goals. An *operation* is a method that performs a calculation or incurs a side effect or both.
- Expose a state that helps the client achieve one of its goals. *State* is the current condition of the system.

Any code that does neither of these two things is an *implementation detail.*

Notice that whether the code is observable behavior depends on who its client is and what the goals of that client are. In order to be a part of observable behavior, the code needs to have an immediate connection to at least one such goal. The word *client* can refer to different things depending on where the code resides. The common examples are client code from the same code base, an external application, or the user interface.

Ideally, the system's public API surface should coincide with its observable behavior, and all its implementation details should be hidden from the eyes of the clients. Such a system has a *well-designed* API (figure 5.4).

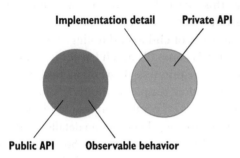

Figure 5.4   In a *well-designed* API, the observable behavior coincides with the public API, while all implementation details are hidden behind the private API.

Often, though, the system's public API extends beyond its observable behavior and starts exposing implementation details. Such a system's implementation details *leak* to its public API surface (figure 5.5).

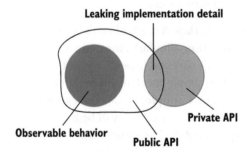

Figure 5.5   A system leaks implementation details when its public API extends beyond the observable behavior.

5.2.2   *Leaking implementation details: An example with an operation*

Let's take a look at examples of code whose implementation details leak to the public API. Listing 5.5 shows a User class with a public API that consists of two members: a Name property and a NormalizeName() method. The class also has an *invariant*: users' names must not exceed 50 characters and should be truncated otherwise.

Listing 5.5   User class with leaking implementation details

```
public class User
{
    public string Name { get; set; }
```

```
    public string NormalizeName(string name)
    {
        string result = (name ?? "").Trim();

        if (result.Length > 50)
            return result.Substring(0, 50);

        return result;
    }
}

public class UserController
{
    public void RenameUser(int userId, string newName)
    {
        User user = GetUserFromDatabase(userId);

        string normalizedName = user.NormalizeName(newName);
        user.Name = normalizedName;

        SaveUserToDatabase(user);
    }
}
```

UserController is client code. It uses the User class in its RenameUser method. The goal of this method, as you have probably guessed, is to change a user's name.

So, why isn't User's API well-designed? Look at its members once again: the Name property and the NormalizeName method. Both of them are public. Therefore, in order for the class's API to be well-designed, these members should be part of the observable behavior. This, in turn, requires them to do one of the following two things (which I'm repeating here for convenience):

- Expose an *operation* that helps the client achieve one of its goals.
- Expose a *state* that helps the client achieve one of its goals.

Only the Name property meets this requirement. It exposes a setter, which is an operation that allows UserController to achieve its goal of changing a user's name. The NormalizeName method is also an operation, but it doesn't have an immediate connection to the client's goal. The only reason UserController calls this method is to satisfy the invariant of User. NormalizeName is therefore an implementation detail that leaks to the class's public API (figure 5.6).

To fix the situation and make the class's API well-designed, User needs to hide NormalizeName() and call it internally as part of the property's setter without relying on the client code to do so. Listing 5.6 shows this approach.

Leaking implementation detail

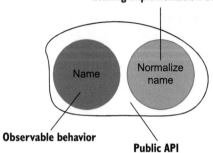

Observable behavior

Public API

Figure 5.6   The API of User is not well-designed: it exposes the NormalizeName method, which is not part of the observable behavior.

Listing 5.6   A version of User with a well-designed API

```
public class User
{
    private string _name;
    public string Name
    {
        get => _name;
        set => _name = NormalizeName(value);
    }

    private string NormalizeName(string name)
    {
        string result = (name ?? "").Trim();

        if (result.Length > 50)
            return result.Substring(0, 50);

        return result;
    }
}

public class UserController
{
    public void RenameUser(int userId, string newName)
    {
        User user = GetUserFromDatabase(userId);
        user.Name = newName;
        SaveUserToDatabase(user);
    }
}
```

User's API in listing 5.6 is well-designed: only the observable behavior (the Name property) is made public, while the implementation details (the NormalizeName method) are hidden behind the private API (figure 5.7).

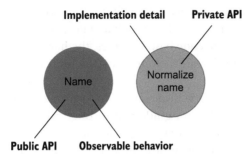

Figure 5.7 `User` with a well-designed API. Only the observable behavior is public; the implementation details are now private.

NOTE Strictly speaking, `Name`'s getter should also be made private, because it's not used by `UserController`. In reality, though, you almost always want to read back changes you make. Therefore, in a real project, there will certainly be another use case that requires seeing users' current names via `Name`'s getter.

There's a good rule of thumb that can help you determine whether a class leaks its implementation details. If the number of operations the client has to invoke on the class to achieve a single goal is greater than one, then that class is likely leaking implementation details. *Ideally, any individual goal should be achieved with a single operation.* In listing 5.5, for example, `UserController` has to use two operations from `User`:

```
string normalizedName = user.NormalizeName(newName);
user.Name = normalizedName;
```

After the refactoring, the number of operations has been reduced to one:

```
user.Name = newName;
```

In my experience, this rule of thumb holds true for the vast majority of cases where business logic is involved. There could very well be exceptions, though. Still, be sure to examine each situation where your code violates this rule for a potential leak of implementation details.

5.2.3 Well-designed API and encapsulation

Maintaining a well-designed API relates to the notion of encapsulation. As you might recall from chapter 3, *encapsulation* is the act of protecting your code against inconsistencies, also known as *invariant violations*. An *invariant* is a condition that should be held true at all times. The `User` class from the previous example had one such invariant: no user could have a name that exceeded 50 characters.

Exposing implementation details goes hand in hand with invariant violations—the former often leads to the latter. Not only did the original version of `User` leak its implementation details, but it also didn't maintain proper encapsulation. It allowed the client to bypass the invariant and assign a new name to a user without normalizing that name first.

Encapsulation is crucial for code base maintainability in the long run. The reason why is *complexity*. Code complexity is one of the biggest challenges you'll face in software development. The more complex the code base becomes, the harder it is to work with, which, in turn, results in slowing down development speed and increasing the number of bugs.

Without encapsulation, you have no practical way to cope with ever-increasing code complexity. When the code's API doesn't guide you through what is and what isn't allowed to be done with that code, you have to keep a lot of information in mind to make sure you don't introduce inconsistencies with new code changes. This brings an additional mental burden to the process of programming. Remove as much of that burden from yourself as possible. *You cannot trust yourself to do the right thing all the time—so, eliminate the very possibility of doing the wrong thing.* The best way to do so is to maintain proper encapsulation so that your code base doesn't even provide an option for you to do anything incorrectly. Encapsulation ultimately serves the same goal as unit testing: it enables sustainable growth of your software project.

There's a similar principle: *tell-don't-ask*. It was coined by Martin Fowler (https://martinfowler.com/bliki/TellDontAsk.html) and stands for bundling data with the functions that operate on that data. You can view this principle as a corollary to the practice of encapsulation. Code encapsulation is a goal, whereas bundling data and functions together, as well as hiding implementation details, are the means to achieve that goal:

- *Hiding implementation details* helps you remove the class's internals from the eyes of its clients, so there's less risk of corrupting those internals.
- *Bundling data and operations* helps to make sure these operations don't violate the class's invariants.

5.2.4 *Leaking implementation details: An example with state*

The example shown in listing 5.5 demonstrated an operation (the `NormalizeName` method) that was an implementation detail leaking to the public API. Let's also look at an example with state. The following listing contains the `MessageRenderer` class you saw in chapter 4. It uses a collection of sub-renderers to generate an HTML representation of a message containing a header, a body, and a footer.

Listing 5.7 State as an implementation detail

```
public class MessageRenderer : IRenderer
{
    public IReadOnlyList<IRenderer> SubRenderers { get; }

    public MessageRenderer()
    {
        SubRenderers = new List<IRenderer>
        {
            new HeaderRenderer(),
            new BodyRenderer(),
```

```
                new FooterRenderer()
        };
    }

    public string Render(Message message)
    {
        return SubRenderers
            .Select(x => x.Render(message))
            .Aggregate("", (str1, str2) => str1 + str2);
    }
}
```

The sub-renderers collection is public. But is it part of observable behavior? Assuming that the client's goal is to render an HTML message, the answer is no. The only class member such a client would need is the Render method itself. Thus SubRenderers is also a leaking implementation detail.

I bring up this example again for a reason. As you may remember, I used it to illustrate a brittle test. That test was brittle precisely because it was tied to this implementation detail—it checked to see the collection's composition. The brittleness was fixed by re-targeting the test at the Render method. The new version of the test verified the resulting message—the only output the client code cared about, the observable behavior.

As you can see, there's an intrinsic connection between good unit tests and a well-designed API. By making all implementation details private, you leave your tests no choice other than to verify the code's observable behavior, which automatically improves their resistance to refactoring.

TIP Making the API well-designed automatically improves unit tests.

Another guideline flows from the definition of a well-designed API: you should expose the absolute minimum number of operations and state. Only code that directly helps clients achieve their goals should be made public. Everything else is implementation details and thus must be hidden behind the private API.

Note that there's no such problem as leaking observable behavior, which would be symmetric to the problem of leaking implementation details. While you can expose an implementation detail (a method or a class that is not supposed to be used by the client), you can't hide an observable behavior. Such a method or class would no longer have an immediate connection to the client goals, because the client wouldn't be able to directly use it anymore. Thus, by definition, this code would cease to be part of observable behavior. Table 5.1 sums it all up.

Table 5.1 The relationship between the code's publicity and purpose. Avoid making implementation details public.

	Observable behavior	Implementation detail
Public	Good	Bad
Private	N/A	Good

5.3   *The relationship between mocks and test fragility*

The previous sections defined a mock and showed the difference between observable behavior and an implementation detail. In this section, you will learn about hexagonal architecture, the difference between internal and external communications, and (finally!) the relationship between mocks and test fragility.

5.3.1   *Defining hexagonal architecture*

A typical application consists of two layers, domain and application services, as shown in figure 5.8. The *domain layer* resides in the middle of the diagram because it's the central part of your application. It contains the *business logic*: the essential functionality your application is built for. The domain layer and its business logic differentiate this application from others and provide a competitive advantage for the organization.

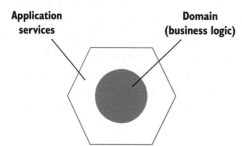

Application
services

Domain
(business logic)

Figure 5.8   A typical application consists of a domain layer and an application services layer. The domain layer contains the application's business logic; application services tie that logic to business use cases.

The application services layer sits on top of the domain layer and orchestrates communication between that layer and the external world. For example, if your application is a RESTful API, all requests to this API hit the application services layer first. This layer then coordinates the work between domain classes and out-of-process dependencies. Here's an example of such coordination for the application service. It does the following:

- Queries the database and uses the data to materialize a domain class instance
- Invokes an operation on that instance
- Saves the results back to the database

The combination of the application services layer and the domain layer forms a *hexagon*, which itself represents your application. It can interact with other applications, which are represented with their own hexagons (see figure 5.9). These other applications could be an SMTP service, a third-party system, a message bus, and so on. A set of interacting hexagons makes up a *hexagonal architecture*.

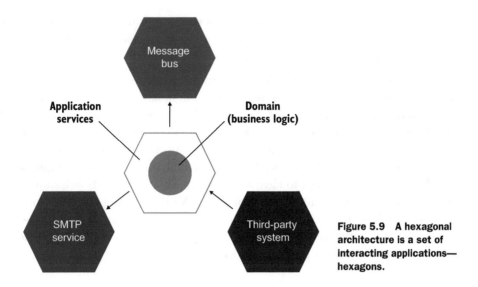

Figure 5.9 A hexagonal architecture is a set of interacting applications— hexagons.

The term *hexagonal architecture* was introduced by Alistair Cockburn. Its purpose is to emphasize three important guidelines:

- *The separation of concerns between the domain and application services layers*—Business logic is the most important part of the application. Therefore, the domain layer should be accountable only for that business logic and exempted from all other responsibilities. Those responsibilities, such as communicating with external applications and retrieving data from the database, must be attributed to application services. Conversely, the application services shouldn't contain any business logic. Their responsibility is to adapt the domain layer by translating the incoming requests into operations on domain classes and then persisting the results or returning them back to the caller. You can view the domain layer as a collection of the application's domain knowledge (*how-to's*) and the application services layer as a set of business use cases (*what-to's*).

- *Communications inside your application*—Hexagonal architecture prescribes a one-way flow of dependencies: from the application services layer to the domain layer. Classes inside the domain layer should only depend on each other; they should not depend on classes from the application services layer. This guideline flows from the previous one. The separation of concerns between the application services layer and the domain layer means that the former knows about the latter, but the opposite is not true. The domain layer should be fully isolated from the external world.

- *Communications between applications*—External applications connect to your application through a common interface maintained by the application services layer. No one has a direct access to the domain layer. Each side in a hexagon represents a connection into or out of the application. Note that although a hexagon has six sides, it doesn't mean your application can only connect to six other applications. The number of connections is arbitrary. The point is that there can be many such connections.

Each layer of your application exhibits observable behavior and contains its own set of implementation details. For example, observable behavior of the domain layer is the sum of this layer's operations and state that helps the application service layer achieve at least one of its goals. The principles of a well-designed API have a fractal nature: they apply equally to as much as a whole layer or as little as a single class.

When you make each layer's API well-designed (that is, hide its implementation details), your tests also start to have a fractal structure; they verify behavior that helps achieve the same goals but at different levels. A test covering an application service checks to see how this service attains an overarching, coarse-grained goal posed by the external client. At the same time, a test working with a domain class verifies a subgoal that is part of that greater goal (figure 5.10).

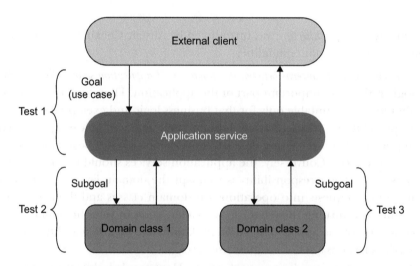

Figure 5.10   Tests working with different layers have a fractal nature: they verify the same behavior at different levels. A test of an application service checks to see how the overall business use case is executed. A test working with a domain class verifies an intermediate subgoal on the way to use-case completion.

You might remember from previous chapters how I mentioned that you should be able to trace any test back to a particular business requirement. Each test should tell a story that is meaningful to a domain expert, and if it doesn't, that's a strong indication that the test couples to implementation details and therefore is brittle. I hope now you can see why.

Observable behavior flows inward from outer layers to the center. The overarching goal posed by the external client gets translated into subgoals achieved by individual domain classes. Each piece of observable behavior in the domain layer therefore preserves the connection to a particular business use case. You can trace this connection recursively from the innermost (domain) layer outward to the application services layer and then to the needs of the external client. This traceability follows from the definition of observable behavior. For a piece of code to be part of observable behavior, it needs to help the client achieve one of its goals. For a domain class, the client is an application service; for the application service, it's the external client itself.

Tests that verify a code base with a well-designed API also have a connection to business requirements because those tests tie to the observable behavior only. A good example is the `User` and `UserController` classes from listing 5.6 (I'm repeating the code here for convenience).

Listing 5.8 A domain class with an application service

```
public class User
{
    private string _name;
    public string Name
    {
        get => _name;
        set => _name = NormalizeName(value);
    }

    private string NormalizeName(string name)
    {
        /* Trim name down to 50 characters */
    }
}

public class UserController
{
    public void RenameUser(int userId, string newName)
    {
        User user = GetUserFromDatabase(userId);
        user.Name = newName;
        SaveUserToDatabase(user);
    }
}
```

`UserController` in this example is an application service. Assuming that the external client doesn't have a specific goal of normalizing user names, and all names are normalized solely due to restrictions from the application itself, the `NormalizeName` method in the `User` class can't be traced to the client's needs. Therefore, it's an implementation detail and should be made private (we already did that earlier in this chapter). Moreover, tests shouldn't check this method directly. They should verify it only as part of the class's observable behavior—the `Name` property's setter in this example.

This guideline of always tracing the code base's public API to business requirements applies to the vast majority of domain classes and application services but less so to utility and infrastructure code. The individual problems such code solves are often too low-level and fine-grained and can't be traced to a specific business use case.

5.3.2   *Intra-system vs. inter-system communications*

There are two types of communications in a typical application: intra-system and inter-system. *Intra-system* communications are communications between classes inside your application. *Inter-system* communications are when your application talks to other applications (figure 5.11).

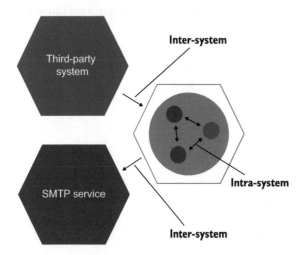

Figure 5.11   **There are two types of communications: intra-system (between classes inside the application) and inter-system (between applications).**

NOTE   Intra-system communications are implementation details; inter-system communications are not.

Intra-system communications are implementation details because the collaborations your domain classes go through in order to perform an operation are not part of their observable behavior. These collaborations don't have an immediate connection to the client's goal. Thus, coupling to such collaborations leads to fragile tests.

Inter-system communications are a different matter. Unlike collaborations between classes inside your application, the way your system talks to the external world forms the observable behavior of that system as a whole. It's part of the contract your application must hold at all times (figure 5.12).

This attribute of inter-system communications stems from the way separate applications evolve together. One of the main principles of such an evolution is maintaining backward compatibility. Regardless of the refactorings you perform inside your system, the communication pattern it uses to talk to external applications should always stay in place, so that external applications can understand it. For example, messages your application emits on a bus should preserve their structure, the calls issued to an SMTP service should have the same number and type of parameters, and so on.

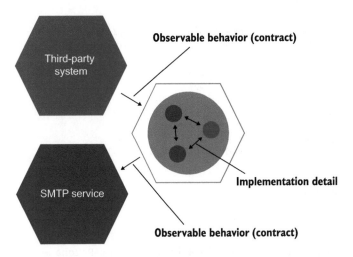

Figure 5.12 Inter-system communications form the observable behavior of your application as a whole. Intra-system communications are implementation details.

The use of mocks is beneficial when verifying the communication pattern between your system and external applications. Conversely, using mocks to verify communications between classes inside your system results in tests that couple to implementation details and therefore fall short of the resistance-to-refactoring metric.

5.3.3 *Intra-system vs. inter-system communications: An example*

To illustrate the difference between intra-system and inter-system communications, I'll expand on the example with the Customer and Store classes that I used in chapter 2 and earlier in this chapter. Imagine the following business use case:

- A customer tries to purchase a product from a store.
- If the amount of the product in the store is sufficient, then
  - The inventory is removed from the store.
  - An email receipt is sent to the customer.
  - A confirmation is returned.

Let's also assume that the application is an API with no user interface.

In the following listing, the CustomerController class is an application service that orchestrates the work between domain classes (Customer, Product, Store) and the external application (EmailGateway, which is a proxy to an SMTP service).

Listing 5.9 Connecting the domain model with external applications

```
public class CustomerController
{
    public bool Purchase(int customerId, int productId, int quantity)
```

```
    {
        Customer customer = _customerRepository.GetById(customerId);
        Product product = _productRepository.GetById(productId);

        bool isSuccess = customer.Purchase(
            _mainStore, product, quantity);

        if (isSuccess)
        {
            _emailGateway.SendReceipt(
                customer.Email, product.Name, quantity);
        }

        return isSuccess;
    }
}
```

Validation of input parameters is omitted for brevity. In the Purchase method, the customer checks to see if there's enough inventory in the store and, if so, decreases the product amount.

The act of making a purchase is a business use case with both intra-system and inter-system communications. The inter-system communications are those between the CustomerController application service and the two external systems: the third-party application (which is also the client initiating the use case) and the email gateway. The intra-system communication is between the Customer and the Store domain classes (figure 5.13).

In this example, the call to the SMTP service is a side effect that is visible to the external world and thus forms the observable behavior of the application as a whole.

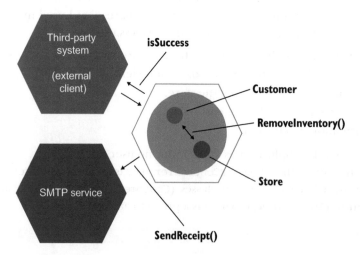

Figure 5.13 The example in listing 5.9 represented using the hexagonal architecture. The communications between the hexagons are inter-system communications. The communication inside the hexagon is intra-system.

It also has a direct connection to the client's goals. The client of the application is the third-party system. This system's goal is to make a purchase, and it expects the customer to receive a confirmation email as part of the successful outcome.

The call to the SMTP service is a legitimate reason to do mocking. It doesn't lead to test fragility because you want to make sure this type of communication stays in place even after refactoring. The use of mocks helps you do exactly that.

The next listing shows an example of a legitimate use of mocks.

Listing 5.10 Mocking that doesn't lead to fragile tests

```
[Fact]
public void Successful_purchase()
{
    var mock = new Mock<IEmailGateway>();
    var sut = new CustomerController(mock.Object);

    bool isSuccess = sut.Purchase(
        customerId: 1, productId: 2, quantity: 5);

    Assert.True(isSuccess);
    mock.Verify(                                    Verifies that the
        x => x.SendReceipt(                         system sent a receipt
            "customer@email.com", "Shampoo", 5),    about the purchase
        Times.Once);
}
```

Note that the isSuccess flag is also observable by the external client and also needs verification. This flag doesn't need mocking, though; a simple value comparison is enough.

Let's now look at a test that mocks the communication between Customer and Store.

Listing 5.11 Mocking that leads to fragile tests

```
[Fact]
public void Purchase_succeeds_when_enough_inventory()
{
    var storeMock = new Mock<IStore>();
    storeMock
        .Setup(x => x.HasEnoughInventory(Product.Shampoo, 5))
        .Returns(true);
    var customer = new Customer();

    bool success = customer.Purchase(
        storeMock.Object, Product.Shampoo, 5);

    Assert.True(success);
    storeMock.Verify(
        x => x.RemoveInventory(Product.Shampoo, 5),
        Times.Once);
}
```

Unlike the communication between `CustomerController` and the SMTP service, the `RemoveInventory()` method call from `Customer` to `Store` doesn't cross the application boundary: both the caller and the recipient reside inside the application. Also, this method is neither an operation nor a state that helps the client achieve its goals. The client of these two domain classes is `CustomerController` with the goal of making a purchase. The only two members that have an immediate connection to this goal are `customer.Purchase()` and `store.GetInventory()`. The `Purchase()` method initiates the purchase, and `GetInventory()` shows the state of the system after the purchase is completed. The `RemoveInventory()` method call is an intermediate step on the way to the client's goal—an implementation detail.

5.4   *The classical vs. London schools of unit testing, revisited*

As a reminder from chapter 2 (table 2.1), table 5.2 sums up the differences between the classical and London schools of unit testing.

Table 5.2   **The differences between the London and classical schools of unit testing**

	Isolation of	A unit is	Uses test doubles for
London school	Units	A class	All but immutable dependencies
Classical school	Unit tests	A class or a set of classes	Shared dependencies

In chapter 2, I mentioned that I prefer the classical school of unit testing over the London school. I hope now you can see why. The London school encourages the use of mocks for all but immutable dependencies and doesn't differentiate between intra-system and inter-system communications. As a result, tests check communications between classes just as much as they check communications between your application and external systems.

This indiscriminate use of mocks is why following the London school often results in tests that couple to implementation details and thus lack resistance to refactoring. As you may remember from chapter 4, the metric of resistance to refactoring (unlike the other three) is mostly a binary choice: a test either has resistance to refactoring or it doesn't. Compromising on this metric renders the test nearly worthless.

The classical school is much better at this issue because it advocates for substituting only dependencies that are shared between tests, which almost always translates into out-of-process dependencies such as an SMTP service, a message bus, and so on. But the classical school is not ideal in its treatment of inter-system communications, either. This school also encourages excessive use of mocks, albeit not as much as the London school.

5.4.1 *Not all out-of-process dependencies should be mocked out*

Before we discuss out-of-process dependencies and mocking, let me give you a quick refresher on types of dependencies (refer to chapter 2 for more details):

- *Shared dependency*—A dependency shared by tests (not production code)
- *Out-of-process dependency*—A dependency hosted by a process other than the program's execution process (for example, a database, a message bus, or an SMTP service)
- *Private dependency*—Any dependency that is not shared

The classical school recommends avoiding shared dependencies because they provide the means for tests to interfere with each other's execution context and thus prevent those tests from running in parallel. The ability for tests to run in parallel, sequentially, and in any order is called *test isolation*.

If a shared dependency is not out-of-process, then it's easy to avoid reusing it in tests by providing a new instance of it on each test run. In cases where the shared dependency is out-of-process, testing becomes more complicated. You can't instantiate a new database or provision a new message bus before each test execution; that would drastically slow down the test suite. The usual approach is to replace such dependencies with test doubles—mocks and stubs.

Not all out-of-process dependencies should be mocked out, though. *If an out-of-process dependency is only accessible through your application, then communications with such a dependency are not part of your system's observable behavior.* An out-of-process dependency that can't be observed externally, in effect, acts as part of your application (figure 5.14).

Remember, the requirement to always preserve the communication pattern between your application and external systems stems from the necessity to maintain backward compatibility. You have to maintain the way your application talks to external

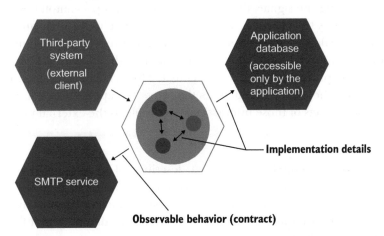

Figure 5.14 Communications with an out-of-process dependency that can't be observed externally are implementation details. They don't have to stay in place after refactoring and therefore shouldn't be verified with mocks.

systems. That's because you can't change those external systems simultaneously with your application; they may follow a different deployment cycle, or you might simply not have control over them.

But when your application acts as a proxy to an external system, and no client can access it directly, the backward-compatibility requirement vanishes. Now you can deploy your application together with this external system, and it won't affect the clients. The communication pattern with such a system becomes an implementation detail.

A good example here is an application database: a database that is used only by your application. No external system has access to this database. Therefore, you can modify the communication pattern between your system and the application database in any way you like, as long as it doesn't break existing functionality. Because that database is completely hidden from the eyes of the clients, you can even replace it with an entirely different storage mechanism, and no one will notice.

The use of mocks for out-of-process dependencies that you have a full control over also leads to brittle tests. You don't want your tests to turn red every time you split a table in the database or modify the type of one of the parameters in a stored procedure. The database and your application must be treated as one system.

This obviously poses an issue. How would you test the work with such a dependency without compromising the feedback speed, the third attribute of a good unit test? You'll see this subject covered in depth in the following two chapters.

5.4.2   *Using mocks to verify behavior*

Mocks are often said to verify behavior. In the vast majority of cases, they don't. The way each individual class interacts with neighboring classes in order to achieve some goal has nothing to do with observable behavior; it's an implementation detail.

Verifying communications between classes is akin to trying to derive a person's behavior by measuring the signals that neurons in the brain pass among each other. Such a level of detail is too granular. What matters is the behavior that can be traced back to the client goals. The client doesn't care what neurons in your brain light up when they ask you to help. The only thing that matters is the help itself—provided by you in a reliable and professional fashion, of course. Mocks have something to do with behavior only when they verify interactions that cross the application boundary and only when the side effects of those interactions are visible to the external world.

Summary

- *Test double* is an overarching term that describes all kinds of non-production-ready, fake dependencies in tests. There are five variations of test doubles—dummy, stub, spy, mock, and fake—that can be grouped in just two types: mocks and stubs. Spies are functionally the same as mocks; dummies and fakes serve the same role as stubs.
- Mocks help emulate and examine *outcoming interactions*: calls from the SUT to its dependencies that change the state of those dependencies. Stubs help

emulate *incoming interactions*: calls the SUT makes to its dependencies to get input data.

- A mock (the tool) is a class from a mocking library that you can use to create a mock (the test double) or a stub.
- Asserting interactions with stubs leads to *fragile tests*. Such an interaction doesn't correspond to the end result; it's an intermediate step on the way to that result, an implementation detail.
- The command query separation (CQS) principle states that every method should be either a command or a query but not both. Test doubles that substitute commands are mocks. Test doubles that substitute queries are stubs.
- All production code can be categorized along two dimensions: public API versus private API, and observable behavior versus implementation details. Code publicity is controlled by access modifiers, such as `private`, `public`, and `internal` keywords. Code is part of observable behavior when it meets one of the following requirements (any other code is an implementation detail):
  - It exposes an operation that helps the client achieve one of its goals. An *operation* is a method that performs a calculation or incurs a side effect.
  - It exposes a state that helps the client achieve one of its goals. *State* is the current condition of the system.
- *Well-designed code* is code whose observable behavior coincides with the public API and whose implementation details are hidden behind the private API. A code *leaks* implementation details when its public API extends beyond the observable behavior.
- *Encapsulation* is the act of protecting your code against invariant violations. Exposing implementation details often entails a breach in encapsulation because clients can use implementation details to bypass the code's invariants.
- *Hexagonal architecture* is a set of interacting applications represented as hexagons. Each hexagon consists of two layers: domain and application services.
- Hexagonal architecture emphasizes three important aspects:
  - Separation of concerns between the domain and application services layers. The domain layer should be responsible for the business logic, while the application services should orchestrate the work between the domain layer and external applications.
  - A one-way flow of dependencies from the application services layer to the domain layer. Classes inside the domain layer should only depend on each other; they should not depend on classes from the application services layer.
  - External applications connect to your application through a common interface maintained by the application services layer. No one has a direct access to the domain layer.
- Each layer in a hexagon exhibits observable behavior and contains its own set of implementation details.

- There are two types of communications in an application: intra-system and inter-system. *Intra-system* communications are communications between classes inside the application. *Inter-system* communication is when the application talks to external applications.
- Intra-system communications are implementation details. Inter-system communications are part of observable behavior, with the exception of external systems that are accessible only through your application. Interactions with such systems are implementation details too, because the resulting side effects are not observed externally.
- Using mocks to assert intra-system communications leads to *fragile* tests. Mocking is legitimate only when it's used for inter-system communications—communications that cross the application boundary—and only when the side effects of those communications are visible to the external world.

Styles of unit testing

6

This chapter covers

- Comparing styles of unit testing
- The relationship between functional and hexagonal architectures
- Transitioning to output-based testing

Chapter 4 introduced the four attributes of a good unit test: protection against regressions, resistance to refactoring, fast feedback, and maintainability. These attributes form a frame of reference that you can use to analyze specific tests and unit testing approaches. We analyzed one such approach in chapter 5: the use of mocks.

In this chapter, I apply the same frame of reference to the topic of unit testing *styles*. There are three such styles: output-based, state-based, and communication-based testing. Among the three, the output-based style produces tests of the highest quality, state-based testing is the second-best choice, and communication-based testing should be used only occasionally.

Unfortunately, you can't use the output-based testing style everywhere. It's only applicable to code written in a purely functional way. But don't worry; there are techniques that can help you transform more of your tests into the output-based style. For that, you'll need to use functional programming principles to restructure the underlying code toward a functional architecture.

119

Note that this chapter doesn't provide a deep dive into the topic of functional programming. Still, by the end of this chapter, I hope you'll have an intuitive understanding of how functional programming relates to output-based testing. You'll also learn how to write more of your tests using the output-based style, as well as the limitations of functional programming and functional architecture.

6.1   *The three styles of unit testing*

As I mentioned in the chapter introduction, there are three styles of unit testing:

- Output-based testing
- State-based testing
- Communication-based testing

You can employ one, two, or even all three styles together in a single test. This section lays the foundation for the whole chapter by defining (with examples) those three styles of unit testing. You'll see how they score against each other in the section after that.

6.1.1   *Defining the output-based style*

The first style of unit testing is the *output-based* style, where you feed an input to the system under test (SUT) and check the output it produces (figure 6.1). This style of unit testing is only applicable to code that doesn't change a global or internal state, so the only component to verify is its return value.

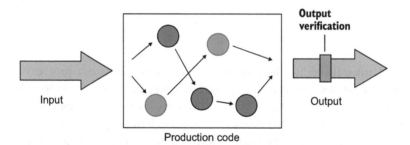

Figure 6.1   In output-based testing, tests verify the output the system generates. This style of testing assumes there are no side effects and the only result of the SUT's work is the value it returns to the caller.

The following listing shows an example of such code and a test covering it. The Price-Engine class accepts an array of products and calculates a discount.

Listing 6.1   Output-based testing

```
public class PriceEngine
{
    public decimal CalculateDiscount(params Product[] products)
```

```
    {
        decimal discount = products.Length * 0.01m;
        return Math.Min(discount, 0.2m);
    }
}

[Fact]
public void Discount_of_two_products()
{
    var product1 = new Product("Hand wash");
    var product2 = new Product("Shampoo");
    var sut = new PriceEngine();

    decimal discount = sut.CalculateDiscount(product1, product2);

    Assert.Equal(0.02m, discount);
}
```

PriceEngine multiplies the number of products by 1% and caps the result at 20%. There's nothing else to this class. It doesn't add the products to any internal collection, nor does it persist them in a database. The only outcome of the `Calculate-Discount()` method is the discount it returns: the *output* value (figure 6.2).

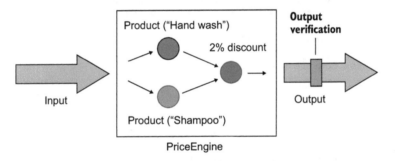

Figure 6.2 `PriceEngine` **represented using input-output notation. Its** `CalculateDiscount()` **method accepts an array of products and calculates a discount.**

The output-based style of unit testing is also known as *functional*. This name takes root in *functional programming*, a method of programming that emphasizes a preference for side-effect-free code. We'll talk more about functional programming and functional architecture later in this chapter.

6.1.2   *Defining the state-based style*

The *state-based* style is about verifying the state of the system after an operation is complete (figure 6.3). The term *state* in this style of testing can refer to the state of the SUT itself, of one of its collaborators, or of an out-of-process dependency, such as the database or the filesystem.

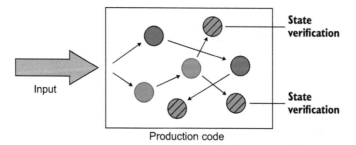

Figure 6.3   In state-based testing, tests verify the final state of the system after an operation is complete. The dashed circles represent that final state.

Here's an example of state-based testing. The `Order` class allows the client to add a new product.

Listing 6.2   State-based testing

```
public class Order
{
    private readonly List<Product> _products = new List<Product>();
    public IReadOnlyList<Product> Products => _products.ToList();

    public void AddProduct(Product product)
    {
        _products.Add(product);
    }
}

[Fact]
public void Adding_a_product_to_an_order()
{
    var product = new Product("Hand wash");
    var sut = new Order();

    sut.AddProduct(product);

    Assert.Equal(1, sut.Products.Count);
    Assert.Equal(product, sut.Products[0]);
}
```

The test verifies the `Products` collection after the addition is completed. Unlike the example of output-based testing in listing 6.1, the outcome of `AddProduct()` is the change made to the order's state.

6.1.3   *Defining the communication-based style*

Finally, the third style of unit testing is *communication-based* testing. This style uses mocks to verify communications between the system under test and its collaborators (figure 6.4).

**Collaboration
verification**

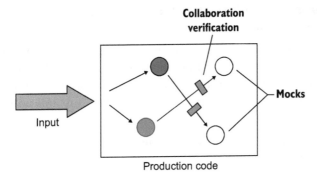

**Figure 6.4 In communication-based
testing, tests substitute the SUT's
collaborators with mocks and verify
that the SUT calls those
collaborators correctly.**

The following listing shows an example of communication-based testing.

Listing 6.3 Communication-based testing

```
[Fact]
public void Sending_a_greetings_email()
{
    var emailGatewayMock = new Mock<IEmailGateway>();
    var sut = new Controller(emailGatewayMock.Object);

    sut.GreetUser("user@email.com");

    emailGatewayMock.Verify(
        x => x.SendGreetingsEmail("user@email.com"),
        Times.Once);
}
```

Styles and schools of unit testing
The classical school of unit testing prefers the state-based style over the communication-based one. The London school makes the opposite choice. Both schools use output-based testing.

6.2 *Comparing the three styles of unit testing*

There's nothing new about output-based, state-based, and communication-based styles of unit testing. In fact, you already saw all of these styles previously in this book. What's interesting is comparing them to each other using the four attributes of a good unit test. Here are those attributes again (refer to chapter 4 for more details):

- Protection against regressions
- Resistance to refactoring
- Fast feedback
- Maintainability

In our comparison, let's look at each of the four separately.

6.2.1   Comparing the styles using the metrics of protection against regressions and feedback speed

Let's first compare the three styles in terms of the protection against regressions and feedback speed attributes, as these attributes are the most straightforward in this particular comparison. The metric of protection against regressions doesn't depend on a particular style of testing. This metric is a product of the following three characteristics:

- The amount of code that is executed during the test
- The complexity of that code
- Its domain significance

Generally, you can write a test that exercises as much or as little code as you like; no particular style provides a benefit in this area. The same is true for the code's complexity and domain significance. The only exception is the communication-based style: overusing it can result in shallow tests that verify only a thin slice of code and mock out everything else. Such shallowness is not a definitive feature of communication-based testing, though, but rather is an extreme case of abusing this technique.

There's little correlation between the styles of testing and the test's feedback speed. As long as your tests don't touch out-of-process dependencies and thus stay in the realm of unit testing, all styles produce tests of roughly equal speed of execution. Communication-based testing can be slightly worse because mocks tend to introduce additional latency at runtime. But the difference is negligible, unless you have tens of thousands of such tests.

6.2.2   Comparing the styles using the metric of resistance to refactoring

When it comes to the metric of resistance to refactoring, the situation is different. *Resistance to refactoring* is the measure of how many *false positives* (false alarms) tests generate during refactorings. False positives, in turn, are a result of tests coupling to code's implementation details as opposed to observable behavior.

Output-based testing provides the best protection against false positives because the resulting tests couple only to the method under test. The only way for such tests to couple to implementation details is when the method under test is itself an implementation detail.

State-based testing is usually more prone to false positives. In addition to the method under test, such tests also work with the class's state. Probabilistically speaking, the greater the coupling between the test and the production code, the greater the chance for this test to tie to a leaking implementation detail. State-based tests tie to a larger API surface, and hence the chances of coupling them to implementation details are also higher.

Communication-based testing is the most vulnerable to false alarms. As you may remember from chapter 5, the vast majority of tests that check interactions with test doubles end up being brittle. This is always the case for interactions with stubs—you should never check such interactions. Mocks are fine only when they verify interactions that cross the application boundary and only when the side effects of those interactions are visible to the external world. As you can see, using communication-based testing requires extra prudence in order to maintain proper resistance to refactoring.

But just like shallowness, brittleness is not a definitive feature of the communication-based style, either. You can reduce the number of false positives to a minimum by maintaining proper encapsulation and coupling tests to observable behavior only. Admittedly, though, the amount of due diligence varies depending on the style of unit testing.

6.2.3 *Comparing the styles using the metric of maintainability*

Finally, the maintainability metric is highly correlated with the styles of unit testing; but, unlike with resistance to refactoring, there's not much you can do to mitigate that. *Maintainability* evaluates the unit tests' maintenance costs and is defined by the following two characteristics:

- How hard it is to understand the test, which is a function of the test's size
- How hard it is to run the test, which is a function of how many out-of-process dependencies the test works with directly

Larger tests are less maintainable because they are harder to grasp or change when needed. Similarly, a test that directly works with one or several out-of-process dependencies (such as the database) is less maintainable because you need to spend time keeping those out-of-process dependencies operational: rebooting the database server, resolving network connectivity issues, and so on.

Maintainability of output-based tests

Compared with the other two types of testing, output-based testing is the most maintainable. The resulting tests are almost always short and concise and thus are easier to maintain. This benefit of the output-based style stems from the fact that this style boils down to only two things: supplying an input to a method and verifying its output, which you can often do with just a couple lines of code.

Because the underlying code in output-based testing must not change the global or internal state, these tests don't deal with out-of-process dependencies. Hence, output-based tests are best in terms of both maintainability characteristics.

Maintainability of state-based tests

State-based tests are normally less maintainable than output-based ones. This is because state verification often takes up more space than output verification. Here's another example of state-based testing.

Listing 6.4   State verification that takes up a lot of space

```
[Fact]
public void Adding_a_comment_to_an_article()
{
    var sut = new Article();
    var text = "Comment text";
    var author = "John Doe";
    var now = new DateTime(2019, 4, 1);

    sut.AddComment(text, author, now);

    Assert.Equal(1, sut.Comments.Count);
    Assert.Equal(text, sut.Comments[0].Text);            Verifies the state
    Assert.Equal(author, sut.Comments[0].Author);        of the article
    Assert.Equal(now, sut.Comments[0].DateCreated);
}
```

This test adds a comment to an article and then checks to see if the comment appears in the article's list of comments. Although this test is simplified and contains just a single comment, its assertion part already spans four lines. State-based tests often need to verify much more data than that and, therefore, can grow in size significantly.

You can mitigate this issue by introducing helper methods that hide most of the code and thus shorten the test (see listing 6.5), but these methods require significant effort to write and maintain. This effort is justified only when those methods are going to be reused across multiple tests, which is rarely the case. I'll explain more about helper methods in part 3 of this book.

Listing 6.5   Using helper methods in assertions

```
[Fact]
public void Adding_a_comment_to_an_article()
{
    var sut = new Article();
    var text = "Comment text";
    var author = "John Doe";
    var now = new DateTime(2019, 4, 1);

    sut.AddComment(text, author, now);

    sut.ShouldContainNumberOfComments(1)         Helper
        .WithComment(text, author, now);         methods
}
```

Another way to shorten a state-based test is to define equality members in the class that is being asserted. In listing 6.6, that's the Comment class. You could turn it into a *value object* (a class whose instances are compared by value and not by reference), as shown next; this would also simplify the test, especially if you combined it with an assertion library like Fluent Assertions.

Listing 6.6   Comment compared by value

```
[Fact]
public void Adding_a_comment_to_an_article()
{
    var sut = new Article();
    var comment = new Comment(
        "Comment text",
        "John Doe",
        new DateTime(2019, 4, 1));

    sut.AddComment(comment.Text, comment.Author, comment.DateCreated);

    sut.Comments.Should().BeEquivalentTo(comment);
}
```

This test uses the fact that comments can be compared as whole values, without the need to assert individual properties in them. It also uses the BeEquivalentTo method from Fluent Assertions, which can compare entire collections, thereby removing the need to check the collection size.

This is a powerful technique, but it works only when the class is inherently a *value* and can be converted into a value object. Otherwise, it leads to *code pollution* (polluting production code base with code whose sole purpose is to enable or, as in this case, simplify unit testing). We'll discuss code pollution along with other unit testing anti-patterns in chapter 11.

As you can see, these two techniques—using helper methods and converting classes into value objects—are applicable only occasionally. And even when these techniques are applicable, state-based tests still take up more space than output-based tests and thus remain less maintainable.

MAINTAINABILITY OF COMMUNICATION-BASED TESTS

Communication-based tests score worse than output-based and state-based tests on the maintainability metric. Communication-based testing requires setting up test doubles and interaction assertions, and that takes up a lot of space. Tests become even larger and less maintainable when you have *mock chains* (mocks or stubs returning other mocks, which also return mocks, and so on, several layers deep).

6.2.4   *Comparing the styles: The results*

Let's now compare the styles of unit testing using the attributes of a good unit test. Table 6.1 sums up the comparison results. As discussed in section 6.2.1, all three styles score equally with the metrics of protection against regressions and feedback speed; hence, I'm omitting these metrics from the comparison.

Output-based testing shows the best results. This style produces tests that rarely couple to implementation details and thus don't require much due diligence to maintain proper resistance to refactoring. Such tests are also the most maintainable due to their conciseness and lack of out-of-process dependencies.

Table 6.1 **The three styles of unit testing: The comparisons**

	Output-based	State-based	Communication-based
Due diligence to maintain resistance to refactoring	Low	Medium	Medium
Maintainability costs	Low	Medium	High

State-based and communication-based tests are worse on both metrics. These are more likely to couple to a leaking implementation detail, and they also incur higher maintenance costs due to being larger in size.

Always prefer output-based testing over everything else. Unfortunately, it's easier said than done. This style of unit testing is only applicable to code that is written in a functional way, which is rarely the case for most object-oriented programming languages. Still, there are techniques you can use to transition more of your tests toward the output-based style.

The rest of this chapter shows how to transition from state-based and collaboration-based testing to output-based testing. The transition requires you to make your code more purely functional, which, in turn, enables the use of output-based tests instead of state- or communication-based ones.

6.3   *Understanding functional architecture*

Some groundwork is needed before I can show how to make the transition. In this section, you'll see what functional programming and functional architecture are and how the latter relates to the hexagonal architecture. Section 6.4 illustrates the transition using an example.

Note that this isn't a deep dive into the topic of functional programming, but rather an explanation of the basic principles behind it. These basic principles should be enough to understand the connection between functional programming and output-based testing. For a deeper look at functional programming, see Scott Wlaschin's website and books at https://fsharpforfunandprofit.com/books.

6.3.1   *What is functional programming?*

As I mentioned in section 6.1.1, the output-based unit testing style is also known as *functional.* That's because it requires the underlying production code to be written in a purely functional way, using functional programming. So, what is functional programming?

Functional programming is programming with mathematical functions. A *mathematical function* (also known as *pure function*) is a function (or method) that doesn't have any hidden inputs or outputs. All inputs and outputs of a mathematical function must be explicitly expressed in its *method signature*, which consists of the method's name, arguments, and return type. A mathematical function produces the same output for a given input regardless of how many times it is called.

Let's take the `CalculateDiscount()` method from listing 6.1 as an example (I'm copying it here for convenience):

```
public decimal CalculateDiscount(Product[] products)
{
    decimal discount = products.Length * 0.01m;
    return Math.Min(discount, 0.2m);
}
```

This method has one input (a `Product` array) and one output (the `decimal` discount), both of which are explicitly expressed in the method's signature. There are no hidden inputs or outputs. This makes `CalculateDiscount()` a mathematical function (figure 6.5).

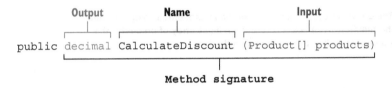

Figure 6.5 `CalculateDiscount()` has one input (a `Product` array) and one output (the `decimal` discount). Both the input and the output are explicitly expressed in the method's signature, which makes `CalculateDiscount()` a mathematical function.

Methods with no hidden inputs and outputs are called mathematical functions because such methods adhere to the definition of a function in mathematics.

DEFINITION In mathematics, a *function* is a relationship between two sets that for each element in the first set, finds exactly one element in the second set.

Figure 6.6 shows how for each input number x, function $f(x) = x + 1$ finds a corresponding number y. Figure 6.7 displays the `CalculateDiscount()` method using the same notation as in figure 6.6.

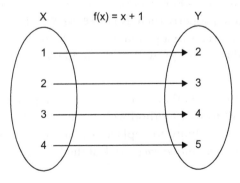

Figure 6.6 A typical example of a function in mathematics is $f(x) = x + 1$. For each input number x in set X, the function finds a corresponding number y in set Y.

CalculateDiscount()

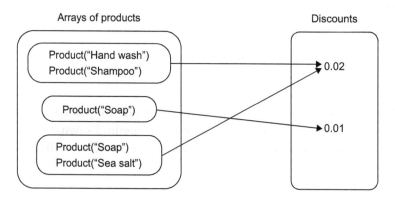

Figure 6.7 The `CalculateDiscount()` method represented using the same notation as the function `f(x) = x + 1`. For each input array of products, the method finds a corresponding discount as an output.

Explicit inputs and outputs make mathematical functions extremely testable because the resulting tests are short, simple, and easy to understand and maintain. Mathematical functions are the only type of methods where you can apply output-based testing, which has the best maintainability and the lowest chance of producing a false positive.

On the other hand, hidden inputs and outputs make the code less testable (and less readable, too). Types of such hidden inputs and outputs include the following:

- *Side effects*—A *side effect* is an output that isn't expressed in the method signature and, therefore, is hidden. An operation creates a side effect when it mutates the state of a class instance, updates a file on the disk, and so on.
- *Exceptions*—When a method throws an exception, it creates a path in the program flow that bypasses the contract established by the method's signature. The thrown exception can be caught anywhere in the call stack, thus introducing an additional output that the method signature doesn't convey.
- *A reference to an internal or external state*—For example, a method can get the current date and time using a static property such as `DateTime.Now`. It can query data from the database, or it can refer to a private mutable field. These are all inputs to the execution flow that aren't present in the method signature and, therefore, are hidden.

A good rule of thumb when determining whether a method is a mathematical function is to see if you can replace a call to that method with its return value without changing the program's behavior. The ability to replace a method call with the corresponding value is known as *referential transparency*. Look at the following method, for example:

```
public int Increment(int x)
{
    return x + 1;
}
```

This method is a mathematical function. These two statements are equivalent to each other:

```
int y = Increment(4);
int y = 5;
```

On the other hand, the following method is *not* a mathematical function. You can't replace it with the return value because that return value doesn't represent all of the method's outputs. In this example, the hidden output is the change to field x (a side effect):

```
int x = 0;
public int Increment()
{
    x++;
    return x;
}
```

Side effects are the most prevalent type of hidden outputs. The following listing shows an AddComment method that looks like a mathematical function on the surface but actually isn't one. Figure 6.8 shows the method graphically.

Listing 6.7 Modification of an internal state

```
public Comment AddComment(string text)
{
    var comment = new Comment(text);
    _comments.Add(comment);            ◁────── Side effect
     return comment;
}
```

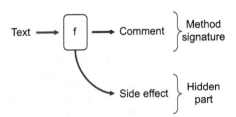

Figure 6.8 Method AddComment (shown as f) has a text input and a Comment output, which are both expressed in the method signature. The side effect is an additional hidden output.

6.3.2   *What is functional architecture?*

You can't create an application that doesn't incur any side effects whatsoever, of course. Such an application would be impractical. After all, side effects are what you create all applications for: updating the user's information, adding a new order line to the shopping cart, and so on.

The goal of functional programming is not to eliminate side effects altogether but rather to introduce a separation between code that handles business logic and code that incurs side effects. These two responsibilities are complex enough on their own; mixing them together multiplies the complexity and hinders code maintainability in the long run. This is where functional architecture comes into play. It separates business logic from side effects by *pushing those side effects to the edges of a business operation*.

> **DEFINITION**   *Functional architecture* maximizes the amount of code written in a purely functional (immutable) way, while minimizing code that deals with side effects. *Immutable* means unchangeable: once an object is created, its state can't be modified. This is in contrast to a *mutable* object (changeable object), which can be modified after it is created.

The separation between business logic and side effects is done by segregating two types of code:

- *Code that makes a decision*—This code doesn't require side effects and thus can be written using mathematical functions.
- *Code that acts upon that decision*—This code converts all the decisions made by the mathematical functions into visible bits, such as changes in the database or messages sent to a bus.

The code that makes decisions is often referred to as a *functional core* (also known as an *immutable core*). The code that acts upon those decisions is a *mutable shell* (figure 6.9).

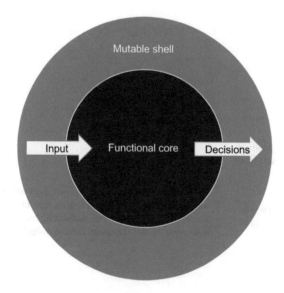

Figure 6.9   In functional architecture, the functional core is implemented using mathematical functions and makes all decisions in the application. The mutable shell provides the functional core with input data and interprets its decisions by applying side effects to out-of-process dependencies such as a database.

The functional core and the mutable shell cooperate in the following way:

- The mutable shell gathers all the inputs.
- The functional core generates decisions.
- The shell converts the decisions into side effects.

To maintain a proper separation between these two layers, you need to make sure the classes representing the decisions contain enough information for the mutable shell to act upon them without additional decision-making. In other words, the mutable shell should be as dumb as possible. The goal is to cover the functional core extensively with output-based tests and leave the mutable shell to a much smaller number of integration tests.

Encapsulation and immutability

Like encapsulation, functional architecture (in general) and immutability (in particular) serve the same goal as unit testing: enabling sustainable growth of your software project. In fact, there's a deep connection between the concepts of encapsulation and immutability.

As you may remember from chapter 5, *encapsulation* is the act of protecting your code against inconsistencies. Encapsulation safeguards the class's internals from corruption by

- Reducing the API surface area that allows for data modification
- Putting the remaining APIs under scrutiny

Immutability tackles this issue of preserving invariants from another angle. With immutable classes, you don't need to worry about state corruption because it's impossible to corrupt something that cannot be changed in the first place. As a consequence, there's no need for encapsulation in functional programming. You only need to validate the class's state once, when you create an instance of it. After that, you can freely pass this instance around. When all your data is immutable, the whole set of issues related to the lack of encapsulation simply vanishes.

There's a great quote from Michael Feathers in that regard:

> *Object-oriented programming makes code understandable by encapsulating moving parts. Functional programming makes code understandable by minimizing moving parts.*

6.3.3 Comparing functional and hexagonal architectures

There are a lot of similarities between functional and hexagonal architectures. Both of them are built around the idea of separation of concerns. The details of that separation vary, though.

As you may remember from chapter 5, the hexagonal architecture differentiates the domain layer and the application services layer (figure 6.10). The *domain layer* is accountable for business logic while the *application services layer*, for communication with

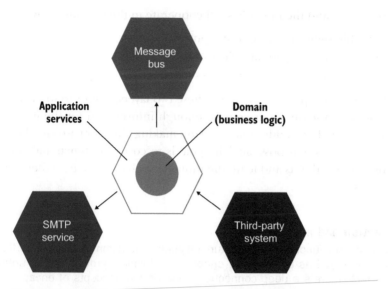

Figure 6.10 Hexagonal architecture is a set of interacting applications—hexagons. Your application consists of a domain layer and an application services layer, which correspond to a functional core and a mutable shell in functional architecture.

external applications such as a database or an SMTP service. This is very similar to functional architecture, where you introduce the separation of decisions and actions.

Another similarity is the one-way flow of dependencies. In the hexagonal architecture, classes inside the domain layer should only depend on each other; they should not depend on classes from the application services layer. Likewise, the immutable core in functional architecture doesn't depend on the mutable shell. It's self-sufficient and can work in isolation from the outer layers. This is what makes functional architecture so testable: you can strip the immutable core from the mutable shell entirely and simulate the inputs that the shell provides using simple values.

The difference between the two is in their treatment of side effects. Functional architecture pushes *all* side effects out of the immutable core to the edges of a business operation. These edges are handled by the mutable shell. On the other hand, the hexagonal architecture is fine with side effects made by the domain layer, as long as they are limited to that domain layer only. All modifications in hexagonal architecture should be contained within the domain layer and *not* cross that layer's boundary. For example, a domain class instance can't persist something to the database directly, but it can change its own state. An application service will then pick up this change and apply it to the database.

> **NOTE** Functional architecture is a subset of the hexagonal architecture. You can view functional architecture as the hexagonal architecture taken to an extreme.

6.4 Transitioning to functional architecture and output-based testing

In this section, we'll take a sample application and refactor it toward functional architecture. You'll see two refactoring stages:

- Moving from using an out-of-process dependency to using mocks
- Moving from using mocks to using functional architecture

The transition affects test code, too! We'll refactor state-based and communication-based tests to the output-based style of unit testing. Before starting the refactoring, let's review the sample project and tests covering it.

6.4.1 Introducing an audit system

The sample project is an audit system that keeps track of all visitors in an organization. It uses flat text files as underlying storage with the structure shown in figure 6.11. The system appends the visitor's name and the time of their visit to the end of the most recent file. When the maximum number of entries per file is reached, a new file with an incremented index is created.

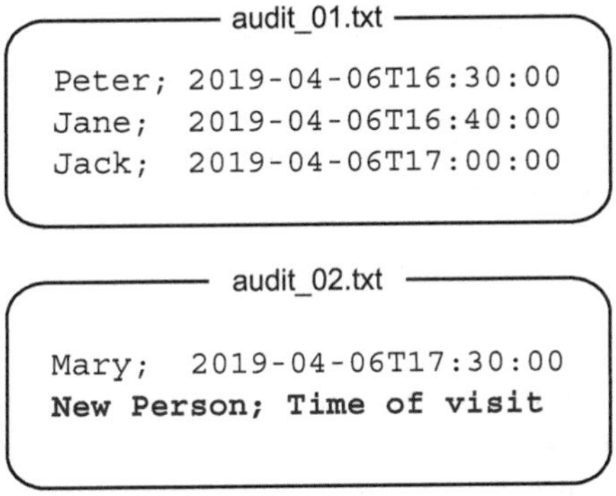

```
——————— audit_01.txt ———————

Peter;  2019-04-06T16:30:00
Jane;   2019-04-06T16:40:00
Jack;   2019-04-06T17:00:00
```

```
——————— audit_02.txt ———————

Mary;   2019-04-06T17:30:00
New Person;  Time of visit
```

Figure 6.11 The audit system stores information about visitors in text files with a specific format. When the maximum number of entries per file is reached, the system creates a new file.

The following listing shows the initial version of the system.

Listing 6.8 Initial implementation of the audit system

```
public class AuditManager
{
    private readonly int _maxEntriesPerFile;
    private readonly string _directoryName;

    public AuditManager(int maxEntriesPerFile, string directoryName)
    {
        _maxEntriesPerFile = maxEntriesPerFile;
        _directoryName = directoryName;
    }
```

```
public void AddRecord(string visitorName, DateTime timeOfVisit)
{
    string[] filePaths = Directory.GetFiles(_directoryName);
    (int index, string path)[] sorted = SortByIndex(filePaths);

    string newRecord = visitorName + ';' + timeOfVisit;

    if (sorted.Length == 0)
    {
        string newFile = Path.Combine(_directoryName, "audit_1.txt");
        File.WriteAllText(newFile, newRecord);
        return;
    }

    (int currentFileIndex, string currentFilePath) = sorted.Last();
    List<string> lines = File.ReadAllLines(currentFilePath).ToList();

    if (lines.Count < _maxEntriesPerFile)
    {
        lines.Add(newRecord);
        string newContent = string.Join("\r\n", lines);
        File.WriteAllText(currentFilePath, newContent);
    }
    else
    {
        int newIndex = currentFileIndex + 1;
        string newName = $"audit_{newIndex}.txt";
        string newFile = Path.Combine(_directoryName, newName);
        File.WriteAllText(newFile, newRecord);
    }
}
```

The code might look a bit large, but it's quite simple. AuditManager is the main class in the application. Its constructor accepts the maximum number of entries per file and the working directory as configuration parameters. The only public method in the class is AddRecord, which does all the work of the audit system:

- Retrieves a full list of files from the working directory
- Sorts them by index (all filenames follow the same pattern: audit_{index}.txt [for example, audit_1.txt])
- If there are no audit files yet, creates a first one with a single record
- If there are audit files, gets the most recent one and either appends the new record to it or creates a new file, depending on whether the number of entries in that file has reached the limit

The AuditManager class is hard to test as-is, because it's tightly coupled to the file-system. Before the test, you'd need to put files in the right place, and after the test finishes, you'd read those files, check their contents, and clear them out (figure 6.12).

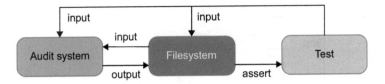

Figure 6.12 Tests covering the initial version of the audit system would have to work directly with the filesystem.

You won't be able to parallelize such tests—at least, not without additional effort that would significantly increase maintenance costs. The bottleneck is the filesystem: it's a shared dependency through which tests can interfere with each other's execution flow.

The filesystem also makes the tests slow. Maintainability suffers, too, because you have to make sure the working directory exists and is accessible to tests—both on your local machine and on the build server. Table 6.2 sums up the scoring.

Table 6.2 The initial version of the audit system scores badly on two out of the four attributes of a good test.

	Initial version
Protection against regressions	Good
Resistance to refactoring	Good
Fast feedback	Bad
Maintainability	Bad

By the way, tests working directly with the filesystem don't fit the definition of a unit test. They don't comply with the second and the third attributes of a unit test, thereby falling into the category of integration tests (see chapter 2 for more details):

- A unit test verifies a single unit of behavior,
- Does it quickly,
- And does it in isolation from other tests.

6.4.2 *Using mocks to decouple tests from the filesystem*

The usual solution to the problem of tightly coupled tests is to mock the filesystem. You can extract all operations on files into a separate class (IFileSystem) and inject that class into AuditManager via the constructor. The tests will then mock this class and capture the writes the audit system do to the files (figure 6.13).

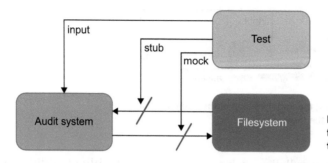

Figure 6.13 **Tests can mock the filesystem and capture the writes the audit system makes to the files.**

The following listing shows how the filesystem is injected into AuditManager.

Listing 6.9 Injecting the filesystem explicitly via the constructor

```
public class AuditManager
{
    private readonly int _maxEntriesPerFile;
    private readonly string _directoryName;
    private readonly IFileSystem _fileSystem;        ◁─────┐

    public AuditManager(
        int maxEntriesPerFile,
        string directoryName,                                 The new interface
        IFileSystem fileSystem)                               represents the
    {                                                         filesystem.

        _maxEntriesPerFile = maxEntriesPerFile;
        _directoryName = directoryName;
        _fileSystem = fileSystem;                    ◁─────┘
    }
}
```

And next is the AddRecord method.

Listing 6.10 Using the new IFileSystem interface

```
public void AddRecord(string visitorName, DateTime timeOfVisit)
{
    string[] filePaths = _fileSystem
        .GetFiles(_directoryName);
    (int index, string path)[] sorted = SortByIndex(filePaths);

    string newRecord = visitorName + ';' + timeOfVisit;

    if (sorted.Length == 0)
    {
        string newFile = Path.Combine(_directoryName, "audit_1.txt");
        _fileSystem.WriteAllText(
            newFile, newRecord);
        return;
    }
```

The new interface in action

```
                    (int currentFileIndex, string currentFilePath) = sorted.Last();
                    List<string> lines = _fileSystem
                        .ReadAllLines(currentFilePath);

                    if (lines.Count < _maxEntriesPerFile)
                    {
                        lines.Add(newRecord);
                        string newContent = string.Join("\r\n", lines);
                        _fileSystem.WriteAllText(
                            currentFilePath, newContent);
                    }
                    else
                    {
                        int newIndex = currentFileIndex + 1;
                        string newName = $"audit_{newIndex}.txt";
                        string newFile = Path.Combine(_directoryName, newName);
                        _fileSystem.WriteAllText(
                            newFile, newRecord);
                    }
                }
```

The new interface in action

In listing 6.10, IFileSystem is a new custom interface that encapsulates the work with the filesystem:

```
public interface IFileSystem
{
    string[] GetFiles(string directoryName);
    void WriteAllText(string filePath, string content);
    List<string> ReadAllLines(string filePath);
}
```

Now that AuditManager is decoupled from the filesystem, the shared dependency is gone, and tests can execute independently from each other. Here's one such test.

Listing 6.11 Checking the audit system's behavior using a mock

```
[Fact]
public void A_new_file_is_created_when_the_current_file_overflows()
{
    var fileSystemMock = new Mock<IFileSystem>();
    fileSystemMock
        .Setup(x => x.GetFiles("audits"))
        .Returns(new string[]
        {
            @"audits\audit_1.txt",
            @"audits\audit_2.txt"
        });
    fileSystemMock
        .Setup(x => x.ReadAllLines(@"audits\audit_2.txt"))
        .Returns(new List<string>
        {
            "Peter; 2019-04-06T16:30:00",
            "Jane; 2019-04-06T16:40:00",
```

```
            "Jack; 2019-04-06T17:00:00"
        });
    var sut = new AuditManager(3, "audits", fileSystemMock.Object);

    sut.AddRecord("Alice", DateTime.Parse("2019-04-06T18:00:00"));

    fileSystemMock.Verify(x => x.WriteAllText(
        @"audits\audit_3.txt",
        "Alice;2019-04-06T18:00:00"));
}
```

This test verifies that when the number of entries in the current file reaches the limit (3, in this example), a new file with a single audit entry is created. Note that this is a legitimate use of mocks. The application creates files that are visible to end users (assuming that those users use another program to read the files, be it specialized software or a simple notepad.exe). Therefore, communications with the filesystem and the side effects of these communications (that is, the changes in files) are part of the application's observable behavior. As you may remember from chapter 5, that's the only legitimate use case for mocking.

This alternative implementation is an improvement over the initial version. Since tests no longer access the filesystem, they execute faster. And because you don't need to look after the filesystem to keep the tests happy, the maintenance costs are also reduced. Protection against regressions and resistance to refactoring didn't suffer from the refactoring either. Table 6.3 shows the differences between the two versions.

Table 6.3 The version with mocks compared to the initial version of the audit system

	Initial version	With mocks
Protection against regressions	Good	Good
Resistance to refactoring	Good	Good
Fast feedback	Bad	Good
Maintainability	Bad	Moderate

We can still do better, though. The test in listing 6.11 contains convoluted setups, which is less than ideal in terms of maintenance costs. Mocking libraries try their best to be helpful, but the resulting tests are still not as readable as those that rely on plain input and output.

6.4.3 *Refactoring toward functional architecture*

Instead of hiding side effects behind an interface and injecting that interface into AuditManager, you can move those side effects out of the class entirely. Audit-Manager is then only responsible for making a decision about what to do with the files. A new class, Persister, acts on that decision and applies updates to the filesystem (figure 6.14).

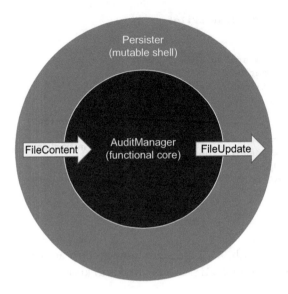

Figure 6.14 `Persister` and `AuditManager` **form the functional architecture.** `Persister` **gathers files and their contents from the working directory, feeds them to** `AuditManager`, **and then converts the return value into changes in the filesystem.**

`Persister` in this scenario acts as a mutable shell, while `AuditManager` becomes a functional (immutable) core. The following listing shows `AuditManager` after the refactoring.

Listing 6.12 The `AuditManager` class after refactoring

```
public class AuditManager
{
    private readonly int _maxEntriesPerFile;

    public AuditManager(int maxEntriesPerFile)
    {
        _maxEntriesPerFile = maxEntriesPerFile;
    }

    public FileUpdate AddRecord(
        FileContent[] files,
        string visitorName,
        DateTime timeOfVisit)
    {
        (int index, FileContent file)[] sorted = SortByIndex(files);

        string newRecord = visitorName + ';' + timeOfVisit;

        if (sorted.Length == 0)
        {
            return new FileUpdate(          │ Returns an update
                "audit_1.txt", newRecord);  │ instruction
        }

        (int currentFileIndex, FileContent currentFile) = sorted.Last();
        List<string> lines = currentFile.Lines.ToList();
```

```
            if (lines.Count < _maxEntriesPerFile)
            {
                lines.Add(newRecord);
                string newContent = string.Join("\r\n", lines);
                return new FileUpdate(
                    currentFile.FileName, newContent);
            }
            else
            {
                int newIndex = currentFileIndex + 1;
                string newName = $"audit_{newIndex}.txt";
                return new FileUpdate(
                    newName, newRecord);
            }
        }
    }
}
```

Returns an update instruction

Instead of the working directory path, `AuditManager` now accepts an array of `File-Content`. This class includes everything `AuditManager` needs to know about the filesystem to make a decision:

```
public class FileContent
{
    public readonly string FileName;
    public readonly string[] Lines;

    public FileContent(string fileName, string[] lines)
    {
        FileName = fileName;
        Lines = lines;
    }
}
```

And, instead of mutating files in the working directory, `AuditManager` now returns an instruction for the side effect it would like to perform:

```
public class FileUpdate
{
    public readonly string FileName;
    public readonly string NewContent;

    public FileUpdate(string fileName, string newContent)
    {
        FileName = fileName;
        NewContent = newContent;
    }
}
```

The following listing shows the `Persister` class.

Listing 6.13   The mutable shell acting on `AuditManager`'s decision

```
public class Persister
{
    public FileContent[] ReadDirectory(string directoryName)
    {
        return Directory
            .GetFiles(directoryName)
            .Select(x => new FileContent(
                Path.GetFileName(x),
                File.ReadAllLines(x)))
            .ToArray();
    }

    public void ApplyUpdate(string directoryName, FileUpdate update)
    {
        string filePath = Path.Combine(directoryName, update.FileName);
        File.WriteAllText(filePath, update.NewContent);
    }
}
```

Notice how trivial this class is. All it does is read content from the working directory and apply updates it receives from `AuditManager` back to that working directory. It has no branching (no `if` statements); all the complexity resides in the `AuditManager` class. *This is the separation between business logic and side effects in action.*

To maintain such a separation, you need to keep the interface of `FileContent` and `FileUpdate` as close as possible to that of the framework's built-in file-interaction commands. All the parsing and preparation should be done in the functional core, so that the code outside of that core remains trivial. For example, if .NET didn't contain the built-in `File.ReadAllLines()` method, which returns the file content as an array of lines, and only has `File.ReadAllText()`, which returns a single string, you'd need to replace the `Lines` property in `FileContent` with a `string` too and do the parsing in `AuditManager`:

```
public class FileContent
{
    public readonly string FileName;
    public readonly string Text; // previously, string[] Lines;
}
```

To glue `AuditManager` and `Persister` together, you need another class: an application service in the hexagonal architecture taxonomy, as shown in the following listing.

Listing 6.14   Gluing together the functional core and mutable shell

```
public class ApplicationService
{
    private readonly string _directoryName;
    private readonly AuditManager _auditManager;
    private readonly Persister _persister;
```

```
public ApplicationService(
    string directoryName, int maxEntriesPerFile)
{
    _directoryName = directoryName;
    _auditManager = new AuditManager(maxEntriesPerFile);
    _persister = new Persister();
}

public void AddRecord(string visitorName, DateTime timeOfVisit)
{
    FileContent[] files = _persister.ReadDirectory(_directoryName);
    FileUpdate update = _auditManager.AddRecord(
        files, visitorName, timeOfVisit);
    _persister.ApplyUpdate(_directoryName, update);
}
}
```

Along with gluing the functional core together with the mutable shell, the application service also provides an entry point to the system for external clients (figure 6.15). With this implementation, it becomes easy to check the audit system's behavior. All tests now boil down to supplying a hypothetical state of the working directory and verifying the decision AuditManager makes.

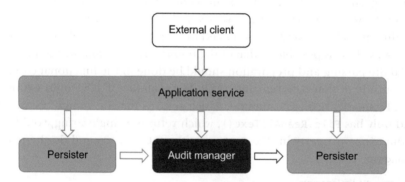

Figure 6.15 ApplicationService glues the functional core (AuditManager) and the mutable shell (Persister) together and provides an entry point for external clients. In the hexagonal architecture taxonomy, ApplicationService and Persister are part of the application services layer, while AuditManager belongs to the domain model.

Listing 6.15   The test without mocks

```
[Fact]
public void A_new_file_is_created_when_the_current_file_overflows()
{
    var sut = new AuditManager(3);
    var files = new FileContent[]
    {
        new FileContent("audit_1.txt", new string[0]),
```

```
        new FileContent("audit_2.txt", new string[]
        {
            "Peter; 2019-04-06T16:30:00",
            "Jane; 2019-04-06T16:40:00",
            "Jack; 2019-04-06T17:00:00"
        })
    };

    FileUpdate update = sut.AddRecord(
        files, "Alice", DateTime.Parse("2019-04-06T18:00:00"));

    Assert.Equal("audit_3.txt", update.FileName);
    Assert.Equal("Alice;2019-04-06T18:00:00", update.NewContent);
}
```

This test retains the improvement the test with mocks made over the initial version (fast feedback) but also further improves on the maintainability metric. There's no need for complex mock setups anymore, only plain inputs and outputs, which helps the test's readability a lot. Table 6.4 compares the output-based test with the initial version and the version with mocks.

Table 6.4 The output-based test compared to the previous two versions

	Initial version	With mocks	Output-based
Protection against regressions	Good	Good	Good
Resistance to refactoring	Good	Good	Good
Fast feedback	Bad	Good	Good
Maintainability	Bad	Moderate	Good

Notice that the instructions generated by a functional core are always a *value* or a *set of values.* Two instances of such a value are interchangeable as long as their contents match. You can take advantage of this fact and improve test readability even further by turning `FileUpdate` into a value object. To do that in .NET, you need to either convert the class into a `struct` or define custom equality members. That will give you comparison by value, as opposed to the comparison by reference, which is the default behavior for classes in C#. Comparison by value also allows you to compress the two assertions from listing 6.15 into one:

```
Assert.Equal(
    new FileUpdate("audit_3.txt", "Alice;2019-04-06T18:00:00"),
    update);
```

Or, using Fluent Assertions,

```
update.Should().Be(
    new FileUpdate("audit_3.txt", "Alice;2019-04-06T18:00:00"));
```

6.4.4 *Looking forward to further developments*

Let's step back for a minute and look at further developments that could be done in our sample project. The audit system I showed you is quite simple and contains only three branches:

- Creating a new file in case of an empty working directory
- Appending a new record to an existing file
- Creating another file when the number of entries in the current file exceeds the limit

Also, there's only one use case: addition of a new entry to the audit log. What if there were another use case, such as deleting all mentions of a particular visitor? And what if the system needed to do validations (say, for the maximum length of the visitor's name)?

Deleting all mentions of a particular visitor could potentially affect several files, so the new method would need to return multiple file instructions:

```
public FileUpdate[] DeleteAllMentions(
    FileContent[] files, string visitorName)
```

Furthermore, business people might require that you not keep empty files in the working directory. If the deleted entry was the last entry in an audit file, you would need to remove that file altogether. To implement this requirement, you could rename FileUpdate to FileAction and introduce an additional ActionType enum field to indicate whether it was an update or a deletion.

Error handling also becomes simpler and more explicit with functional architecture. You could embed errors into the method's signature, either in the FileUpdate class or as a separate component:

```
public (FileUpdate update, Error error) AddRecord(
    FileContent[] files,
    string visitorName,
    DateTime timeOfVisit)
```

The application service would then check for this error. If it was there, the service wouldn't pass the update instruction to the persister, instead propagating an error message to the user.

6.5 *Understanding the drawbacks of functional architecture*

Unfortunately, functional architecture isn't always attainable. And even when it is, the maintainability benefits are often offset by a performance impact and increase in the size of the code base. In this section, we'll explore the costs and the trade-offs attached to functional architecture.

6.5.1 Applicability of functional architecture

Functional architecture worked for our audit system because this system could gather all the inputs up front, before making a decision. Often, though, the execution flow is less straightforward. You might need to query additional data from an out-of-process dependency, based on an intermediate result of the decision-making process.

Here's an example. Let's say the audit system needs to check the visitor's access level if the number of times they have visited during the last 24 hours exceeds some threshold. And let's also assume that all visitors' access levels are stored in a database. You can't pass an `IDatabase` instance to `AuditManager` like this:

```
public FileUpdate AddRecord(
    FileContent[] files, string visitorName,
    DateTime timeOfVisit, IDatabase database
)
```

Such an instance would introduce a hidden input to the `AddRecord()` method. This method would, therefore, cease to be a mathematical function (figure 6.16), which means you would no longer be able to apply output-based testing.

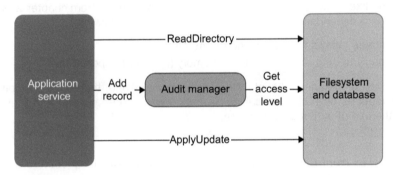

Figure 6.16   A dependency on the database introduces a hidden input to `AuditManager`. Such a class is no longer purely functional, and the whole application no longer follows the functional architecture.

There are two solutions in such a situation:

- You can gather the visitor's access level in the application service up front, along with the directory content.
- You can introduce a new method such as `IsAccessLevelCheckRequired()` in `AuditManager`. The application service would call this method before `Add-Record()`, and if it returned `true`, the service would get the access level from the database and pass it to `AddRecord()`.

Both approaches have drawbacks. The first one concedes performance—it unconditionally queries the database, even in cases when the access level is not required. But this approach keeps the separation of business logic and communication with external systems fully intact: all decision-making resides in `AuditManager` as before. The second approach concedes a degree of that separation for performance gains: the decision as to whether to call the database now goes to the application service, not `AuditManager`.

Note that, unlike these two options, making the domain model (`AuditManager`) depend on the database isn't a good idea. I'll explain more about keeping the balance between performance and separation of concerns in the next two chapters.

Collaborators vs. values

You may have noticed that `AuditManager`'s `AddRecord()` method has a dependency that's not present in its signature: the `_maxEntriesPerFile` field. The audit manager refers to this field to make a decision to either append an existing audit file or create a new one.

Although this dependency isn't present among the method's arguments, it's not hidden. It can be derived from the class's constructor signature. And because the `_maxEntriesPerFile` field is immutable, it stays the same between the class instantiation and the call to `AddRecord()`. In other words, that field is a *value*.

The situation with the `IDatabase` dependency is different because it's a *collaborator*, not a value like `_maxEntriesPerFile`. As you may remember from chapter 2, a collaborator is a dependency that is one or the other of the following:

- Mutable (allows for modification of its state)
- A proxy to data that is not yet in memory (a shared dependency)

The `IDatabase` instance falls into the second category and, therefore, is a collaborator. It requires an additional call to an out-of-process dependency and thus precludes the use of output-based testing.

NOTE   A class from the functional core should work not with a collaborator, but with the product of its work, a value.

6.5.2   *Performance drawbacks*

The performance impact on the system as a whole is a common argument against functional architecture. Note that it's not the performance of tests that suffers. The output-based tests we ended up with work as fast as the tests with mocks. It's that the system itself now has to do more calls to out-of-process dependencies and becomes less performant. The initial version of the audit system didn't read all files from the working directory, and neither did the version with mocks. But the final version does in order to comply with the read-decide-act approach.

The choice between a functional architecture and a more traditional one is a trade-off between performance and code maintainability (both production and test code). In some systems where the performance impact is not as noticeable, it's better to go with functional architecture for additional gains in maintainability. In others, you might need to make the opposite choice. There's no one-size-fits-all solution.

6.5.3 *Increase in the code base size*

The same is true for the size of the code base. Functional architecture requires a clear separation between the functional (immutable) core and the mutable shell. This necessitates additional coding initially, although it ultimately results in reduced code complexity and gains in maintainability.

Not all projects exhibit a high enough degree of complexity to justify such an initial investment, though. Some code bases aren't that significant from a business perspective or are just plain too simple. It doesn't make sense to use functional architecture in such projects because the initial investment will never pay off. Always apply functional architecture strategically, taking into account the complexity and importance of your system.

Finally, don't go for purity of the functional approach if that purity comes at too high a cost. In most projects, you won't be able to make the domain model fully immutable and thus can't rely solely on output-based tests, at least not when using an OOP language like C# or Java. In most cases, you'll have a combination of output-based and state-based styles, with a small mix of communication-based tests, and that's fine. The goal of this chapter is not to incite you to transition *all* your tests toward the output-based style; the goal is to transition as many of them as reasonably possible. The difference is subtle but important.

Summary

- *Output-based* testing is a style of testing where you feed an input to the SUT and check the output it produces. This style of testing assumes there are no hidden inputs or outputs, and the only result of the SUT's work is the value it returns.
- *State-based* testing verifies the state of the system after an operation is completed.
- In *communication-based* testing, you use mocks to verify communications between the system under test and its collaborators.
- The classical school of unit testing prefers the state-based style over the communication-based one. The London school has the opposite preference. Both schools use output-based testing.
- Output-based testing produces tests of the highest quality. Such tests rarely couple to implementation details and thus are resistant to refactoring. They are also small and concise and thus are more maintainable.
- State-based testing requires extra prudence to avoid brittleness: you need to make sure you don't expose a private state to enable unit testing. Because state-based tests tend to be larger than output-based tests, they are also less maintainable. Maintainability issues can sometimes be mitigated (but not eliminated) with the use of helper methods and value objects.
- Communication-based testing also requires extra prudence to avoid brittleness. You should only verify communications that cross the application boundary and whose side effects are visible to the external world. Maintainability of

communication-based tests is worse compared to output-based and state-based tests. Mocks tend to occupy a lot of space, and that makes tests less readable.

- *Functional programming* is programming with mathematical functions.
- A *mathematical function* is a function (or method) that doesn't have any hidden inputs or outputs. Side effects and exceptions are hidden outputs. A reference to an internal or external state is a hidden input. Mathematical functions are explicit, which makes them extremely testable.
- The goal of functional programming is to introduce a separation between business logic and side effects.
- Functional architecture helps achieve that separation by pushing side effects to the edges of a business operation. This approach maximizes the amount of code written in a purely functional way while minimizing code that deals with side effects.
- Functional architecture divides all code into two categories: functional core and mutable shell. The *functional core* makes decisions. The *mutable shell* supplies input data to the functional core and converts decisions the core makes into side effects.
- The difference between functional and hexagonal architectures is in their treatment of side effects. Functional architecture pushes *all* side effects out of the domain layer. Conversely, hexagonal architecture is fine with side effects made by the domain layer, as long as they are limited to that domain layer only. Functional architecture is hexagonal architecture taken to an extreme.
- The choice between a functional architecture and a more traditional one is a trade-off between performance and code maintainability. Functional architecture concedes performance for maintainability gains.
- Not all code bases are worth converting into functional architecture. Apply functional architecture strategically. Take into account the complexity and the importance of your system. In code bases that are simple or not that important, the initial investment required for functional architecture won't pay off.

Refactoring toward valuable unit tests

This chapter covers

- Recognizing the four types of code
- Understanding the Humble Object pattern
- Writing valuable tests

In chapter 1, I defined the properties of a good unit test suite:

- It is integrated into the development cycle.
- It targets only the most important parts of your code base.
- It provides maximum value with minimum maintenance costs. To achieve this last attribute, you need to be able to:
  - Recognize a valuable test (and, by extension, a test of low value).
  - Write a valuable test.

Chapter 4 covered the topic of recognizing a valuable test using the four attributes: protection against regressions, resistance to refactoring, fast feedback, and maintainability. And chapter 5 expanded on the most important one of the four: resistance to refactoring.

As I mentioned earlier, it's not enough to *recognize* valuable tests, you should also be able to *write* such tests. The latter skill requires the former, but it also requires that you know code design techniques. Unit tests and the underlying code are highly intertwined, and it's impossible to create valuable tests without putting effort into the code base they cover.

You saw an example of a code base transformation in chapter 6, where we refactored an audit system toward a functional architecture and, as a result, were able to apply output-based testing. This chapter generalizes this approach onto a wider spectrum of applications, including those that can't use a functional architecture. You'll see practical guidelines on how to write valuable tests in almost any software project.

7.1   *Identifying the code to refactor*

It's rarely possible to significantly improve a test suite without refactoring the underlying code. There's no way around it—test and production code are intrinsically connected. In this section, you'll see how to categorize your code into the four types in order to outline the direction of the refactoring. The subsequent sections show a comprehensive example.

7.1.1   *The four types of code*

In this section, I describe the four types of code that serve as a foundation for the rest of this chapter.

All production code can be categorized along two dimensions:

- Complexity or domain significance
- The number of collaborators

Code complexity is defined by the number of decision-making (branching) points in the code. The greater that number, the higher the complexity.

How to calculate cyclomatic complexity

In computer science, there's a special term that describes code complexity: *cyclomatic complexity*. Cyclomatic complexity indicates the number of branches in a given program or method. This metric is calculated as

```
1 + <number of branching points>
```

Thus, a method with no control flow statements (such as `if` statements or conditional loops) has a cyclomatic complexity of $1 + 0 = 1$.

There's another meaning to this metric. You can think of it in terms of the number of independent paths through the method from an entry to an exit, or the number of tests needed to get a 100% branch coverage.

Note that the number of branching points is counted as the number of simplest predicates involved. For instance, a statement like `IF condition1 AND condition2 THEN ...` is equivalent to `IF condition1 THEN IF condition2 THEN ...` Therefore, its complexity would be $1 + 2 = 3$.

Domain significance shows how significant the code is for the problem domain of your project. Normally, all code in the domain layer has a direct connection to the end users' goals and thus exhibits a high domain significance. On the other hand, utility code doesn't have such a connection.

Complex code and code that has domain significance benefit from unit testing the most because the corresponding tests have great protection against regressions. Note that the domain code doesn't have to be complex, and complex code doesn't have to exhibit domain significance to be test-worthy. The two components are independent of each other. For example, a method calculating an order price can contain no conditional statements and thus have the cyclomatic complexity of 1. Still, it's important to test such a method because it represents business-critical functionality.

The second dimension is the number of collaborators a class or a method has. As you may remember from chapter 2, a *collaborator* is a dependency that is either mutable or out-of-process (or both). Code with a large number of collaborators is expensive to test. That's due to the maintainability metric, which depends on the size of the test. It takes space to bring collaborators to an expected condition and then check their state or interactions with them afterward. And the more collaborators there are, the larger the test becomes.

The type of the collaborators also matters. Out-of-process collaborators are a no-go when it comes to the domain model. They add additional maintenance costs due to the necessity to maintain complicated mock machinery in tests. You also have to be extra prudent and only use mocks to verify interactions that cross the application boundary in order to maintain proper resistance to refactoring (refer to chapter 5 for more details). It's better to delegate all communications with out-of-process dependencies to classes outside the domain layer. The domain classes then will only work with in-process dependencies.

Notice that both implicit and explicit collaborators count toward this number. It doesn't matter if the system under test (SUT) accepts a collaborator as an argument or refers to it implicitly via a static method, you still have to set up this collaborator in tests. Conversely, immutable dependencies (values or value objects) don't count. Such dependencies are much easier to set up and assert against.

The combination of code complexity, its domain significance, and the number of collaborators give us the four types of code shown in figure 7.1:

- *Domain model and algorithms (figure 7.1, top left)*—Complex code is often part of the domain model but not in 100% of all cases. You might have a complex algorithm that's not directly related to the problem domain.
- *Trivial code (figure 7.1, bottom left)*—Examples of such code in C# are parameterless constructors and one-line properties: they have few (if any) collaborators and exhibit little complexity or domain significance.
- *Controllers (figure 7.1, bottom right)*—This code doesn't do complex or business-critical work by itself but coordinates the work of other components like domain classes and external applications.

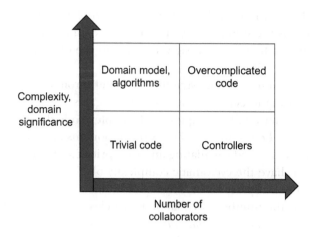

Figure 7.1   **The four types of code,
categorized by code complexity and
domain significance (the vertical
axis) and the number of collaborators
(the horizontal axis).**

- *Overcomplicated code (figure 7.1, top right)*—Such code scores highly on both metrics: it has a lot of collaborators, and it's also complex or important. An example here are *fat controllers* (controllers that don't delegate complex work anywhere and do everything themselves).

Unit testing the top-left quadrant (domain model and algorithms) gives you the best return for your efforts. The resulting unit tests are highly valuable and cheap. They're valuable because the underlying code carries out complex or important logic, thus increasing tests' protection against regressions. And they're cheap because the code has few collaborators (ideally, none), thus decreasing tests' maintenance costs.

Trivial code shouldn't be tested at all; such tests have a close-to-zero value. As for controllers, you should test them briefly as part of a much smaller set of the overarching integration tests (I cover this topic in part 3).

The most problematic type of code is the overcomplicated quadrant. It's hard to unit test but too risky to leave without test coverage. Such code is one of the main reasons many people struggle with unit testing. This whole chapter is primarily devoted to how you can bypass this dilemma. The general idea is to split overcomplicated code into two parts: algorithms and controllers (figure 7.2), although the actual implementation can be tricky at times.

> **TIP**   The more important or complex the code, the fewer collaborators it should have.

Getting rid of the overcomplicated code and unit testing only the domain model and algorithms is the path to a highly valuable, easily maintainable test suite. With this approach, you won't have 100% test coverage, but you don't need to—100% coverage shouldn't ever be your goal. Your goal is a test suite where each test adds significant value to the project. Refactor or get rid of all other tests. Don't allow them to inflate the size of your test suite.

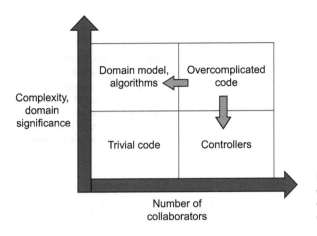

Figure 7.2 Refactor overcomplicated code by splitting it into algorithms and controllers. Ideally, you should have no code in the top-right quadrant.

NOTE Remember that it's better to not write a test at all than to write a bad test.

Of course, getting rid of overcomplicated code is easier said than done. Still, there are techniques that can help you do that. I'll first explain the theory behind those techniques and then demonstrate them using a close-to-real-world example.

7.1.2 *Using the Humble Object pattern to split overcomplicated code*

To split overcomplicated code, you need to use the Humble Object design pattern. This pattern was introduced by Gerard Meszaros in his book *xUnit Test Patterns: Refactoring Test Code* (Addison-Wesley, 2007) as one of the ways to battle code coupling, but it has a much broader application. You'll see why shortly.

We often find that code is hard to test because it's coupled to a framework dependency (see figure 7.3). Examples include asynchronous or multi-threaded execution, user interfaces, communication with out-of-process dependencies, and so on.

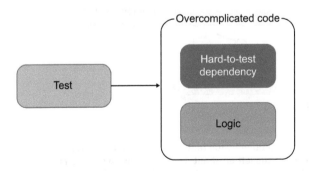

Figure 7.3 It's hard to test code that couples to a difficult dependency. Tests have to deal with that dependency, too, which increases their maintenance cost.

To bring the logic of this code under test, you need to extract a testable part out of it. As a result, the code becomes a thin, *humble* wrapper around that testable part: it glues

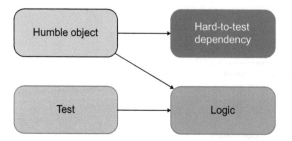

Figure 7.4   The Humble Object pattern extracts the logic out of the overcomplicated code, making that code so humble that it doesn't need to be tested. The extracted logic is moved into another class, decoupled from the hard-to-test dependency.

the hard-to-test dependency and the newly extracted component together, but itself contains little or no logic and thus doesn't need to be tested (figure 7.4).

If this approach looks familiar, it's because you already saw it in this book. In fact, both hexagonal and functional architectures implement this exact pattern. As you may remember from previous chapters, hexagonal architecture advocates for the separation of business logic and communications with out-of-process dependencies. This is what the domain and application services layers are responsible for, respectively.

Functional architecture goes even further and separates business logic from communications with *all* collaborators, not just out-of-process ones. This is what makes functional architecture so testable: its functional core has no collaborators. All dependencies in a functional core are immutable, which brings it very close to the vertical axis on the types-of-code diagram (figure 7.5).

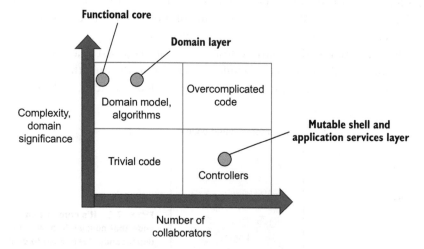

Figure 7.5   The functional core in a functional architecture and the domain layer in a hexagonal architecture reside in the top-left quadrant: they have few collaborators and exhibit high complexity and domain significance. The functional core is closer to the vertical axis because it has no collaborators. The mutable shell (functional architecture) and the application services layer (hexagonal architecture) belong to the controllers' quadrant.

Another way to view the Humble Object pattern is as a means to adhere to the Single Responsibility principle, which states that each class should have only a single responsibility.[1] One such responsibility is always business logic; the pattern can be applied to segregate that logic from pretty much anything.

In our particular situation, we are interested in the separation of business logic and orchestration. You can think of these two responsibilities in terms of *code depth* versus *code width.* Your code can be either deep (complex or important) or wide (work with many collaborators), but never both (figure 7.6).

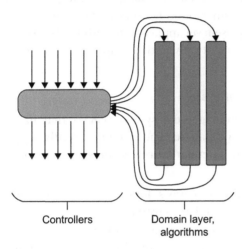

Controllers   Domain layer,
                     algorithms

Figure 7.6 Code depth versus code width is a useful metaphor to apply when you think of the separation between the business logic and orchestration responsibilities. Controllers orchestrate many dependencies (represented as arrows in the figure) but aren't complex on their own (complexity is represented as block height). Domain classes are the opposite of that.

I can't stress enough how important this separation is. In fact, many well-known principles and patterns can be described as a form of the Humble Object pattern: they are designed specifically to segregate complex code from the code that does orchestration.

You already saw the relationship between this pattern and hexagonal and functional architectures. Other examples include the Model-View-Presenter (MVP) and the Model-View-Controller (MVC) patterns. These two patterns help you decouple business logic (the *Model* part), UI concerns (the *View*), and the coordination between them (*Presenter* or *Controller*). The Presenter and Controller components are *humble objects*: they glue the view and the model together.

Another example is the Aggregate pattern from *Domain-Driven Design.*[2] One of its goals is to reduce connectivity between classes by grouping them into clusters—*aggregates.* The classes are highly connected inside those clusters, but the clusters themselves are loosely coupled. Such a structure decreases the total number of communications in the code base. The reduced connectivity, in turn, improves testability.

---

[1] See *Agile Principles, Patterns, and Practices in C#* by Robert C. Martin and Micah Martin (Prentice Hall, 2006).
[2] See *Domain-Driven Design: Tackling Complexity in the Heart of Software* by Eric Evans (Addison-Wesley, 2003).

Note that improved testability is not the only reason to maintain the separation between business logic and orchestration. Such a separation also helps tackle code complexity, which is crucial for project growth, too, especially in the long run. I personally always find it fascinating how a testable design is not only testable but also easy to maintain.

7.2   *Refactoring toward valuable unit tests*

In this section, I'll show a comprehensive example of splitting overcomplicated code into algorithms and controllers. You saw a similar example in the previous chapter, where we talked about output-based testing and functional architecture. This time, I'll generalize this approach to all enterprise-level applications, with the help of the Humble Object pattern. I'll use this project not only in this chapter but also in the subsequent chapters of part 3.

7.2.1   *Introducing a customer management system*

The sample project is a customer management system (CRM) that handles user registrations. All users are stored in a database. The system currently supports only one use case: changing a user's email. There are three business rules involved in this operation:

- If the user's email belongs to the company's domain, that user is marked as an employee. Otherwise, they are treated as a customer.
- The system must track the number of employees in the company. If the user's type changes from employee to customer, or vice versa, this number must change, too.
- When the email changes, the system must notify external systems by sending a message to a message bus.

The following listing shows the initial implementation of the CRM system.

Listing 7.1   Initial implementation of the CRM system

```
public class User
{
    public int UserId { get; private set; }
    public string Email { get; private set; }
    public UserType Type { get; private set; }

    public void ChangeEmail(int userId, string newEmail)
    {
        object[] data = Database.GetUserById(userId);        ◁──┐ Retrieves the user's
        UserId = userId;                                         current email and
        Email = (string)data[1];                                 type from the
        Type = (UserType)data[2];                                database

        if (Email == newEmail)
            return;
```

```
object[] companyData = Database.GetCompany();
string companyDomainName = (string)companyData[0];
int numberOfEmployees = (int)companyData[1];

string emailDomain = newEmail.Split('@')[1];
bool isEmailCorporate = emailDomain == companyDomainName;
UserType newType = isEmailCorporate
    ? UserType.Employee
    : UserType.Customer;

if (Type != newType)
{
    int delta = newType == UserType.Employee ? 1 : -1;
    int newNumber = numberOfEmployees + delta;
    Database.SaveCompany(newNumber);
}

Email = newEmail;
Type = newType;

Database.SaveUser(this);
MessageBus.SendEmailChangedMessage(UserId, newEmail);
    }
}

public enum UserType
{
    Customer = 1,
    Employee = 2
}
```

> **Retrieves the organization's domain name and the number of employees from the database**

> **Sets the user type depending on the new email's domain name**

> **Updates the number of employees in the organization, if needed**

> **Persists the user in the database**

> **Sends a notification to the message bus**

The User class changes a user email. Note that, for brevity, I omitted simple validations such as checks for email correctness and user existence in the database. Let's analyze this implementation from the perspective of the types-of-code diagram.

The code's complexity is not too high. The ChangeEmail method contains only a couple of explicit decision-making points: whether to identify the user as an employee or a customer, and how to update the company's number of employees. Despite being simple, these decisions are important: they are the application's core business logic. Hence, the class scores highly on the complexity and domain significance dimension.

On the other hand, the User class has four dependencies, two of which are explicit and the other two of which are implicit. The explicit dependencies are the userId and newEmail arguments. These are values, though, and thus don't count toward the class's number of collaborators. The implicit ones are Database and MessageBus. These two are out-of-process collaborators. As I mentioned earlier, out-of-process collaborators are a no-go for code with high domain significance. Hence, the User class scores highly on the collaborators dimension, which puts this class into the overcomplicated category (figure 7.7).

This approach—when a domain class retrieves and persists itself to the database—is called the Active Record pattern. It works fine in simple or short-lived projects but

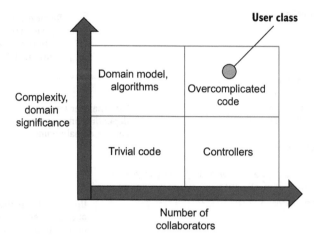

Figure 7.7   **The initial implementation of the** `User` **class scores highly on both dimensions and thus falls into the category of overcomplicated code.**

often fails to scale as the code base grows. The reason is precisely this lack of separation between these two responsibilities: business logic and communication with out-of-process dependencies.

7.2.2   *Take 1: Making implicit dependencies explicit*

The usual approach to improve testability is to make implicit dependencies explicit: that is, introduce interfaces for `Database` and `MessageBus`, inject those interfaces into `User`, and then mock them in tests. This approach does help, and that's exactly what we did in the previous chapter when we introduced the implementation with mocks for the audit system. However, it's not enough.

From the perspective of the types-of-code diagram, it doesn't matter if the domain model refers to out-of-process dependencies directly or via an interface. Such dependencies are still *out-of-process*; they are proxies to data that is not yet in memory. You still need to maintain complicated mock machinery in order to test such classes, which increases the tests' maintenance costs. Moreover, using mocks for the database dependency would lead to test fragility (we'll discuss this in the next chapter).

Overall, it's much cleaner for the domain model not to depend on out-of-process collaborators at all, directly or indirectly (via an interface). That's what the hexagonal architecture advocates as well—the domain model shouldn't be responsible for communications with external systems.

7.2.3   *Take 2: Introducing an application services layer*

To overcome the problem of the domain model directly communicating with external systems, we need to shift this responsibility to another class, a *humble* controller (an application service, in the hexagonal architecture taxonomy). As a general rule, domain classes should only depend on in-process dependencies, such as other domain classes, or plain values. Here's what the first version of that application service looks like.

Listing 7.2   Application service, version 1

```
public class UserController
{
    private readonly Database _database = new Database();
    private readonly MessageBus _messageBus = new MessageBus();

    public void ChangeEmail(int userId, string newEmail)
    {
        object[] data = _database.GetUserById(userId);
        string email = (string)data[1];
        UserType type = (UserType)data[2];
        var user = new User(userId, email, type);

        object[] companyData = _database.GetCompany();
        string companyDomainName = (string)companyData[0];
        int numberOfEmployees = (int)companyData[1];

        int newNumberOfEmployees = user.ChangeEmail(
            newEmail, companyDomainName, numberOfEmployees);

        _database.SaveCompany(newNumberOfEmployees);
        _database.SaveUser(user);
        _messageBus.SendEmailChangedMessage(userId, newEmail);
    }
}
```

This is a good first try; the application service helped offload the work with out-of-process dependencies from the User class. But there are some issues with this implementation:

- The out-of-process dependencies (Database and MessageBus) are instantiated directly, not injected. That's going to be a problem for the integration tests we'll be writing for this class.
- The controller reconstructs a User instance from the raw data it receives from the database. This is complex logic and thus shouldn't belong to the application service, whose sole role is orchestration, not logic of any complexity or domain significance.
- The same is true for the company's data. The other problem with that data is that User now returns an updated number of employees, which doesn't look right. The number of company employees has nothing to do with a specific user. This responsibility should belong elsewhere.
- The controller persists modified data and sends notifications to the message bus unconditionally, regardless of whether the new email is different than the previous one.

The User class has become quite easy to test because it no longer has to communicate with out-of-process dependencies. In fact, it has no collaborators whatsoever—out-of-process or not. Here's the new version of User's ChangeEmail method:

```
public int ChangeEmail(string newEmail,
    string companyDomainName, int numberOfEmployees)
{
    if (Email == newEmail)
        return numberOfEmployees;

    string emailDomain = newEmail.Split('@')[1];
    bool isEmailCorporate = emailDomain == companyDomainName;
    UserType newType = isEmailCorporate
        ? UserType.Employee
        : UserType.Customer;

    if (Type != newType)
    {
        int delta = newType == UserType.Employee ? 1 : -1;
        int newNumber = numberOfEmployees + delta;
        numberOfEmployees = newNumber;
    }

    Email = newEmail;
    Type = newType;

    return numberOfEmployees;
}
```

Figure 7.8 shows where `User` and `UserController` currently stand in our diagram. `User` has moved to the domain model quadrant, close to the vertical axis, because it no longer has to deal with collaborators. `UserController` is more problematic. Although I've put it into the controllers quadrant, it almost crosses the boundary into overcomplicated code because it contains logic that is quite complex.

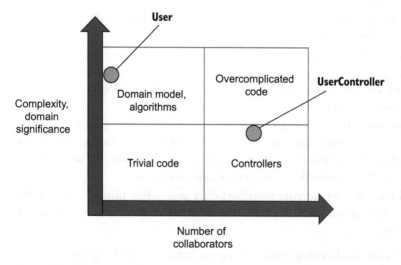

Figure 7.8 Take 2 puts `User` in the domain model quadrant, close to the vertical axis. `UserController` almost crosses the boundary with the overcomplicated quadrant because it contains complex logic.

7.2.4   *Take 3: Removing complexity from the application service*

To put `UserController` firmly into the controllers quadrant, we need to extract the reconstruction logic from it. If you use an object-relational mapping (ORM) library to map the database into the domain model, that would be a good place to which to attribute the reconstruction logic. Each ORM library has a dedicated place where you can specify how your database tables should be mapped to domain classes, such as attributes on top of those domain classes, XML files, or files with fluent mappings.

If you don't want to or can't use an ORM, create a factory in the domain model that will instantiate the domain classes using raw database data. This factory can be a separate class or, for simpler cases, a static method in the existing domain classes. The reconstruction logic in our sample application is not too complicated, but it's good to keep such things separated, so I'm putting it in a separate `UserFactory` class as shown in the following listing.

Listing 7.3   User factory

```
public class UserFactory
{
    public static User Create(object[] data)
    {
        Precondition.Requires(data.Length >= 3);

        int id = (int)data[0];
        string email = (string)data[1];
        UserType type = (UserType)data[2];

        return new User(id, email, type);
    }
}
```

This code is now fully isolated from all collaborators and therefore easily testable. Notice that I've put a safeguard in this method: a requirement to have at least three elements in the data array. `Precondition` is a simple custom class that throws an exception if the Boolean argument is false. The reason for this class is the more succinct code and the condition inversion: affirmative statements are more readable than negative ones. In our example, the `data.Length >= 3` requirement reads better than

```
if (data.Length < 3)
    throw new Exception();
```

Note that while this reconstruction logic is somewhat complex, it doesn't have domain significance: it isn't directly related to the client's goal of changing the user email. It's an example of the utility code I refer to in previous chapters.

> ### How is the reconstruction logic complex?
>
> How is the reconstruction logic complex, given that there's only a single branching point in the `UserFactory.Create()` method? As I mentioned in chapter 1, there could be a lot of hidden branching points in the underlying libraries used by the code and thus a lot of potential for something to go wrong. This is exactly the case for the `UserFactory.Create()` method.
>
> Referring to an array element by index (`data[0]`) entails an internal decision made by the .NET Framework as to what data element to access. The same is true for the conversion from `object` to `int` or `string`. Internally, the .NET Framework decides whether to throw a cast exception or allow the conversion to proceed. All these hidden branches make the reconstruction logic test-worthy, despite the lack of decision points in it.

7.2.5   *Take 4: Introducing a new Company class*

Look at this code in the controller once again:

```
object[] companyData = _database.GetCompany();
string companyDomainName = (string)companyData[0];
int numberOfEmployees = (int)companyData[1];

int newNumberOfEmployees = user.ChangeEmail(
    newEmail, companyDomainName, numberOfEmployees);
```

The awkwardness of returning an updated number of employees from `User` is a sign of a misplaced responsibility, which itself is a sign of a missing abstraction. To fix this, we need to introduce another domain class, `Company`, that bundles the company-related logic and data together, as shown in the following listing.

Listing 7.4   The new class in the domain layer

```
public class Company
{
    public string DomainName { get; private set; }
    public int NumberOfEmployees { get; private set; }

    public void ChangeNumberOfEmployees(int delta)
    {
        Precondition.Requires(NumberOfEmployees + delta >= 0);

        NumberOfEmployees += delta;
    }

    public bool IsEmailCorporate(string email)
    {
        string emailDomain = email.Split('@')[1];
        return emailDomain == DomainName;
    }
}
```

There are two methods in this class: ChangeNumberOfEmployees() and IsEmail-Corporate(). These methods help adhere to the tell-don't-ask principle I mentioned in chapter 5. This principle advocates for bundling together data and operations on that data. A User instance will *tell* the company to change its number of employees or figure out whether a particular email is corporate; it won't *ask* for the raw data and do everything on its own.

There's also a new CompanyFactory class, which is responsible for the reconstruction of Company objects, similar to UserFactory. This is how the controller now looks.

Listing 7.5   Controller after refactoring

```
public class UserController
{
    private readonly Database _database = new Database();
    private readonly MessageBus _messageBus = new MessageBus();

    public void ChangeEmail(int userId, string newEmail)
    {
        object[] userData = _database.GetUserById(userId);
        User user = UserFactory.Create(userData);

        object[] companyData = _database.GetCompany();
        Company company = CompanyFactory.Create(companyData);

        user.ChangeEmail(newEmail, company);

        _database.SaveCompany(company);
        _database.SaveUser(user);
        _messageBus.SendEmailChangedMessage(userId, newEmail);
    }
}
```

And here's the User class.

Listing 7.6   User after refactoring

```
public class User
{
    public int UserId { get; private set; }
    public string Email { get; private set; }
    public UserType Type { get; private set; }

    public void ChangeEmail(string newEmail, Company company)
    {
        if (Email == newEmail)
            return;

        UserType newType = company.IsEmailCorporate(newEmail)
            ? UserType.Employee
            : UserType.Customer;
```

```
        if (Type != newType)
        {
            int delta = newType == UserType.Employee ? 1 : -1;
            company.ChangeNumberOfEmployees(delta);
        }

        Email = newEmail;
        Type = newType;
    }
}
```

Notice how the removal of the misplaced responsibility made User much cleaner. Instead of operating on company data, it accepts a Company instance and delegates two important pieces of work to that instance: determining whether an email is corporate and changing the number of employees in the company.

Figure 7.9 shows where each class stands in the diagram. The factories and both domain classes reside in the domain model and algorithms quadrant. User has moved to the right because it now has one collaborator, Company, whereas previously it had none. That has made User less testable, but not much.

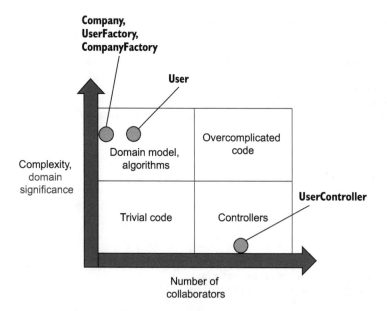

Figure 7.9 User **has shifted to the right because it now has the** Company **collaborator.** UserController **firmly stands in the controllers quadrant; all its complexity has moved to the factories.**

UserController now firmly stands in the controllers quadrant because all of its complexity has moved to the factories. The only thing this class is responsible for is gluing together all the collaborating parties.

Note the similarities between this implementation and the functional architecture from the previous chapter. Neither the functional core in the audit system nor the domain layer in this CRM (the User and Company classes) communicates with out-of-process dependencies. In both implementations, the application services layer is responsible for such communication: it gets the raw data from the filesystem or from the database, passes that data to stateless algorithms or the domain model, and then persists the results back to the data storage.

The difference between the two implementations is in their treatment of side effects. The functional core doesn't incur any side effects whatsoever. The CRM's domain model does, but all those side effects remain inside the domain model in the form of the changed user email and the number of employees. The side effects only cross the domain model's boundary when the controller persists the User and Company objects in the database.

The fact that all side effects are contained in memory until the very last moment improves testability a lot. Your tests don't need to examine out-of-process dependencies, nor do they need to resort to communication-based testing. All the verification can be done using output-based and state-based testing of objects in memory.

7.3 Analysis of optimal unit test coverage

Now that we've completed the refactoring with the help of the Humble Object pattern, let's analyze which parts of the project fall into which code category and how those parts should be tested. Table 7.1 shows all the code from the sample project grouped by position in the types-of-code diagram.

Table 7.1 Types of code in the sample project after refactoring using the Humble Object pattern

	Few collaborators	**Many collaborators**
High complexity or domain significance	`ChangeEmail(newEmail, company)` in User; `ChangeNumberOfEmployees(delta)` and `IsEmailCorporate(email)` in Company; and `Create(data)` in UserFactory and CompanyFactory	
Low complexity and domain significance	Constructors in User and Company	`ChangeEmail(userId, newEmail)` in UserController

With the full separation of business logic and orchestration at hand, it's easy to decide which parts of the code base to unit test.

7.3.1 Testing the domain layer and utility code

Testing methods in the top-left quadrant in table 7.1 provides the best results in cost-benefit terms. The code's high complexity or domain significance guarantees great protection against regressions, while having few collaborators ensures the lowest maintenance costs. This is an example of how User could be tested:

```
[Fact]
public void Changing_email_from_non_corporate_to_corporate()
{
    var company = new Company("mycorp.com", 1);
    var sut = new User(1, "user@gmail.com", UserType.Customer);

    sut.ChangeEmail("new@mycorp.com", company);

    Assert.Equal(2, company.NumberOfEmployees);
    Assert.Equal("new@mycorp.com", sut.Email);
    Assert.Equal(UserType.Employee, sut.Type);
}
```

To achieve full coverage, you'd need another three such tests:

```
public void Changing_email_from_corporate_to_non_corporate()
public void Changing_email_without_changing_user_type()
public void Changing_email_to_the_same_one()
```

Tests for the other three classes would be even shorter, and you could use parameterized tests to group several test cases together:

```
[InlineData("mycorp.com", "email@mycorp.com", true)]
[InlineData("mycorp.com", "email@gmail.com", false)]
[Theory]
public void Differentiates_a_corporate_email_from_non_corporate(
    string domain, string email, bool expectedResult)
{
    var sut = new Company(domain, 0);

    bool isEmailCorporate = sut.IsEmailCorporate(email);

    Assert.Equal(expectedResult, isEmailCorporate);
}
```

7.3.2   *Testing the code from the other three quadrants*

Code with low complexity and few collaborators (bottom-left quadrant in table 7.1) is represented by the constructors in User and Company, such as

```
public User(int userId, string email, UserType type)
{
    UserId = userId;
    Email = email;
    Type = type;
}
```

These constructors are trivial and aren't worth the effort. The resulting tests wouldn't provide great enough protection against regressions.

The refactoring has eliminated all code with high complexity and a large number of collaborators (top-right quadrant in table 7.1), so we have nothing to test there, either. As for the controllers quadrant (bottom-right in table 7.1), we'll discuss testing it in the next chapter.

7.3.3   *Should you test preconditions?*

Let's take a look at a special kind of branching points—preconditions—and see whether you should test them. For example, look at this method from Company once again:

```
public void ChangeNumberOfEmployees(int delta)
{
    Precondition.Requires(NumberOfEmployees + delta >= 0);

    NumberOfEmployees += delta;
}
```

It has a precondition stating that the number of employees in the company should never become negative. This precondition is a safeguard that's activated only in exceptional cases. Such exceptional cases are usually the result of bugs. The only possible reason for the number of employees to go below zero is if there's an error in code. The safeguard provides a mechanism for your software to fail fast and to prevent the error from spreading and being persisted in the database, where it would be much harder to deal with. Should you test such preconditions? In other words, would such tests be valuable enough to have in the test suite?

There's no hard rule here, but the general guideline I recommend is to test all preconditions that have domain significance. The requirement for the non-negative number of employees is such a precondition. It's part of the Company class's invariants: conditions that should be held true at all times. But don't spend time testing preconditions that don't have domain significance. For example, UserFactory has the following safeguard in its Create method:

```
public static User Create(object[] data)
{
    Precondition.Requires(data.Length >= 3);

    /* Extract id, email, and type out of data */
}
```

There's no domain meaning to this precondition and therefore not much value in testing it.

7.4   *Handling conditional logic in controllers*

Handling conditional logic and simultaneously maintaining the domain layer free of out-of-process collaborators is often tricky and involves trade-offs. In this section, I'll show what those trade-offs are and how to decide which of them to choose in your own project.

The separation between business logic and orchestration works best when a business operation has three distinct stages:

- Retrieving data from storage
- Executing business logic
- Persisting data back to the storage (figure 7.10)

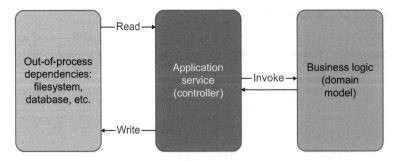

Figure 7.10 Hexagonal and functional architectures work best when all references to out-of-process dependencies can be pushed to the edges of business operations.

There are a lot of situations where these stages aren't as clearcut, though. As we discussed in chapter 6, you might need to query additional data from an out-of-process dependency based on an intermediate result of the decision-making process (figure 7.11). Writing to the out-of-process dependency often depends on that result, too.

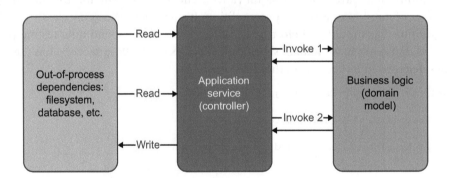

Figure 7.11 A hexagonal architecture doesn't work as well when you need to refer to out-of-process dependencies in the middle of the business operation.

As also discussed in the previous chapter, you have three options in such a situation:

- *Push all external reads and writes to the edges anyway*. This approach preserves the read-decide-act structure but concedes performance: the controller will call out-of-process dependencies even when there's no need for that.
- *Inject the out-of-process dependencies into the domain model* and allow the business logic to directly decide when to call those dependencies.
- *Split the decision-making process into more granular steps* and have the controller act on each of those steps separately.

The challenge is to balance the following three attributes:

- *Domain model testability,* which is a function of the number and type of collaborators in domain classes
- *Controller simplicity,* which depends on the presence of decision-making (branching) points in the controller
- *Performance,* as defined by the number of calls to out-of-process dependencies

Each option only gives you two out of the three attributes (figure 7.12):

- *Pushing all external reads and writes to the edges of a business operation*—Preserves controller simplicity and keeps the domain model isolated from out-of-process dependencies (thus allowing it to remain testable) but concedes performance.
- *Injecting out-of-process dependencies into the domain model*—Keeps performance and the controller's simplicity intact but damages domain model testability.
- *Splitting the decision-making process into more granular steps*—Helps with both performance and domain model testability but concedes controller simplicity. You'll need to introduce decision-making points in the controller in order to manage these granular steps.

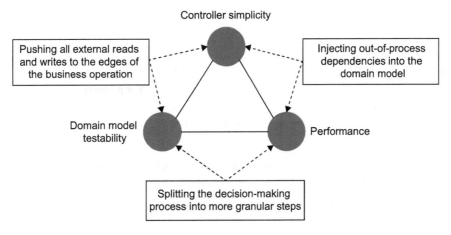

Figure 7.12   There's no single solution that satisfies all three attributes: controller simplicity, domain model testability, and performance. You have to choose two out of the three.

In most software projects, performance *is* important, so the first approach (pushing external reads and writes to the edges of a business operation) is out of the question. The second option (injecting out-of-process dependencies into the domain model) brings most of your code into the overcomplicated quadrant on the types-of-code diagram. This is exactly what we refactored the initial CRM implementation away from. I recommend that you avoid this approach: such code no longer preserves the separation between business logic and communication with out-of-process dependencies and thus becomes much harder to test and maintain.

That leaves you with the third option: splitting the decision-making process into smaller steps. With this approach, you will have to make your controllers more complex, which will also push them closer to the overcomplicated quadrant. But there are ways to mitigate this problem. Although you will rarely be able to factor *all* the complexity out of controllers as we did previously in the sample project, you *can* keep that complexity manageable.

7.4.1   *Using the CanExecute/Execute pattern*

The first way to mitigate the growth of the controllers' complexity is to use the CanExecute/Execute pattern, which helps avoid leaking of business logic from the domain model to controllers. This pattern is best explained with an example, so let's expand on our sample project.

Let's say that a user can change their email only until they confirm it. If a user tries to change the email after the confirmation, they should be shown an error message. To accommodate this new requirement, we'll add a new property to the User class.

Listing 7.7   User with a new property

```
public class User
{
    public int UserId { get; private set; }
    public string Email { get; private set; }
    public UserType Type { get; private set; }
    public bool IsEmailConfirmed
        { get; private set; }                    New property

    /* ChangeEmail(newEmail, company) method */
}
```

There are two options for where to put this check. First, you could put it in User's ChangeEmail method:

```
public string ChangeEmail(string newEmail, Company company)
{
    if (IsEmailConfirmed)
        return "Can't change a confirmed email";

    /* the rest of the method */
}
```

Then you could make the controller either return an error or incur all necessary side effects, depending on this method's output.

Listing 7.8   The controller, still stripped of all decision-making

```
public string ChangeEmail(int userId, string newEmail)
{
```

```
                      object[] userData = _database.GetUserById(userId);
                      User user = UserFactory.Create(userData);
```
Prepares the data
```
                      object[] companyData = _database.GetCompany();
                      Company company = CompanyFactory.Create(companyData);
```

Makes a decision ⌐→
```
                      string error = user.ChangeEmail(newEmail, company);
                      if (error != null)
                          return error;
```

```
                      _database.SaveCompany(company);
                      _database.SaveUser(user);
                      _messageBus.SendEmailChangedMessage(userId, newEmail);
```
Acts on the decision

```
                      return "OK";
                  }
```

This implementation keeps the controller free of decision-making, but it does so at the expense of a performance drawback. The Company instance is retrieved from the database unconditionally, even when the email is confirmed and thus can't be changed. This is an example of pushing all external reads and writes to the edges of a business operation.

NOTE I don't consider the new if statement analyzing the error string an increase in complexity because it belongs to the acting phase; it's not part of the decision-making process. All the decisions are made by the User class, and the controller merely acts on those decisions.

The second option is to move the check for IsEmailConfirmed from User to the controller.

Listing 7.9 Controller deciding whether to change the user's email

```
public string ChangeEmail(int userId, string newEmail)
{
    object[] userData = _database.GetUserById(userId);
    User user = UserFactory.Create(userData);

    if (user.IsEmailConfirmed)                         Decision-making
        return "Can't change a confirmed email";       moved here from User.

    object[] companyData = _database.GetCompany();
    Company company = CompanyFactory.Create(companyData);

    user.ChangeEmail(newEmail, company);

    _database.SaveCompany(company);
    _database.SaveUser(user);
    _messageBus.SendEmailChangedMessage(userId, newEmail);

    return "OK";
}
```

With this implementation, the performance stays intact: the `Company` instance is retrieved from the database only after it is certain that the email can be changed. But now the decision-making process is split into two parts:

- Whether to proceed with the change of email (performed by the controller)
- What to do during that change (performed by `User`)

Now it's also possible to change the email without verifying the `IsEmailConfirmed` flag first, which diminishes the domain model's encapsulation. Such fragmentation hinders the separation between business logic and orchestration and moves the controller closer to the overcomplicated danger zone.

To prevent this fragmentation, you can introduce a new method in `User`, `CanChange-Email()`, and make its successful execution a precondition for changing an email. The modified version in the following listing follows the CanExecute/Execute pattern.

Listing 7.10   Changing an email using the CanExecute/Execute pattern

```
public string CanChangeEmail()
{
    if (IsEmailConfirmed)
        return "Can't change a confirmed email";

    return null;
}

public void ChangeEmail(string newEmail, Company company)
{
    Precondition.Requires(CanChangeEmail() == null);

    /* the rest of the method */
}
```

This approach provides two important benefits:

- The controller no longer needs to know anything about the process of changing emails. All it needs to do is call the `CanChangeEmail()` method to see if the operation can be done. Notice that this method can contain multiple validations, all encapsulated away from the controller.
- The additional precondition in `ChangeEmail()` guarantees that the email won't ever be changed without checking for the confirmation first.

This pattern helps you to consolidate all decisions in the domain layer. The controller no longer has an option not to check for the email confirmation, which essentially eliminates the new decision-making point from that controller. Thus, although the controller still contains the `if` statement calling `CanChangeEmail()`, you don't need to test that `if` statement. Unit testing the precondition in the `User` class itself is enough.

> **NOTE**   For simplicity's sake, I'm using a `string` to denote an error. In a real-world project, you may want to introduce a custom `Result` class to indicate the success or failure of an operation.

7.4.2 Using domain events to track changes in the domain model

It's sometimes hard to deduce what steps led the domain model to the current state. Still, it might be important to know these steps because you need to inform external systems about what exactly has happened in your application. Putting this responsibility on the controllers would make them more complicated. To avoid that, you can track important changes in the domain model and then convert those changes into calls to out-of-process dependencies after the business operation is complete. *Domain events* help you implement such tracking.

> **DEFINITION** A *domain event* describes an event in the application that is meaningful to domain experts. The meaningfulness for domain experts is what differentiates domain events from regular events (such as button clicks). Domain events are often used to inform external applications about important changes that have happened in your system.

Our CRM has a tracking requirement, too: it has to notify external systems about changed user emails by sending messages to the message bus. The current implementation has a flaw in the notification functionality: it sends messages even when the email is not changed, as shown in the following listing.

Listing 7.11 Sends a notification even when the email has not changed

```
// User
public void ChangeEmail(string newEmail, Company company)
{
    Precondition.Requires(CanChangeEmail() == null);

    if (Email == newEmail)          ◁──┐ User email may
        return;                         │ not change.

    /* the rest of the method */
}

// Controller
public string ChangeEmail(int userId, string newEmail)
{
    /* preparations */

    user.ChangeEmail(newEmail, company);

    _database.SaveCompany(company);
    _database.SaveUser(user);              │ The controller sends
    _messageBus.SendEmailChangedMessage(   │ a message anyway.
        userId, newEmail);

    return "OK";
}
```

You could resolve this bug by moving the check for email sameness to the controller, but then again, there are issues with the business logic fragmentation. And you can't put this check to `CanChangeEmail()` because the application shouldn't return an error if the new email is the same as the old one.

Note that this particular check probably doesn't introduce too much business logic fragmentation, so I personally wouldn't consider the controller overcomplicated if it contained that check. But you may find yourself in a more difficult situation in which it's hard to prevent your application from making unnecessary calls to out-of-process dependencies without passing those dependencies to the domain model, thus over-complicating that domain model. The only way to prevent such overcomplication is the use of domain events.

From an implementation standpoint, a *domain event* is a class that contains data needed to notify external systems. In our specific example, it is the user's ID and email:

```
public class EmailChangedEvent
{
    public int UserId { get; }
    public string NewEmail { get; }
}
```

NOTE Domain events should always be named in the past tense because they represent things that already happened. Domain events are values—they are immutable and interchangeable.

`User` will have a collection of such events to which it will add a new element when the email changes. This is how its `ChangeEmail()` method looks after the refactoring.

Listing 7.12   `User` adding an event when the email changes

```
public void ChangeEmail(string newEmail, Company company)
{
    Precondition.Requires(CanChangeEmail() == null);

    if (Email == newEmail)
        return;

    UserType newType = company.IsEmailCorporate(newEmail)
        ? UserType.Employee
        : UserType.Customer;

    if (Type != newType)
    {
        int delta = newType == UserType.Employee ? 1 : -1;
        company.ChangeNumberOfEmployees(delta);
    }

    Email = newEmail;
    Type = newType;
    EmailChangedEvents.Add(                            │  A new event indicates
        new EmailChangedEvent(UserId, newEmail));      │  the change of email.
}
```

The controller then will convert the events into messages on the bus.

Listing 7.13 The controller processing domain events

```
public string ChangeEmail(int userId, string newEmail)
{
    object[] userData = _database.GetUserById(userId);
    User user = UserFactory.Create(userData);

    string error = user.CanChangeEmail();
    if (error != null)
        return error;

    object[] companyData = _database.GetCompany();
    Company company = CompanyFactory.Create(companyData);

    user.ChangeEmail(newEmail, company);

    _database.SaveCompany(company);
    _database.SaveUser(user);
    foreach (var ev in user.EmailChangedEvents)
    {
        _messageBus.SendEmailChangedMessage(          Domain event
            ev.UserId, ev.NewEmail);                  processing
    }

    return "OK";
}
```

Notice that the `Company` and `User` instances are still persisted in the database unconditionally: the persistence logic doesn't depend on domain events. This is due to the difference between changes in the database and messages in the bus.

Assuming that no application has access to the database other than the CRM, communications with that database are not part of the CRM's observable behavior—they
are implementation details. As long as the final state of the database is correct, it
doesn't matter how many calls your application makes to that database. On the other
hand, communications with the message bus *are* part of the application's observable
behavior. In order to maintain the contract with external systems, the CRM should put
messages on the bus only when the email changes.

There are performance implications to persisting data in the database unconditionally, but they are relatively insignificant. The chances that after all the validations
the new email is the same as the old one are quite small. The use of an ORM can also
help. Most ORMs won't make a round trip to the database if there are no changes to
the object state.

You can generalize the solution with domain events: extract a `DomainEvent` base
class and introduce a base class for all domain classes, which would contain a collection of such events: `List<DomainEvent>` events. You can also write a separate event
dispatcher instead of dispatching domain events manually in controllers. Finally, in
larger projects, you might need a mechanism for merging domain events before

dispatching them. That topic is outside the scope of this book, though. You can read about it in my article "Merging domain events before dispatching" at http://mng .bz/YeVe.

Domain events remove the decision-making responsibility from the controller and put that responsibility into the domain model, thus simplifying unit testing communications with external systems. Instead of verifying the controller itself and using mocks to substitute out-of-process dependencies, you can test the domain event creation directly in unit tests, as shown next.

Listing 7.14   Testing the creation of a domain event

```
[Fact]
public void Changing_email_from_corporate_to_non_corporate()
{
    var company = new Company("mycorp.com", 1);
    var sut = new User(1, "user@mycorp.com", UserType.Employee, false);

    sut.ChangeEmail("new@gmail.com", company);

    company.NumberOfEmployees.Should().Be(0);
    sut.Email.Should().Be("new@gmail.com");
    sut.Type.Should().Be(UserType.Customer);
    sut.EmailChangedEvents.Should().Equal(
        new EmailChangedEvent(1, "new@gmail.com"));
}
```

> Simultaneously asserts the collection size and the element in the collection

---

Of course, you'll still need to test the controller to make sure it does the orchestration correctly, but doing so requires a much smaller set of tests. That's the topic of the next chapter.

7.5   Conclusion

Notice a theme that has been present throughout this chapter: abstracting away the application of side effects to external systems. You achieve such abstraction by keeping those side effects in memory until the very end of the business operation, so that they can be tested with plain unit tests without involving out-of-process dependencies. Domain events are abstractions on top of upcoming messages in the bus. Changes in domain classes are abstractions on top of upcoming modifications in the database.

NOTE   It's easier to test abstractions than the things they abstract.

Although we were able to successfully contain all the decision-making in the domain model with the help of domain events and the CanExecute/Execute pattern, you won't be able to always do that. There are situations where business logic fragmentation is inevitable.

For example, there's no way to verify email uniqueness outside the controller without introducing out-of-process dependencies in the domain model. Another example is failures in out-of-process dependencies that should alter the course of the business operation. The decision about which way to go can't reside in the domain layer because it's not the domain layer that calls those out-of-process dependencies. You will have to put this logic into controllers and then cover it with integration tests. Still, even with the potential fragmentation, there's a lot of value in separating business logic from orchestration because this separation drastically simplifies the unit testing process.

Just as you can't avoid having some business logic in controllers, you will rarely be able to remove all collaborators from domain classes. And that's fine. One, two, or even three collaborators won't turn a domain class into overcomplicated code, as long as these collaborators don't refer to out-of-process dependencies.

Don't use mocks to verify interactions with such collaborators, though. These interactions have nothing to do with the domain model's observable behavior. Only the very first call, which goes from a controller to a domain class, has an immediate connection to that controller's goal. All the subsequent calls the domain class makes to its neighbor domain classes within the same operation are implementation details.

Figure 7.13 illustrates this idea. It shows the communications between components in the CRM and their relationship to observable behavior. As you may remember from chapter 5, whether a method is part of the class's observable behavior depends on whom the client is and what the goals of that client are. To be part of the observable behavior, the method must meet one of the following two criteria:

- Have an immediate connection to one of the client's goals
- Incur a side effect in an out-of-process dependency that is visible to external applications

The controller's `ChangeEmail()` method is part of its observable behavior, and so is the call it makes to the message bus. The first method is the entry point for the external client, thereby meeting the first criterion. The call to the bus sends messages to external applications, thereby meeting the second criterion. You should verify both of

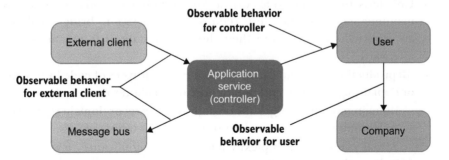

Figure 7.13 A map that shows communications among components in the CRM and the relationship between these communications and observable behavior

these method calls (which is the topic of the next chapter). However, the subsequent call from the controller to User doesn't have an immediate connection to the goals of the external client. That client doesn't care how the controller decides to implement the change of email as long as the final state of the system is correct and the call to the message bus is in place. Therefore, you shouldn't verify calls the controller makes to User when testing that controller's behavior.

When you step one level down the call stack, you get a similar situation. Now it's the controller who is the client, and the ChangeEmail method in User has an immediate connection to that client's goal of changing the user email and thus should be tested. But the subsequent calls from User to Company are implementation details from the controller's point of view. Therefore, the test that covers the ChangeEmail method in User shouldn't verify what methods User calls on Company. The same line of reasoning applies when you step one more level down and test the two methods in Company from User's point of view.

Think of the observable behavior and implementation details as onion layers. Test each layer from the outer layer's point of view, and disregard how that layer talks to the underlying layers. As you peel these layers one by one, you switch perspective: what previously was an implementation detail now becomes an observable behavior, which you then cover with another set of tests.

Summary

- Code complexity is defined by the number of decision-making points in the code, both explicit (made by the code itself) and implicit (made by the libraries the code uses).
- Domain significance shows how significant the code is for the problem domain of your project. Complex code often has high domain significance and vice versa, but not in 100% of all cases.
- Complex code and code that has domain significance benefit from unit testing the most because the corresponding tests have greater protection against regressions.
- Unit tests that cover code with a large number of collaborators have high maintenance costs. Such tests require a lot of space to bring collaborators to an expected condition and then check their state or interactions with them afterward.
- All production code can be categorized into four types of code by its complexity or domain significance and the number of collaborators:
  - Domain model and algorithms (high complexity or domain significance, few collaborators) provide the best return on unit testing efforts.
  - Trivial code (low complexity and domain significance, few collaborators) isn't worth testing at all.

- – Controllers (low complexity and domain significance, large number of collaborators) should be tested briefly by integration tests.
  - – Overcomplicated code (high complexity or domain significance, large number of collaborators) should be split into controllers and complex code.
- The more important or complex the code is, the fewer collaborators it should have.
- The Humble Object pattern helps make overcomplicated code testable by extracting business logic out of that code into a separate class. As a result, the remaining code becomes a controller—a thin, *humble* wrapper around the business logic.
- The hexagonal and functional architectures implement the Humble Object pattern. *Hexagonal architecture* advocates for the separation of business logic and communications with out-of-process dependencies. *Functional architecture* separates business logic from communications with *all* collaborators, not just out-of-process ones.
- Think of the business logic and orchestration responsibilities in terms of code depth versus code width. Your code can be either deep (complex or important) or wide (work with many collaborators), but never both.
- Test preconditions if they have a domain significance; don't test them otherwise.
- There are three important attributes when it comes to separating business logic from orchestration:
  - – *Domain model testability*—A function of the number and the type of collaborators in domain classes
  - – *Controller simplicity*—Depends on the presence of decision-making points in the controller
  - – *Performance*—Defined by the number of calls to out-of-process dependencies
- You can have a maximum of two of these three attributes at any given moment:
  - – *Pushing all external reads and writes to the edges of a business operation*—Preserves controller simplicity and keeps the domain model testability, but concedes performance
  - – *Injecting out-of-process dependencies into the domain model*—Keeps performance and the controller's simplicity, but damages domain model testability
  - – *Splitting the decision-making process into more granular steps*—Preserves performance and domain model testability, but gives up controller simplicity
- *Splitting the decision-making process into more granular steps*—Is a trade-off with the best set of pros and cons. You can mitigate the growth of controller complexity using the following two patterns:
  - – The CanExecute/Execute pattern introduces a CanDo() for each Do() method and makes its successful execution a precondition for Do(). This pattern essentially eliminates the controller's decision-making because there's no option not to call CanDo() before Do().

- Domain events help track important changes in the domain model, and then convert those changes to calls to out-of-process dependencies. This pattern removes the tracking responsibility from the controller.
- It's easier to test abstractions than the things they abstract. Domain events are abstractions on top of upcoming calls to out-of-process dependencies. Changes in domain classes are abstractions on top of upcoming modifications in the data storage.

Part 3

Integration testing

Have you ever been in a situation where all the unit tests pass but the application still doesn't work? Validating software components in isolation from each other is important, but it's equally important to check how those components work in integration with external systems. This is where integration testing comes into play.

In chapter 8, we'll look at integration testing in general and revisit the Test Pyramid concept. You'll learn the trade-offs inherent to integration testing and how to navigate them. Chapters 9 and 10 will then discuss more specific topics. Chapter 9 will teach you how to get the most out of your mocks. Chapter 10 is a deep dive into working with relational databases in tests.

Why integration testing?

You can never be sure your system works as a whole if you rely on unit tests exclusively. Unit tests are great at verifying business logic, but it's not enough to check that logic in a vacuum. You have to validate how different parts of it integrate with each other and external systems: the database, the message bus, and so on.

In this chapter, you'll learn the role of integration tests: when you should apply them and when it's better to rely on plain old unit tests or even other techniques such as the Fail Fast principle. You will see which out-of-process dependencies to use as-is in integration tests and which to replace with mocks. You will also see integration testing best practices that will help improve the health of your code base in general: making domain model boundaries explicit, reducing the number of layers in the application, and eliminating circular dependencies. Finally, you'll learn why interfaces with a single implementation should be used sporadically, and how and when to test logging functionality.

185

8.1   *What is an integration test?*

Integration tests play an important role in your test suite. It's also crucial to balance the number of unit and integration tests. You will see shortly what that role is and how to maintain the balance, but first, let me give you a refresher on what differentiates an integration test from a unit test.

8.1.1   *The role of integration tests*

As you may remember from chapter 2, a *unit test* is a test that meets the following three requirements:

- Verifies a single unit of behavior,
- Does it quickly,
- And does it in isolation from other tests.

A test that doesn't meet at least one of these three requirements falls into the category of integration tests. An *integration test* then is any test that is not a unit test.

In practice, integration tests almost always verify how your system works in integration with out-of-process dependencies. In other words, these tests cover the code from the controllers quadrant (see chapter 7 for more details about code quadrants). The diagram in figure 8.1 shows the typical responsibilities of unit and integration tests. Unit tests cover the domain model, while integration tests check the code that glues that domain model with out-of-process dependencies.

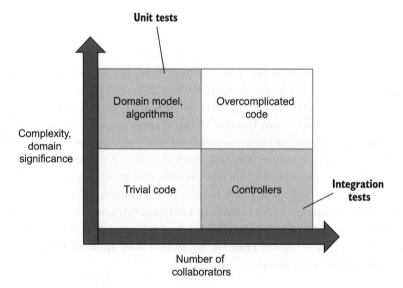

Figure 8.1   Integration tests cover controllers, while unit tests cover the domain model and algorithms. Trivial and overcomplicated code shouldn't be tested at all.

Note that tests covering the controllers quadrant can sometimes be unit tests too. If all out-of-process dependencies are replaced with mocks, there will be no dependencies shared between tests, which will allow those tests to remain fast and maintain their isolation from each other. Most applications do have an out-of-process dependency that can't be replaced with a mock, though. It's usually a database—a dependency that is not visible to other applications.

As you may also remember from chapter 7, the other two quadrants from figure 8.1 (trivial code and overcomplicated code) shouldn't be tested at all. Trivial code isn't worth the effort, while overcomplicated code should be refactored into algorithms and controllers. Thus, all your tests must focus on the domain model and the controllers quadrants exclusively.

8.1.2 The Test Pyramid revisited

It's important to maintain a balance between unit and integration tests. Working directly with out-of-process dependencies makes integration tests slow. Such tests are also more expensive to maintain. The increase in maintainability costs is due to

- The necessity to keep the out-of-process dependencies operational
- The greater number of collaborators involved, which inflates the test's size

On the other hand, integration tests go through a larger amount of code (both your code and the code of the libraries used by the application), which makes them better than unit tests at protecting against regressions. They are also more detached from the production code and therefore have better resistance to refactoring.

The ratio between unit and integration tests can differ depending on the project's specifics, but the general rule of thumb is the following: check as many of the business scenario's edge cases as possible with unit tests; use integration tests to cover one happy path, as well as any edge cases that can't be covered by unit tests.

> **DEFINITION** A *happy path* is a successful execution of a business scenario. An *edge case* is when the business scenario execution results in an error.

Shifting the majority of the workload to unit tests helps keep maintenance costs low. At the same time, having one or two overarching integration tests per business scenario ensures the correctness of your system as a whole. This guideline forms the pyramid-like ratio between unit and integration tests, as shown in figure 8.2 (as discussed in chapter 2, end-to-end tests are a subset of integration tests).

The Test Pyramid can take different shapes depending on the project's complexity. Simple applications have little (if any) code in the domain model and algorithms quadrant. As a result, tests form a rectangle instead of a pyramid, with an equal number of unit and integration tests (figure 8.3). In the most trivial cases, you might have no unit tests whatsoever.

Note that integration tests retain their value even in simple applications. Regardless of how simple your code is, it's still important to verify how it works in integration with other subsystems.

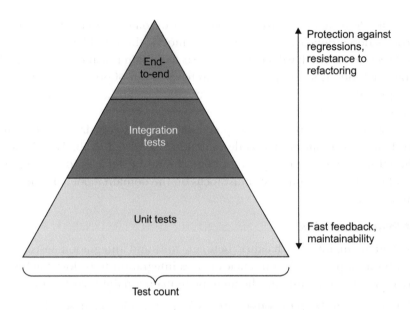

Figure 8.2   **The Test Pyramid represents a trade-off that works best for most applications. Fast, cheap unit tests cover the majority of edge cases, while a smaller number of slow, more expensive integration tests ensure the correctness of the system as a whole.**

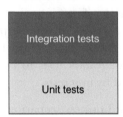

Figure 8.3   **The Test Pyramid of a simple project. Little complexity requires a smaller number of unit tests compared to a normal pyramid.**

8.1.3   *Integration testing vs. failing fast*

This section elaborates on the guideline of using integration tests to cover one happy path per business scenario and any edge cases that can't be covered by unit tests.

For an integration test, select the longest happy path in order to verify interactions with *all* out-of-process dependencies. If there's no one path that goes through all such interactions, write additional integration tests—as many as needed to capture communications with *every* external system.

As with the edge cases that can't be covered by unit tests, there are exceptions to this part of the guideline, too. There's no need to test an edge case if an incorrect execution of that edge case immediately fails the entire application. For example, you saw in chapter 7 how `User` from the sample CRM system implemented a `CanChange-Email` method and made its successful execution a precondition for `ChangeEmail()`:

```
public void ChangeEmail(string newEmail, Company company)
{
    Precondition.Requires(CanChangeEmail() == null);

    /* the rest of the method */
}
```

The controller invokes `CanChangeEmail()` and interrupts the operation if that method returns an error:

```
// UserController
public string ChangeEmail(int userId, string newEmail)
{
    object[] userData = _database.GetUserById(userId);
    User user = UserFactory.Create(userData);

    string error = user.CanChangeEmail();
    if (error != null)
        return error;                          Edge case

    /* the rest of the method */
}
```

This example shows the edge case you could theoretically cover with an integration test. Such a test doesn't provide a significant enough value, though. If the controller tries to change the email without consulting with `CanChangeEmail()` first, the application crashes. This bug reveals itself with the first execution and thus is easy to notice and fix. It also doesn't lead to data corruption.

> **TIP** It's better to not write a test at all than to write a bad test. A test that doesn't provide significant value is a *bad* test.

Unlike the call from the controller to `CanChangeEmail()`, the presence of the precondition in `User` *should* be tested. But that is better done with a unit test; there's no need for an integration test.

Making bugs manifest themselves quickly is called the *Fail Fast principle*, and it's a viable alternative to integration testing.

The Fail Fast principle

The *Fail Fast principle* stands for stopping the current operation as soon as any unexpected error occurs. This principle makes your application more stable by

- *Shortening the feedback loop*—The sooner you detect a bug, the easier it is to fix. A bug that is already in production is orders of magnitude more expensive to fix compared to a bug found during development.
- *Protecting the persistence state*—Bugs lead to corruption of the application's state. Once that state penetrates into the database, it becomes much harder to fix. Failing fast helps you prevent the corruption from spreading.

(continued)

Stopping the current operation is normally done by throwing exceptions, because exceptions have semantics that are perfectly suited for the Fail Fast principle: they interrupt the program flow and pop up to the highest level of the execution stack, where you can log them and shut down or restart the operation.

Preconditions are one example of the Fail Fast principle in action. A failing precondition signifies an incorrect assumption made about the application state, which is always a bug. Another example is reading data from a configuration file. You can arrange the reading logic such that it will throw an exception if the data in the configuration file is incomplete or incorrect. You can also put this logic close to the application startup, so that the application doesn't launch if there's a problem with its configuration.

8.2   *Which out-of-process dependencies to test directly*

As I mentioned earlier, integration tests verify how your system integrates with out-of-process dependencies. There are two ways to implement such verification: use the real out-of-process dependency, or replace that dependency with a mock. This section shows when to apply each of the two approaches.

8.2.1   *The two types of out-of-process dependencies*

All out-of-process dependencies fall into two categories:

- *Managed dependencies (out-of-process dependencies you have full control over)*—These dependencies are only accessible through your application; interactions with them aren't visible to the external world. A typical example is a database. External systems normally don't access your database directly; they do that through the API your application provides.
- *Unmanaged dependencies (out-of-process dependencies you don't have full control over)*— Interactions with such dependencies *are* observable externally. Examples include an SMTP server and a message bus: both produce side effects visible to other applications.

I mentioned in chapter 5 that communications with managed dependencies are implementation details. Conversely, communications with unmanaged dependencies are part of your system's observable behavior (figure 8.4). This distinction leads to the difference in treatment of out-of-process dependencies in integration tests.

> **IMPORTANT**   Use real instances of managed dependencies; replace unmanaged dependencies with mocks.

As discussed in chapter 5, the requirement to preserve the communication pattern with unmanaged dependencies stems from the necessity to maintain backward compatibility with those dependencies. Mocks are perfect for this task. With mocks, you can ensure communication pattern permanence in light of any possible refactorings.

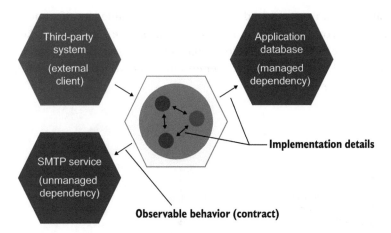

Figure 8.4 Communications with managed dependencies are implementation details; use such dependencies as-is in integration tests. Communications with unmanaged dependencies are part of your system's observable behavior. Such dependencies should be mocked out.

However, there's no need to maintain backward compatibility in communications with managed dependencies, because your application is the only one that talks to them. External clients don't care how you organize your database; the only thing that matters is the final state of your system. Using real instances of managed dependencies in integration tests helps you verify that final state from the external client's point of view. It also helps during database refactorings, such as renaming a column or even migrating from one database to another.

8.2.2 *Working with both managed and unmanaged dependencies*

Sometimes you'll encounter an out-of-process dependency that exhibits attributes of both managed and unmanaged dependencies. A good example is a database that other applications have access to.

The story usually goes like this. A system begins with its own dedicated database. After a while, another system begins to require data from the same database. And so the team decides to share access to a limited number of tables just for ease of integration with that other system. As a result, the database becomes a dependency that is both managed and unmanaged. It still contains parts that are visible to your application only; but, in addition to those parts, it also has a number of tables accessible by other applications.

The use of a database is a poor way to implement integration between systems because it couples these systems to each other and complicates their further development. Only resort to this approach when all other options are exhausted. A better way to do the integration is via an API (for synchronous communications) or a message bus (for asynchronous communications).

But what do you do when you already have a shared database and can't do anything about it in the foreseeable future? In this case, treat tables that are visible to other applications as an unmanaged dependency. Such tables in effect act as a message bus, with their rows playing the role of messages. Use mocks to make sure the communication pattern with these tables remains unchanged. At the same time, treat the rest of your database as a managed dependency and verify its final state, not the interactions with it (figure 8.5).

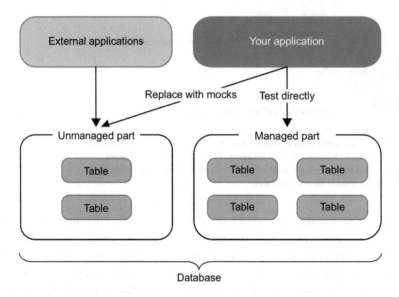

Figure 8.5   Treat the part of the database that is visible to external applications as an unmanaged dependency. Replace it with mocks in integration tests. Treat the rest of the database as a managed dependency. Verify its final state, not interactions with it.

It's important to differentiate these two parts of your database because, again, the shared tables are observable externally, and you need to be careful about how your application communicates with them. Don't change the way your system interacts with those tables unless absolutely necessary! You never know how other applications will react to such a change.

8.2.3   *What if you can't use a real database in integration tests?*

Sometimes, for reasons outside of your control, you just can't use a real version of a managed dependency in integration tests. An example would be a legacy database that you can't deploy to a test automation environment, not to mention a developer machine, because of some IT security policy, or because the cost of setting up and maintaining a test database instance is prohibitive.

What should you do in such a situation? Should you mock out the database anyway, despite it being a managed dependency? No, because mocking out a managed dependency compromises the integration tests' resistance to refactoring. Furthermore, such tests no longer provide as good protection against regressions. And if the database is the only out-of-process dependency in your project, the resulting integration tests would deliver no additional protection compared to the existing set of unit tests (assuming these unit tests follow the guidelines from chapter 7).

The only thing such integration tests would do, in addition to unit tests, is check what repository methods the controller calls. In other words, you wouldn't really gain confidence about anything other than those three lines of code in your controller being correct, while still having to do a lot of plumbing.

If you can't test the database as-is, don't write integration tests at all, and instead, focus exclusively on unit testing of the domain model. Remember to always put all your tests under close scrutiny. Tests that don't provide a high enough value should have no place in your test suite.

8.3 Integration testing: An example

Let's get back to the sample CRM system from chapter 7 and see how it can be covered with integration tests. As you may recall, this system implements one feature: changing the user's email. It retrieves the user and the company from the database, delegates the decision-making to the domain model, and then saves the results back to the database and puts a message on the bus if needed (figure 8.6).

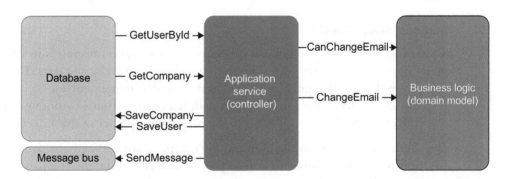

Figure 8.6   The use case of changing the user's email. The controller orchestrates the work between the database, the message bus, and the domain model.

The following listing shows how the controller currently looks.

Listing 8.1   The user controller

```
public class UserController
{
    private readonly Database _database = new Database();
    private readonly MessageBus _messageBus = new MessageBus();

    public string ChangeEmail(int userId, string newEmail)
    {
```

```
        object[] userData = _database.GetUserById(userId);
        User user = UserFactory.Create(userData);

        string error = user.CanChangeEmail();
        if (error != null)
            return error;

        object[] companyData = _database.GetCompany();
        Company company = CompanyFactory.Create(companyData);

        user.ChangeEmail(newEmail, company);

        _database.SaveCompany(company);
        _database.SaveUser(user);
        foreach (EmailChangedEvent ev in user.EmailChangedEvents)
        {
            _messageBus.SendEmailChangedMessage(ev.UserId, ev.NewEmail);
        }

        return "OK";
    }
}
```

In the following section, I'll first outline scenarios to verify using integration tests. Then I'll show you how to work with the database and the message bus in tests.

8.3.1   *What scenarios to test?*

As I mentioned earlier, the general guideline for integration testing is to cover the longest happy path and any edge cases that can't be exercised by unit tests. The *longest happy path* is the one that goes through all out-of-process dependencies.

In the CRM project, the longest happy path is a change from a corporate to a non-corporate email. Such a change leads to the maximum number of side effects:

- In the database, both the user and the company are updated: the user changes its type (from corporate to non-corporate) and email, and the company changes its number of employees.
- A message is sent to the message bus.

As for the edge cases that aren't tested by unit tests, there's only one such edge case: the scenario where the email can't be changed. There's no need to test this scenario, though, because the application will fail fast if this check isn't present in the controller. That leaves us with a single integration test:

```
public void Changing_email_from_corporate_to_non_corporate()
```

8.3.2 Categorizing the database and the message bus

Before writing the integration test, you need to categorize the two out-of-process dependencies and decide which of them to test directly and which to replace with a mock. The application database is a managed dependency because no other system can access it. Therefore, you should use a real instance of it. The integration test will

- Insert a user and a company into the database.
- Run the change of email scenario on that database.
- Verify the database state.

On the other hand, the message bus is an unmanaged dependency—its sole purpose is to enable communication with other systems. The integration test will mock out the message bus and verify the interactions between the controller and the mock afterward.

8.3.3 What about end-to-end testing?

There will be no end-to-end tests in our sample project. An end-to-end test in a scenario with an API would be a test running against a deployed, fully functioning version of that API, which means no mocks for any of the out-of-process dependencies (figure 8.7). On the other hand, integration tests host the application within the same process and substitute unmanaged dependencies with mocks (figure 8.8).

As I mentioned in chapter 2, whether to use end-to-end tests is a judgment call. For the most part, when you include managed dependencies in the integration testing scope and mock out only unmanaged dependencies, integration tests provide a level

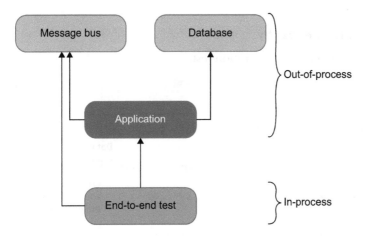

Figure 8.7   End-to-end tests emulate the external client and therefore test a deployed version of the application with all out-of-process dependencies included in the testing scope. End-to-end tests shouldn't check managed dependencies (such as the database) directly, only indirectly through the application.

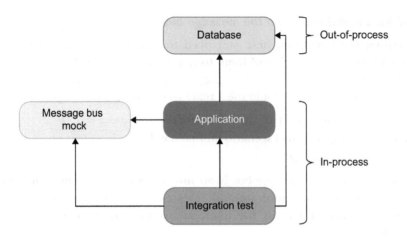

Figure 8.8 Integration tests host the application within the same process. Unlike end-to-end tests, integration tests substitute unmanaged dependencies with mocks. The only out-of-process components for integration tests are managed dependencies.

of protection that is close enough to that of end-to-end tests, so you can skip end-to-end testing. However, you could still create one or two overarching end-to-end tests that would provide a sanity check for the project after deployment. Make such tests go through the longest happy path, too, to ensure that your application communicates with all out-of-process dependencies properly. To emulate the external client's behavior, check the message bus directly, but verify the database's state through the application itself.

8.3.4   *Integration testing: The first try*

Here's the first version of the integration test.

Listing 8.2   The integration test

```
[Fact]
public void Changing_email_from_corporate_to_non_corporate()
{
    // Arrange                                              Database
    var db = new Database(ConnectionString);                repository
    User user = CreateUser(                                 Creates the user
        "user@mycorp.com", UserType.Employee, db);          and company in
    CreateCompany("mycorp.com", 1, db);                     the database

    var messageBusMock = new Mock<IMessageBus>();           Sets up a
    var sut = new UserController(db, messageBusMock.Object); mock for the
                                                            message bus
    // Act
    string result = sut.ChangeEmail(user.UserId, "new@gmail.com");
```

```
// Assert
Assert.Equal("OK", result);

object[] userData = db.GetUserById(user.UserId);        Asserts the
User userFromDb = UserFactory.Create(userData);         user's state
Assert.Equal("new@gmail.com", userFromDb.Email);
Assert.Equal(UserType.Customer, userFromDb.Type);

object[] companyData = db.GetCompany();                 Asserts the
Company companyFromDb = CompanyFactory                  company's
    .Create(companyData);                               state
Assert.Equal(0, companyFromDb.NumberOfEmployees);

messageBusMock.Verify(                                  Checks the
    x => x.SendEmailChangedMessage(                     interactions
        user.UserId, "new@gmail.com"),                  with the mock
    Times.Once);
}
```

TIP Notice that in the arrange section, the test doesn't insert the user and the company into the database on its own but instead calls the `CreateUser` and `CreateCompany` helper methods. These methods can be reused across multiple integration tests.

It's important to check the state of the database independently of the data used as input parameters. To do that, the integration test queries the user and company data separately in the assert section, creates new `userFromDb` and `companyFromDb` instances, and only then asserts their state. This approach ensures that the test exercises both writes to and reads from the database and thus provides the maximum protection against regressions. The reading itself must be implemented using the same code the controller uses internally: in this example, using the `Database`, `UserFactory`, and `CompanyFactory` classes.

This integration test, while it gets the job done, can still benefit from some improvement. For instance, you could use helper methods in the assertion section, too, in order to reduce this section's size. Also, `messageBusMock` doesn't provide as good protection against regressions as it potentially could. We'll talk about these improvements in the subsequent two chapters where we discuss mocking and database testing best practices.

8.4 *Using interfaces to abstract dependencies*

One of the most misunderstood subjects in the sphere of unit testing is the use of interfaces. Developers often ascribe invalid reasons to why they introduce interfaces and, as a result, tend to overuse them. In this section, I'll expand on those invalid reasons and show in what circumstances the use of interfaces is and isn't preferable.

8.4.1 *Interfaces and loose coupling*

Many developers introduce interfaces for out-of-process dependencies, such as the database or the message bus, even when these interfaces have only one implementation. This practice has become so widespread nowadays that hardly anyone questions it. You'll often see class-interface pairs similar to the following:

```
public interface IMessageBus
public class MessageBus : IMessageBus

public interface IUserRepository
public class UserRepository : IUserRepository
```

The common reasoning behind the use of such interfaces is that they help to

- Abstract out-of-process dependencies, thus achieving loose coupling
- Add new functionality without changing the existing code, thus adhering to the Open-Closed principle (OCP)

Both of these reasons are misconceptions. Interfaces with a single implementation are not abstractions and don't provide loose coupling any more than concrete classes that implement those interfaces. Genuine abstractions are *discovered*, not *invented*. The discovery, by definition, takes place post factum, when the abstraction already exists but is not yet clearly defined in the code. Thus, for an interface to be a genuine abstraction, it must have at least two implementations.

The second reason (the ability to add new functionality without changing the existing code) is a misconception because it violates a more foundational principle: YAGNI. *YAGNI* stands for "You aren't gonna need it" and advocates against investing time in functionality that's not needed right now. You shouldn't develop this functionality, nor should you modify your existing code to account for the appearance of such functionality in the future. The two major reasons are as follows:

- *Opportunity cost*—If you spend time on a feature that business people don't need at the moment, you steer that time away from features they do need right now. Moreover, when the business people finally come to require the developed functionality, their view on it will most likely have evolved, and you will still need to adjust the already-written code. Such activity is wasteful. It's more beneficial to implement the functionality from scratch when the actual need for it emerges.
- *The less code in the project, the better.* Introducing code *just in case* without an immediate need unnecessarily increases your code base's cost of ownership. It's better to postpone introducing new functionality until as late a stage of your project as possible.

  TIP Writing code is an expensive way to solve problems. The less code the solution requires and the simpler that code is, the better.

There are exceptional cases where YAGNI doesn't apply, but these are few and far between. For those cases, see my article "OCP vs YAGNI," at https://enterprise-craftsmanship.com/posts/ocp-vs-yagni.

8.4.2 Why use interfaces for out-of-process dependencies?

So, why use interfaces for out-of-process dependencies at all, assuming that each of those interfaces has only one implementation? The real reason is much more practical and down-to-earth. It's to enable mocking—as simple as that. Without an interface, you can't create a test double and thus can't verify interactions between the system under test and the out-of-process dependency.

Therefore, *don't introduce interfaces for out-of-process dependencies unless you need to mock out those dependencies.* You only mock out unmanaged dependencies, so the guideline can be boiled down to this: *use interfaces for unmanaged dependencies only.* Still inject managed dependencies into the controller explicitly, but use concrete classes for that.

Note that genuine abstractions (abstractions that have more than one implementation) can be represented with interfaces regardless of whether you mock them out. Introducing an interface with a single implementation for reasons other than mocking is a violation of YAGNI, however.

And you might have noticed in listing 8.2 that `UserController` now accepts both the message bus and the database explicitly via the constructor, but only the message bus has a corresponding interface. The database is a managed dependency and thus doesn't require such an interface. Here's the controller:

```
public class UserController
{
    private readonly Database _database;          // A concrete class
    private readonly IMessageBus _messageBus;     // The interface

    public UserController(Database database, IMessageBus messageBus)
    {
        _database = database;
        _messageBus = messageBus;
    }

    public string ChangeEmail(int userId, string newEmail)
    {
        /* the method uses _database and _messageBus */
    }
}
```

NOTE You can mock out a dependency without resorting to an interface by making methods in that dependency virtual and using the class itself as a base for the mock. This approach is inferior to the one with interfaces, though. I explain more on this topic of interfaces versus base classes in chapter 11.

8.4.3 Using interfaces for in-process dependencies

You sometimes see code bases where interfaces back not only out-of-process dependencies but in-process dependencies as well. For example:

```
public interface IUser
{
    int UserId { get; set; }
```

```
    string Email { get; }
    string CanChangeEmail();
    void ChangeEmail(string newEmail, Company company);
}

public class User : IUser
{
    /* ... */
}
```

Assuming that IUser has only one implementation (and such specific interfaces always have only one implementation), this is a huge red flag. Just like with out-of-process dependencies, the only reason to introduce an interface with a single implementation for a domain class is to enable mocking. But unlike out-of-process dependencies, you should never check interactions between domain classes, because doing so results in brittle tests: tests that couple to implementation details and thus fail on the metric of resisting to refactoring (see chapter 5 for more details about mocks and test fragility).

8.5   Integration testing best practices

There are some general guidelines that can help you get the most out of your integration tests:

- Making domain model boundaries explicit
- Reducing the number of layers in the application
- Eliminating circular dependencies

As usual, best practices that are beneficial for tests also tend to improve the health of your code base in general.

8.5.1   Making domain model boundaries explicit

Try to always have an explicit, well-known place for the domain model in your code base. The *domain model* is the collection of domain knowledge about the problem your project is meant to solve. Assigning the domain model an explicit boundary helps you better visualize and reason about that part of your code.

This practice also helps with testing. As I mentioned earlier in this chapter, unit tests target the domain model and algorithms, while integration tests target controllers. The explicit boundary between domain classes and controllers makes it easier to tell the difference between unit and integration tests.

The boundary itself can take the form of a separate assembly or a namespace. The particulars aren't that important as long as all of the domain logic is put under a single, distinct umbrella and not scattered across the code base.

8.5.2   Reducing the number of layers

Most programmers naturally gravitate toward abstracting and generalizing the code by introducing additional layers of indirection. In a typical enterprise-level application, you can easily observe several such layers (figure 8.9).

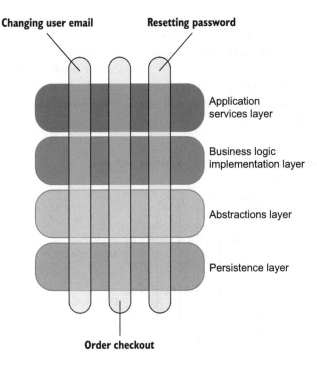

Figure 8.9 Various application concerns are often addressed by separate layers of indirection. A typical feature takes up a small portion of each layer.

In extreme cases, an application gets so many abstraction layers that it becomes too hard to navigate the code base and understand the logic behind even the simplest operations. At some point, you just want to get to the specific solution of the problem at hand, not some generalization of that solution in a vacuum.

> *All problems in computer science can be solved by another layer of indirection, except for the problem of too many layers of indirection.*
>
> —David J. Wheeler

Layers of indirection negatively affect your ability to reason about the code. When every feature has a representation in each of those layers, you have to expend significant effort assembling all the pieces into a cohesive picture. This creates an additional mental burden that handicaps the entire development process.

An excessive number of abstractions doesn't help unit or integration testing, either. Code bases with many layers of indirections tend not to have a clear boundary between controllers and the domain model (which, as you might remember from chapter 7, is a precondition for effective tests). There's also a much stronger tendency to verify each layer separately. This tendency results in a lot of low-value integration tests, each of which exercises only the code from a specific layer and mocks out layers underneath. The end result is always the same: insufficient protection against regressions combined with low resistance to refactoring.

Try to have as few layers of indirection as possible. In most backend systems, you can get away with just three: the domain model, application services layer (controllers), and infrastructure layer. The infrastructure layer typically consists of algorithms that don't belong to the domain model, as well as code that enables access to out-of-process dependencies (figure 8.10).

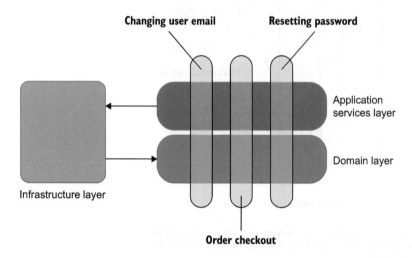

Figure 8.10   You can get away with just three layers: the domain layer (contains domain logic), application services layers (provides an entry point for the external client, and coordinates the work between domain classes and out-of-process dependencies), and infrastructure layer (works with out-of-process dependencies; database repositories, ORM mappings, and SMTP gateways reside in this layer).

8.5.3   *Eliminating circular dependencies*

Another practice that can drastically improve the maintainability of your code base and make testing easier is eliminating circular dependencies.

> **DEFINITION**   A *circular dependency* (also known as *cyclic dependency*) is two or more classes that directly or indirectly depend on each other to function properly.

A typical example of a circular dependency is a callback:

```
public class CheckOutService
{
    public void CheckOut(int orderId)
    {
        var service = new ReportGenerationService();
        service.GenerateReport(orderId, this);
```

```
        /* other code */
    }
}

public class ReportGenerationService
{
    public void GenerateReport(
        int orderId,
        CheckOutService checkOutService)
    {
        /* calls checkOutService when generation is completed */
    }
}
```

Here, CheckOutService creates an instance of ReportGenerationService and passes itself to that instance as an argument. ReportGenerationService calls CheckOut-Service back to notify it about the result of the report generation.

Just like an excessive number of abstraction layers, circular dependencies add tremendous cognitive load when you try to read and understand the code. The reason is that circular dependencies don't give you a clear starting point from which you can begin exploring the solution. To understand just one class, you have to read and understand the whole graph of its siblings all at once. Even a small set of interdependent classes can quickly become too hard to grasp.

Circular dependencies also interfere with testing. You often have to resort to interfaces and mocking in order to split the class graph and isolate a single unit of behavior, which, again, is a no-go when it comes to testing the domain model (more on that in chapter 5).

Note that the use of interfaces only masks the problem of circular dependencies. If you introduce an interface for CheckOutService and make ReportGenerationService depend on that interface instead of the concrete class, you remove the circular dependency at compile time (figure 8.11), but the cycle still persists at runtime. Even though the compiler no longer regards this class composition as a circular reference, the cognitive load required to understand the code doesn't become any smaller. If anything, it increases due to the additional interface.

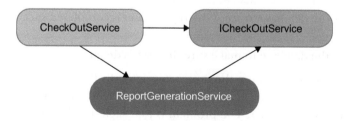

Figure 8.11 With an interface, you remove the circular dependency at compile time, but not at runtime. The cognitive load required to understand the code doesn't become any smaller.

A better approach to handle circular dependencies is to get rid of them. Refactor ReportGenerationService such that it depends on neither CheckOutService nor the ICheckOutService interface, and make ReportGenerationService return the result of its work as a plain value instead of calling CheckOutService:

```
public class CheckOutService
{
    public void CheckOut(int orderId)
    {
        var service = new ReportGenerationService();
        Report report = service.GenerateReport(orderId);

        /* other work */
    }
}

public class ReportGenerationService
{
    public Report GenerateReport(int orderId)
    {
        /* ... */
    }
}
```

It's rarely possible to eliminate all circular dependencies in your code base. But even then, you can minimize the damage by making the remaining graphs of interdependent classes as small as possible.

8.5.4 *Using multiple act sections in a test*

As you might remember from chapter 3, having more than one arrange, act, or assert section in a test is a code smell. It's a sign that this test checks multiple units of behavior, which, in turn, hinders the test's maintainability. For example, if you have two related use cases—say, user registration and user deletion—it might be tempting to check both of these use cases in a single integration test. Such a test could have the following structure:

- *Arrange*—Prepare data with which to register a user.
- *Act*—Call UserController.RegisterUser().
- *Assert*—Query the database to see if the registration is completed successfully.
- *Act*—Call UserController.DeleteUser().
- *Assert*—Query the database to make sure the user is deleted.

This approach is compelling because the user states naturally flow from one another, and the first act (registering a user) can simultaneously serve as an arrange phase for the subsequent act (user deletion). The problem is that such tests lose focus and can quickly become too bloated.

It's best to split the test by extracting each act into a test of its own. It may seem like unnecessary work (after all, why create two tests where one would suffice?), but this work pays off in the long run. Having each test focus on a single unit of behavior makes those tests easier to understand and modify when necessary.

The exception to this guideline is tests working with out-of-process dependencies that are hard to bring to a desirable state. Let's say for example that registering a user results in creating a bank account in an external banking system. The bank has provisioned a sandbox for your organization, and you want to use that sandbox in an end-to-end test. The problem is that the sandbox is too slow, or maybe the bank limits the number of calls you can make to that sandbox. In such a scenario, it becomes beneficial to combine multiple acts into a single test and thus reduce the number of interactions with the problematic out-of-process dependency.

Hard-to-manage out-of-process dependencies are the only legitimate reason to write a test with more than one act section. This is why you should never have multiple acts in a unit test—unit tests don't work with out-of-process dependencies. Even integration tests should rarely have several acts. In practice, multistep tests almost always belong to the category of end-to-end tests.

8.6 How to test logging functionality

Logging is a gray area, and it isn't obvious what to do with it when it comes to testing. This is a complex topic that I'll split into the following questions:

- Should you test logging at all?
- If so, how should you test it?
- How much logging is enough?
- How do you pass around logger instances?

We'll use our sample CRM project as an example.

8.6.1 Should you test logging?

Logging is a cross-cutting functionality, which you can require in any part of your code base. Here's an example of logging in the `User` class.

Listing 8.3 An example of logging in `User`

```
public class User
{
    public void ChangeEmail(string newEmail, Company company)
    {
        _logger.Info(
            $"Changing email for user {UserId} to {newEmail}");

        Precondition.Requires(CanChangeEmail() == null);

        if (Email == newEmail)
            return;

        UserType newType = company.IsEmailCorporate(newEmail)
            ? UserType.Employee
            : UserType.Customer;
```

Start of the method →

```
        if (Type != newType)
        {
            int delta = newType == UserType.Employee ? 1 : -1;
            company.ChangeNumberOfEmployees(delta);
            _logger.Info(
                $"User {UserId} changed type " +
                $"from {Type} to {newType}");
        }

        Email = newEmail;
        Type = newType;
        EmailChangedEvents.Add(new EmailChangedEvent(UserId, newEmail));

        _logger.Info(
            $"Email is changed for user {UserId}");
    }
}
```

> **Changes the user type** (annotation for the first `if` block)

> **End of the method** (annotation pointing to the `_logger.Info` call)

The User class records in a log file each beginning and ending of the ChangeEmail method, as well as the change of the user type. Should you test this functionality?

On the one hand, logging generates important information about the application's behavior. But on the other hand, logging can be so ubiquitous that it's not obvious whether this functionality is worth the additional, quite significant, testing effort. The answer to the question of whether you should test logging comes down to this: *Is logging part of the application's observable behavior, or is it an implementation detail?*

In that sense, it isn't different from any other functionality. Logging ultimately results in side effects in an out-of-process dependency such as a text file or a database. If these side effects are meant to be observed by your customer, the application's clients, or anyone else other than the developers themselves, then logging *is* an observable behavior and thus must be tested. If the only audience is the developers, then it's an implementation detail that can be freely modified without anyone noticing, in which case it shouldn't be tested.

For example, if you write a logging library, then the logs this library produces are the most important (and the only) part of its observable behavior. Another example is when business people insist on logging key application workflows. In this case, logs also become a business requirement and thus have to be covered by tests. However, in the latter example, you might also have separate logging just for developers.

Steve Freeman and Nat Pryce, in their book *Growing Object-Oriented Software, Guided by Tests* (Addison-Wesley Professional, 2009), call these two types of logging *support logging* and *diagnostic logging*:

- *Support logging* produces messages that are intended to be tracked by support staff or system administrators.
- *Diagnostic logging* helps developers understand what's going on inside the application.

8.6.2 How should you test logging?

Because logging involves out-of-process dependencies, when it comes to testing it, the same rules apply as with any other functionality that touches out-of-process dependencies. You need to use mocks to verify interactions between your application and the log storage.

INTRODUCING A WRAPPER ON TOP OF ILOGGER

But don't just mock out the `ILogger` interface. Because support logging is a business requirement, reflect that requirement explicitly in your code base. Create a special `DomainLogger` class where you explicitly list all the support logging needed for the business; verify interactions with that class instead of the raw `ILogger`.

For example, let's say that business people require you to log all changes of the users' types, but the logging at the beginning and the end of the method is there just for debugging purposes. The next listing shows the `User` class after introducing a `DomainLogger` class.

Listing 8.4 Extracting support logging into the `DomainLogger` class

```
public void ChangeEmail(string newEmail, Company company)
{
    _logger.Info(                                         ◁── Diagnostic logging
        $"Changing email for user {UserId} to {newEmail}");

    Precondition.Requires(CanChangeEmail() == null);

    if (Email == newEmail)
        return;

    UserType newType = company.IsEmailCorporate(newEmail)
        ? UserType.Employee
        : UserType.Customer;

    if (Type != newType)
    {
        int delta = newType == UserType.Employee ? 1 : -1;
        company.ChangeNumberOfEmployees(delta);
        _domainLogger.UserTypeHasChanged(          ◁── Support logging
            UserId, Type, newType);
    }

    Email = newEmail;
    Type = newType;
    EmailChangedEvents.Add(new EmailChangedEvent(UserId, newEmail));

    _logger.Info(                                  ◁── Diagnostic logging
        $"Email is changed for user {UserId}");
}
```

The diagnostic logging still uses the old `logger` (which is of type `ILogger`), but the support logging now uses the new `domainLogger` instance of type `IDomainLogger`. The following listing shows the implementation of `IDomainLogger`.

Listing 8.5 `DomainLogger` **as a wrapper on top of** `ILogger`

```
public class DomainLogger : IDomainLogger
{
    private readonly ILogger _logger;

    public DomainLogger(ILogger logger)
    {
        _logger = logger;
    }

    public void UserTypeHasChanged(
        int userId, UserType oldType, UserType newType)
    {
        _logger.Info(
            $"User {userId} changed type " +
            $"from {oldType} to {newType}");
    }
}
```

DomainLogger works on top of ILogger: it uses the domain language to declare specific log entries required by the business, thus making support logging easier to understand and maintain. In fact, this implementation is very similar to the concept of structured logging, which enables great flexibility when it comes to log file post-processing and analysis.

UNDERSTANDING STRUCTURED LOGGING

Structured logging is a logging technique where capturing log data is decoupled from the rendering of that data. Traditional logging works with simple text. A call like

```
logger.Info("User Id is " + 12);
```

first forms a string and then writes that string to a log storage. The problem with this approach is that the resulting log files are hard to analyze due to the lack of structure. For example, it's not easy to see how many messages of a particular type there are and how many of those relate to a specific user ID. You'd need to use (or even write your own) special tooling for that.

On the other hand, structured logging introduces structure to your log storage. The use of a structured logging library looks similar on the surface:

```
logger.Info("User Id is {UserId}", 12);
```

But its underlying behavior differs significantly. Behind the scenes, this method computes a hash of the message template (the message itself is stored in a lookup storage for space efficiency) and combines that hash with the input parameters to form a set of *captured data*. The next step is the rendering of that data. You can still have a flat log file, as with traditional logging, but that's just one possible rendering. You could also configure the logging library to render the captured data as a JSON or a CSV file, where it would be easier to analyze (figure 8.12).

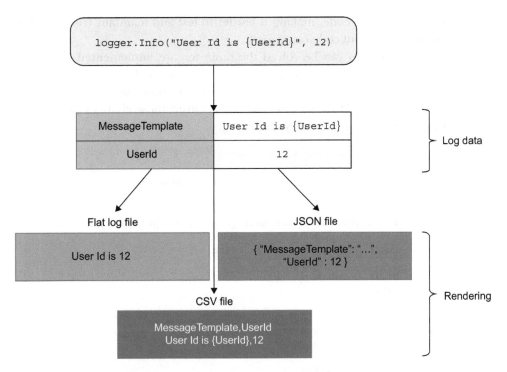

Figure 8.12 **Structured logging decouples log data from renderings of that data. You can set up multiple renderings, such as a flat log file, JSON, or CSV file.**

DomainLogger in listing 8.5 isn't a structured logger per se, but it operates in the same spirit. Look at this method once again:

```
public void UserTypeHasChanged(
    int userId, UserType oldType, UserType newType)
{
    _logger.Info(
        $"User {userId} changed type " +
        $"from {oldType} to {newType}");
}
```

You can view UserTypeHasChanged() as the message template's hash. Together with the userId, oldType, and newType parameters, that hash forms the log data. The method's implementation renders the log data into a flat log file. And you can easily create additional renderings by also writing the log data into a JSON or a CSV file.

WRITING TESTS FOR SUPPORT AND DIAGNOSTIC LOGGING
As I mentioned earlier, DomainLogger represents an out-of-process dependency—the log storage. This poses a problem: User now interacts with that dependency and thus violates the separation between business logic and communication with out-of-process dependencies. The use of DomainLogger has transitioned User to the category of

overcomplicated code, making it harder to test and maintain (refer to chapter 7 for more details about code categories).

This problem can be solved the same way we implemented the notification of external systems about changed user emails: with the help of domain events (again, see chapter 7 for details). You can introduce a separate domain event to track changes in the user type. The controller will then convert those changes into calls to Domain-Logger, as shown in the following listing.

Listing 8.6 Replacing `DomainLogger` in `User` with a domain event

```
public void ChangeEmail(string newEmail, Company company)
{
    _logger.Info(
        $"Changing email for user {UserId} to {newEmail}");

    Precondition.Requires(CanChangeEmail() == null);

    if (Email == newEmail)
        return;

    UserType newType = company.IsEmailCorporate(newEmail)
        ? UserType.Employee
        : UserType.Customer;

    if (Type != newType)
    {
        int delta = newType == UserType.Employee ? 1 : -1;
        company.ChangeNumberOfEmployees(delta);
        AddDomainEvent(                          ◁── Uses a domain
            new UserTypeChangedEvent(                event instead of
                UserId, Type, newType));             DomainLogger
    }

    Email = newEmail;
    Type = newType;
    AddDomainEvent(new EmailChangedEvent(UserId, newEmail));

    _logger.Info($"Email is changed for user {UserId}");
}
```

Notice that there are now two domain events: `UserTypeChangedEvent` and `Email-ChangedEvent`. Both of them implement the same interface (`IDomainEvent`) and thus can be stored in the same collection.

And here is how the controller looks.

Listing 8.7 Latest version of `UserController`

```
public string ChangeEmail(int userId, string newEmail)
{
    object[] userData = _database.GetUserById(userId);
    User user = UserFactory.Create(userData);
```

```
        string error = user.CanChangeEmail();
        if (error != null)
            return error;

        object[] companyData = _database.GetCompany();
        Company company = CompanyFactory.Create(companyData);

        user.ChangeEmail(newEmail, company);

        _database.SaveCompany(company);
        _database.SaveUser(user);                              Dispatches user
        _eventDispatcher.Dispatch(user.DomainEvents);   ◁───┘  domain events

        return "OK";
}
```

EventDispatcher is a new class that converts domain events into calls to out-of-process dependencies:

- EmailChangedEvent translates into _messageBus.SendEmailChangedMessage().
- UserTypeChangedEvent translates into _domainLogger.UserTypeHasChanged().

The use of UserTypeChangedEvent has restored the separation between the two responsibilities: domain logic and communication with out-of-process dependencies. Testing support logging now isn't any different from testing the other *unmanaged* dependency, the message bus:

- Unit tests should check an instance of UserTypeChangedEvent in the User under test.
- The single integration test should use a mock to ensure the interaction with DomainLogger is in place.

Note that if you need to do support logging in the controller and not one of the domain classes, there's no need to use domain events. As you may remember from chapter 7, controllers orchestrate the collaboration between the domain model and out-of-process dependencies. DomainLogger is one of such dependencies, and thus UserController can use that logger directly.

Also notice that I didn't change the way the User class does diagnostic logging. User still uses the logger instance directly in the beginning and at the end of its ChangeEmail method. This is by design. Diagnostic logging is for developers only; you don't need to unit test this functionality and thus don't have to keep it out of the domain model.

Still, refrain from the use of diagnostic logging in User or other domain classes when possible. I explain why in the next section.

8.6.3   How much logging is enough?

Another important question is about the optimum amount of logging. How much logging is enough? Support logging is out of the question here because it's a business requirement. You do have control over diagnostic logging, though.

It's important not to overuse diagnostic logging, for the following two reasons:

- *Excessive logging clutters the code.* This is especially true for the domain model. That's why I don't recommend using diagnostic logging in `User` even though such a use is fine from a unit testing perspective: it obscures the code.
- *Logs' signal-to-noise ratio is key.* The more you log, the harder it is to find relevant information. Maximize the signal; minimize the noise.

Try not to use diagnostic logging in the domain model at all. In most cases, you can safely move that logging from domain classes to controllers. And even then, resort to diagnostic logging only temporarily when you need to debug something. Remove it once you finish debugging. Ideally, you should use diagnostic logging for unhandled exceptions only.

8.6.4   How do you pass around logger instances?

Finally, the last question is how to pass logger instances in the code. One way to resolve these instances is using static methods, as shown in the following listing.

> **Listing 8.8   Storing `ILogger` in a static field**

```
public class User                                    Resolves ILogger through a
{                                                    static method, and stores it
    private static readonly ILogger _logger =        in a private static field
        LogManager.GetLogger(typeof(User));

    public void ChangeEmail(string newEmail, Company company)
    {
        _logger.Info(
            $"Changing email for user {UserId} to {newEmail}");

        /* ... */

        _logger.Info($"Email is changed for user {UserId}");
    }
}
```

Steven van Deursen and Mark Seeman, in their book *Dependency Injection Principles, Practices, Patterns* (Manning Publications, 2018), call this type of dependency acquisition *ambient context.* This is an anti-pattern. Two of their arguments are that

- The dependency is hidden and hard to change.
- Testing becomes more difficult.

I fully agree with this analysis. To me, though, the main drawback of ambient context is that it masks potential problems in code. If injecting a logger explicitly into a domain class becomes so inconvenient that you have to resort to ambient context, that's a certain sign of trouble. You either log too much or use too many layers of indirection. In any case, ambient context is not a solution. Instead, tackle the root cause of the problem.

The following listing shows one way to explicitly inject the logger: as a method argument. Another way is through the class constructor.

Listing 8.9 Injecting the logger explicitly

```
public void ChangeEmail(
    string newEmail,
    Company company,           Method
    ILogger logger)            injection
{
    logger.Info(
        $"Changing email for user {UserId} to {newEmail}");

    /* ... */

    logger.Info($"Email is changed for user {UserId}");
}
```

8.7 Conclusion

View communications with all out-of-process dependencies through the lens of whether this communication is part of the application's observable behavior or an implementation detail. The log storage isn't any different in that regard. Mock logging functionality if the logs are observable by non-programmers; don't test it otherwise. In the next chapter, we'll dive deeper into the topic of mocking and best practices related to it.

Summary

- An *integration test* is any test that is not a unit test. Integration tests verify how your system works in integration with out-of-process dependencies:
  - Integration tests cover controllers; unit tests cover algorithms and the domain model.
  - Integration tests provide better protection against regressions and resistance to refactoring; unit tests have better maintainability and feedback speed.
- The bar for integration tests is higher than for unit tests: the score they have in the metrics of protection against regressions and resistance to refactoring must be higher than that of a unit test to offset the worse maintainability and feedback speed. The *Test Pyramid* represents this trade-off: the majority of tests should be fast and cheap unit tests, with a smaller number of slow and more expensive integration tests that check correctness of the system as a whole:
  - Check as many of the business scenario's edge cases as possible with unit tests. Use integration tests to cover one happy path, as well as any edge cases that can't be covered by unit tests.

- – The shape of the Test Pyramid depends on the project's complexity. Simple projects have little code in the domain model and thus can have an equal number of unit and integration tests. In the most trivial cases, there might be no unit tests.
- The *Fail Fast principle* advocates for making bugs manifest themselves quickly and is a viable alternative to integration testing.
- *Managed dependencies* are out-of-process dependencies that are only accessible through your application. Interactions with managed dependencies aren't observable externally. A typical example is the application database.
- *Unmanaged dependencies* are out-of-process dependencies that other applications have access to. Interactions with unmanaged dependencies are observable externally. Typical examples include an SMTP server and a message bus.
- Communications with managed dependencies are implementation details; communications with unmanaged dependencies are part of your system's observable behavior.
- Use real instances of managed dependencies in integration tests; replace unmanaged dependencies with mocks.
- Sometimes an out-of-process dependency exhibits attributes of both managed and unmanaged dependencies. A typical example is a database that other applications have access to. Treat the observable part of the dependency as an unmanaged dependency: replace that part with mocks in tests. Treat the rest of the dependency as a managed dependency: verify its final state, not interactions with it.
- An integration test must go through all layers that work with a managed dependency. In an example with a database, this means checking the state of that database independently of the data used as input parameters.
- Interfaces with a single implementation are not abstractions and don't provide loose coupling any more than the concrete classes that implement those interfaces. Trying to anticipate future implementations for such interfaces violates the YAGNI (you aren't gonna need it) principle.
- The only legitimate reason to use interfaces with a single implementation is to enable mocking. Use such interfaces only for unmanaged dependencies. Use concrete classes for managed dependencies.
- Interfaces with a single implementation used for in-process dependencies are a red flag. Such interfaces hint at using mocks to check interactions between domain classes, which leads to coupling tests to the code's implementation details.
- Have an explicit and well-known place for the domain model in your code base. The explicit boundary between domain classes and controllers makes it easier to tell unit and integration tests apart.
- An excessive number of layers of indirection negatively affects your ability to reason about the code. Have as few layers of indirections as possible. In most

backend systems, you can get away with just three of them: the domain model, an application services layer (controllers), and an infrastructure layer.

- Circular dependencies add cognitive load when you try to understand the code. A typical example is a callback (when a callee notifies the caller about the result of its work). Break the cycle by introducing a value object; use that value object to return the result from the callee to the caller.

- Multiple act sections in a test are only justified when that test works with out-of-process dependencies that are hard to bring into a desirable state. You should never have multiple acts in a unit test, because unit tests don't work with out-of-process dependencies. Multistep tests almost always belong to the category of end-to-end tests.

- Support logging is intended for support staff and system administrators; it's part of the application's observable behavior. Diagnostic logging helps developers understand what's going on inside the application: it's an implementation detail.

- Because support logging is a business requirement, reflect that requirement explicitly in your code base. Introduce a special `DomainLogger` class where you list all the support logging needed for the business.

- Treat support logging like any other functionality that works with an out-of-process dependency. Use domain events to track changes in the domain model; convert those domain events into calls to `DomainLogger` in controllers.

- Don't test diagnostic logging. Unlike support logging, you can do diagnostic logging directly in the domain model.

- Use diagnostic logging sporadically. Excessive diagnostic logging clutters the code and damages the logs' signal-to-noise ratio. Ideally, you should only use diagnostic logging for unhandled exceptions.

- Always inject all dependencies explicitly (including loggers), either via the constructor or as a method argument.

Mocking best practices

As you might remember from chapter 5, a mock is a test double that helps to emulate and examine interactions between the system under test and its dependencies. As you might also remember from chapter 8, mocks should only be applied to *unmanaged dependencies* (interactions with such dependencies are observable by external applications). Using mocks for anything else results in *brittle tests* (tests that lack the metric of resistance to refactoring). When it comes to mocks, adhering to this one guideline will get you about two-thirds of the way to success.

This chapter shows the remaining guidelines that will help you develop integration tests that have the greatest possible value by maxing out mocks' resistance to refactoring and protection against regressions. I'll first show a typical use of mocks, describe its drawbacks, and then demonstrate how you can overcome those drawbacks.

216

9.1 *Maximizing mocks' value*

It's important to limit the use of mocks to unmanaged dependencies, but that's only the first step on the way to maximizing the value of mocks. This topic is best explained with an example, so I'll continue using the CRM system from earlier chapters as a sample project. I'll remind you of its functionality and show the integration test we ended up with. After that, you'll see how that test can be improved with regard to mocking.

As you might recall, the CRM system currently supports only one use case: changing a user's email. The following listing shows where we left off with the controller.

Listing 9.1 User controller

```
public class UserController
{
    private readonly Database _database;
    private readonly EventDispatcher _eventDispatcher;

    public UserController(
        Database database,
        IMessageBus messageBus,
        IDomainLogger domainLogger)
    {
        _database = database;
        _eventDispatcher = new EventDispatcher(
            messageBus, domainLogger);
    }

    public string ChangeEmail(int userId, string newEmail)
    {
        object[] userData = _database.GetUserById(userId);
        User user = UserFactory.Create(userData);

        string error = user.CanChangeEmail();
        if (error != null)
            return error;

        object[] companyData = _database.GetCompany();
        Company company = CompanyFactory.Create(companyData);

        user.ChangeEmail(newEmail, company);

        _database.SaveCompany(company);
        _database.SaveUser(user);
        _eventDispatcher.Dispatch(user.DomainEvents);

        return "OK";
    }
}
```

Note that there's no longer any diagnostic logging, but support logging (the IDomain-Logger interface) is still in place (see chapter 8 for more details). Also, listing 9.1 introduces a new class: the EventDispatcher. It converts domain events generated by the domain model into calls to *unmanaged* dependencies (something that the controller previously did by itself), as shown next.

Listing 9.2   Event dispatcher

```
public class EventDispatcher
{
    private readonly IMessageBus _messageBus;
    private readonly IDomainLogger _domainLogger;

    public EventDispatcher(
        IMessageBus messageBus,
        IDomainLogger domainLogger)
    {
        _domainLogger = domainLogger;
        _messageBus = messageBus;
    }

    public void Dispatch(List<IDomainEvent> events)
    {
        foreach (IDomainEvent ev in events)
        {
            Dispatch(ev);
        }
    }

    private void Dispatch(IDomainEvent ev)
    {
        switch (ev)
        {
            case EmailChangedEvent emailChangedEvent:
                _messageBus.SendEmailChangedMessage(
                    emailChangedEvent.UserId,
                    emailChangedEvent.NewEmail);
                break;

            case UserTypeChangedEvent userTypeChangedEvent:
                _domainLogger.UserTypeHasChanged(
                    userTypeChangedEvent.UserId,
                    userTypeChangedEvent.OldType,
                    userTypeChangedEvent.NewType);
                break;
        }
    }
}
```

Finally, the following listing shows the integration test. This test goes through all out-of-process dependencies (both managed and unmanaged).

Listing 9.3   Integration test

```
[Fact]
public void Changing_email_from_corporate_to_non_corporate()
{
```

```
// Arrange
var db = new Database(ConnectionString);
User user = CreateUser("user@mycorp.com", UserType.Employee, db);
CreateCompany("mycorp.com", 1, db);

var messageBusMock = new Mock<IMessageBus>();          Sets up the
var loggerMock = new Mock<IDomainLogger>();            mocks
var sut = new UserController(
    db, messageBusMock.Object, loggerMock.Object);

// Act
string result = sut.ChangeEmail(user.UserId, "new@gmail.com");

// Assert
Assert.Equal("OK", result);

object[] userData = db.GetUserById(user.UserId);
User userFromDb = UserFactory.Create(userData);
Assert.Equal("new@gmail.com", userFromDb.Email);
Assert.Equal(UserType.Customer, userFromDb.Type);

object[] companyData = db.GetCompany();
Company companyFromDb = CompanyFactory.Create(companyData);
Assert.Equal(0, companyFromDb.NumberOfEmployees);

messageBusMock.Verify(
    x => x.SendEmailChangedMessage(
        user.UserId, "new@gmail.com"),
    Times.Once);                              Verifies the
loggerMock.Verify(                            interactions
    x => x.UserTypeHasChanged(                with the mocks
        user.UserId,
        UserType.Employee,
        UserType.Customer),
    Times.Once);
}
```

This test mocks out two unmanaged dependencies: IMessageBus and IDomainLogger. I'll focus on IMessageBus first. We'll discuss IDomainLogger later in this chapter.

9.1.1 Verifying interactions at the system edges

Let's discuss why the mocks used by the integration test in listing 9.3 aren't ideal in terms of their protection against regressions and resistance to refactoring and how we can fix that.

> **TIP** When mocking, always adhere to the following guideline: verify interactions with unmanaged dependencies at the very edges of your system.

The problem with messageBusMock in listing 9.3 is that the IMessageBus interface doesn't reside at the system's edge. Look at that interface's implementation.

Listing 9.4   Message bus

```
public interface IMessageBus
{
    void SendEmailChangedMessage(int userId, string newEmail);
}

public class MessageBus : IMessageBus
{
    private readonly IBus _bus;

    public void SendEmailChangedMessage(
        int userId, string newEmail)
    {
        _bus.Send("Type: USER EMAIL CHANGED; " +
            $"Id: {userId}; " +
            $"NewEmail: {newEmail}");
    }
}

public interface IBus
{
    void Send(string message);
}
```

Both the IMessageBus and IBus interfaces (and the classes implementing them) belong to our project's code base. IBus is a wrapper on top of the message bus SDK library (provided by the company that develops that message bus). This wrapper encapsulates non-essential technical details, such as connection credentials, and exposes a nice, clean interface for sending arbitrary text messages to the bus. IMessageBus is a wrapper on top of IBus; it defines messages specific to your domain. IMessageBus helps you keep all such messages in one place and reuse them across the application.

It's possible to merge the IBus and IMessageBus interfaces together, but that would be a suboptimal solution. These two responsibilities—hiding the external library's complexity and holding all application messages in one place—are best kept separated. This is the same situation as with ILogger and IDomainLogger, which you saw in chapter 8. IDomainLogger implements specific logging functionality required by the business, and it does that by using the generic ILogger behind the scenes.

Figure 9.1 shows where IBus and IMessageBus stand from a hexagonal architecture perspective: IBus is the last link in the chain of types between the controller and the message bus, while IMessageBus is only an intermediate step on the way.

Mocking IBus instead of IMessageBus maximizes the mock's protection against regressions. As you might remember from chapter 4, protection against regressions is a function of the amount of code that is executed during the test. Mocking the very last type that communicates with the unmanaged dependency increases the number of classes the integration test goes through and thus improves the protection. This guideline is also the reason you don't want to mock EventDispatcher. It resides even further away from the edge of the system, compared to IMessageBus.

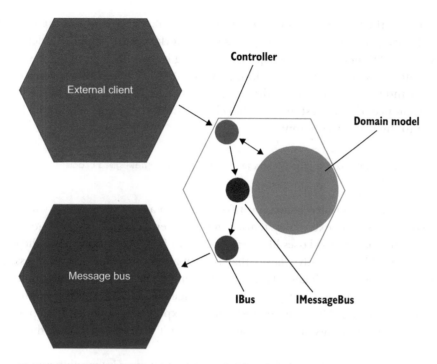

Figure 9.1 IBus resides at the system's edge; IMessageBus is only an intermediate link in the chain of types between the controller and the message bus. Mocking IBus instead of IMessageBus achieves the best protection against regressions.

Here's the integration test after retargeting it from IMessageBus to IBus. I'm omitting the parts that didn't change from listing 9.3.

Listing 9.5   Integration test targeting IBus

```
[Fact]
public void Changing_email_from_corporate_to_non_corporate()
{
    var busMock = new Mock<IBus>();
    var messageBus = new MessageBus(busMock.Object);        ◁── Uses a concrete
    var loggerMock = new Mock<IDomainLogger>();                  class instead of
    var sut = new UserController(db, messageBus, loggerMock.Object);   the interface

    /* ... */

    busMock.Verify(
        x => x.Send(
            "Type: USER EMAIL CHANGED; " +      Verifies the actual
            $"Id: {user.UserId}; " +            message sent to
            "NewEmail: new@gmail.com"),         the bus
        Times.Once);
}
```

Notice how the test now uses the concrete `MessageBus` class and not the corresponding `IMessageBus` interface. `IMessageBus` is an interface with a single implementation, and, as you'll remember from chapter 8, mocking is the only legitimate reason to have such interfaces. Because we no longer mock `IMessageBus`, this interface can be deleted and its usages replaced with `MessageBus`.

Also notice how the test in listing 9.5 checks the text message sent to the bus. Compare it to the previous version:

```
messageBusMock.Verify(
    x => x.SendEmailChangedMessage(user.UserId, "new@gmail.com"),
    Times.Once);
```

There's a huge difference between verifying a call to a custom class that you wrote and the actual text sent to external systems. External systems expect text messages from your application, not calls to classes like `MessageBus`. In fact, text messages are the only side effect observable externally; classes that participate in producing those messages are mere implementation details. Thus, in addition to the increased protection against regressions, verifying interactions at the very edges of your system also improves resistance to refactoring. The resulting tests are less exposed to potential false positives; no matter what refactorings take place, such tests won't turn red as long as the message's structure is preserved.

The same mechanism is at play here as the one that gives integration and end-to-end tests additional resistance to refactoring compared to unit tests. They are more detached from the code base and, therefore, aren't affected as much during low-level refactorings.

> **TIP** A call to an unmanaged dependency goes through several stages before it leaves your application. Pick the last such stage. It is the best way to ensure backward compatibility with external systems, which is the goal that mocks help you achieve.

9.1.2 *Replacing mocks with spies*

As you may remember from chapter 5, a *spy* is a variation of a test double that serves the same purpose as a mock. The only difference is that spies are written manually, whereas mocks are created with the help of a mocking framework. Indeed, spies are often called *handwritten mocks*.

It turns out that, when it comes to classes residing at the system edges, *spies are superior to mocks*. Spies help you reuse code in the assertion phase, thereby reducing the test's size and improving readability. The next listing shows an example of a spy that works on top of `IBus`.

Listing 9.6 A spy (also known as a handwritten mock)

```
public interface IBus
{
    void Send(string message);
}
```

```
public class BusSpy : IBus
{
    private List<string> _sentMessages =          ┐   Stores all sent
        new List<string>();                        │   messages
                                                   │   locally
    public void Send(string message)              │
    {                                             │
        _sentMessages.Add(message);               │
    }                                             ┘

    public BusSpy ShouldSendNumberOfMessages(int number)
    {
        Assert.Equal(number, _sentMessages.Count);
        return this;
    }

    public BusSpy WithEmailChangedMessage(int userId, string newEmail)
    {
        string message = "Type: USER EMAIL CHANGED; " +
            $"Id: {userId}; " +
            $"NewEmail: {newEmail}";
        Assert.Contains(                                Asserts that the
            _sentMessages, x => x == message);          message has been sent

        return this;
    }
}
```

The following listing is a new version of the integration test. Again, I'm showing only the relevant parts.

Listing 9.7   Using the spy from listing 6.43

```
[Fact]
public void Changing_email_from_corporate_to_non_corporate()
{
    var busSpy = new BusSpy();
    var messageBus = new MessageBus(busSpy);
    var loggerMock = new Mock<IDomainLogger>();
    var sut = new UserController(db, messageBus, loggerMock.Object);

    /* ... */

    busSpy.ShouldSendNumberOfMessages(1)
        .WithEmailChangedMessage(user.UserId, "new@gmail.com");
}
```

Verifying the interactions with the message bus is now succinct and expressive, thanks to the fluent interface that BusSpy provides. With that fluent interface, you can chain together several assertions, thus forming cohesive, almost plain-English sentences.

TIP   You can rename BusSpy into BusMock. As I mentioned earlier, the difference between a mock and a spy is an implementation detail. Most programmers aren't familiar with the term *spy*, though, so renaming the spy as BusMock can save your colleagues unnecessary confusion.

There's a reasonable question to be asked here: didn't we just make a full circle and come back to where we started? The version of the test in listing 9.7 looks a lot like the earlier version that mocked IMessageBus:

```
messageBusMock.Verify(                    Same as WithEmailChanged-
    x => x.SendEmailChangedMessage(       Message(user.UserId,
        user.UserId, "new@gmail.com"),    "new@gmail.com")
    Times.Once);                          Same as
                                          ShouldSendNumberOfMessages(1)
```

These assertions are similar because both BusSpy and MessageBus are wrappers on top of IBus. But there's a crucial difference between the two: BusSpy is part of the test code, whereas MessageBus belongs to the production code. This difference is important because *you shouldn't rely on the production code when making assertions in tests.*

Think of your tests as auditors. A good auditor wouldn't just take the auditee's words at face value; they would double-check everything. The same is true with the spy: it provides an independent checkpoint that raises an alarm when the message structure is changed. On the other hand, a mock on IMessageBus puts too much trust in the production code.

9.1.3 What about IDomainLogger?

The mock that previously verified interactions with IMessageBus is now targeted at IBus, which resides at the system's edge. Here are the current mock assertions in the integration test.

Listing 9.8   Mock assertions

```
busSpy.ShouldSendNumberOfMessages(1)      Checks
    .WithEmailChangedMessage(             interactions
        user.UserId, "new@gmail.com");    with IBus

loggerMock.Verify(
    x => x.UserTypeHasChanged(
        user.UserId,                      Checks
        UserType.Employee,                interactions with
        UserType.Customer),               IDomainLogger
    Times.Once);
```

Note that just as MessageBus is a wrapper on top of IBus, DomainLogger is a wrapper on top of ILogger (see chapter 8 for more details). Shouldn't the test be retargeted at ILogger, too, because this interface also resides at the application boundary?

In most projects, such retargeting isn't necessary. While the logger and the message bus are unmanaged dependencies and, therefore, both require maintaining backward compatibility, the accuracy of that compatibility doesn't have to be the same. With the message bus, it's important not to allow *any* changes to the structure of the messages, because you never know how external systems will react to such changes. But the exact structure of text logs is not that important for the intended audience (support staff and system administrators). What's important is the existence of those logs and the information they carry. Thus, mocking IDomainLogger alone provides the necessary level of protection.

9.2 *Mocking best practices*

You've learned two major mocking best practices so far:

- Applying mocks to unmanaged dependencies only
- Verifying the interactions with those dependencies at the very edges of your system

In this section, I explain the remaining best practices:

- Using mocks in integration tests only, not in unit tests
- Always verifying the number of calls made to the mock
- Mocking only types that you own

9.2.1 *Mocks are for integration tests only*

The guideline saying that mocks are for integration tests only, and that you shouldn't use mocks in unit tests, stems from the foundational principle described in chapter 7: the separation of business logic and orchestration. Your code should either communicate with out-of-process dependencies or be complex, but never both. This principle naturally leads to the formation of two distinct layers: the domain model (that handles complexity) and controllers (that handle the communication).

Tests on the domain model fall into the category of unit tests; tests covering controllers are integration tests. Because mocks are for unmanaged dependencies only, and because controllers are the only code working with such dependencies, you should only apply mocking when testing controllers—in integration tests.

9.2.2 *Not just one mock per test*

You might sometimes hear the guideline of having only one mock per test. According to this guideline, if you have more than one mock, you are likely testing several things at a time.

This is a misconception that follows from a more foundational misunderstanding covered in chapter 2: that a *unit* in a unit test refers to a *unit of code*, and all such units must be tested in isolation from each other. On the contrary: the term *unit* means a *unit of behavior*, not a unit of code. The amount of code it takes to implement such a unit of behavior is irrelevant. It could span across multiple classes, a single class, or take up just a tiny method.

With mocks, the same principle is at play: *it's irrelevant how many mocks it takes to verify a unit of behavior.* Earlier in this chapter, it took us two mocks to check the scenario of changing the user email from corporate to non-corporate: one for the logger and the other for the message bus. That number could have been larger. In fact, you don't have control over how many mocks to use in an integration test. The number of mocks depends solely on the number of unmanaged dependencies participating in the operation.

9.2.3 *Verifying the number of calls*

When it comes to communications with unmanaged dependencies, it's important to ensure both of the following:

- The existence of expected calls
- The absence of unexpected calls

This requirement, once again, stems from the need to maintain backward compatibility with unmanaged dependencies. The compatibility must go both ways: your application shouldn't omit messages that external systems expect, and it also shouldn't produce unexpected messages. It's not enough to check that the system under test sends a message like this:

```
messageBusMock.Verify(
    x => x.SendEmailChangedMessage(user.UserId, "new@gmail.com"));
```

You also need to ensure that this message is sent exactly once:

```
messageBusMock.Verify(
    x => x.SendEmailChangedMessage(user.UserId, "new@gmail.com"),
    Times.Once);          ⟵ ┐ Ensures that the method
                             │ is called only once
```

With most mocking libraries, you can also explicitly verify that no other calls are made on the mock. In Moq (the mocking library of my choice), this verification looks as follows:

```
messageBusMock.Verify(
    x => x.SendEmailChangedMessage(user.UserId, "new@gmail.com"),
    Times.Once);
messageBusMock.VerifyNoOtherCalls();          ⟵ ┤ The additional
                                                 │ check
```

BusSpy implements this functionality, too:

```
busSpy
    .ShouldSendNumberOfMessages(1)
    .WithEmailChangedMessage(user.UserId, "new@gmail.com");
```

The spy's check ShouldSendNumberOfMessages(1) encompasses both Times.Once and VerifyNoOtherCalls() verifications from the mock.

9.2.4   *Only mock types that you own*

The last guideline I'd like to talk about is mocking only types that you own. It was first introduced by Steve Freeman and Nat Pryce.[1] The guideline states that you should always write your own adapters on top of third-party libraries and mock those adapters instead of the underlying types. A few of their arguments are as follows:

- You often don't have a deep understanding of how the third-party code works.
- Even if that code already provides built-in interfaces, it's risky to mock those interfaces, because you have to be sure the behavior you mock matches what the external library actually does.
- Adapters abstract non-essential technical details of the third-party code and define the relationship with the library in your application's terms.

I fully agree with this analysis. Adapters, in effect, act as an anti-corruption layer between your code and the external world.[2] These help you to

- Abstract the underlying library's complexity
- Only expose features you need from the library
- Do that using your project's domain language

The IBus interface in our sample CRM project serves exactly that purpose. Even if the underlying message bus's library provides as nice and clean an interface as IBus, you are still better off introducing your own wrapper on top of it. You never know how the third-party code will change when you upgrade the library. Such an upgrade could cause a ripple effect across the whole code base! The additional abstraction layer restricts that ripple effect to just one class: the adapter itself.

Note that the "mock your own types" guideline *doesn't* apply to in-process dependencies. As I explained previously, mocks are for unmanaged dependencies only. Thus, there's no need to abstract in-memory or managed dependencies. For instance, if a library provides a date and time API, you can use that API as-is, because it doesn't reach out to unmanaged dependencies. Similarly, there's no need to abstract an ORM as long as it's used for accessing a database that isn't visible to external applications. Of course, you can introduce your own wrapper on top of any library, but it's rarely worth the effort for anything other than unmanaged dependencies.

Summary

- Verify interactions with an unmanaged dependency at the very edges of your system. Mock the last type in the chain of types between the controller and the unmanaged dependency. This helps you increase both protection against regressions (due to more code being validated by the integration test) and

---

[1] See page 69 in *Growing Object-Oriented Software, Guided by Tests* by Steve Freeman and Nat Pryce (Addison-Wesley Professional, 2009).

[2] See *Domain-Driven Design: Tackling Complexity in the Heart of Software* by Eric Evans (Addison-Wesley, 2003).

resistance to refactoring (due to detaching the mock from the code's implementation details).

- *Spies* are handwritten mocks. When it comes to classes residing at the system's edges, spies are superior to mocks. They help you reuse code in the assertion phase, thereby reducing the test's size and improving readability.

- Don't rely on production code when making assertions. Use a separate set of literals and constants in tests. Duplicate those literals and constants from the production code if necessary. Tests should provide a checkpoint independent of the production code. Otherwise, you risk producing *tautology tests* (tests that don't verify anything and contain semantically meaningless assertions).

- Not all unmanaged dependencies require the same level of backward compatibility. If the exact structure of the message isn't important, and you only want to verify the existence of that message and the information it carries, you can ignore the guideline of verifying interactions with unmanaged dependencies at the very edges of your system. The typical example is logging.

- Because mocks are for unmanaged dependencies only, and because controllers are the only code working with such dependencies, you should only apply mocking when testing controllers—in integration tests. Don't use mocks in unit tests.

- The number of mocks used in a test is irrelevant. That number depends solely on the number of unmanaged dependencies participating in the operation.

- Ensure both the existence of *expected* calls and the absence of *unexpected* calls to mocks.

- Only mock types that you own. Write your own adapters on top of third-party libraries that provide access to unmanaged dependencies. Mock those adapters instead of the underlying types.

Testing the database

This chapter covers

- Prerequisites for testing the database
- Database testing best practices
- Test data life cycle
- Managing database transactions in tests

The last piece of the puzzle in integration testing is *managed* out-of-process dependencies. The most common example of a managed dependency is an application database—a database no other application has access to.

Running tests against a real database provides bulletproof protection against regressions, but those tests aren't easy to set up. This chapter shows the preliminary steps you need to take before you can start testing your database: it covers keeping track of the database schema, explains the difference between the state-based and migration-based database delivery approaches, and demonstrates why you should choose the latter over the former.

After learning the basics, you'll see how to manage transactions during the test, clean up leftover data, and keep tests small by eliminating insignificant parts and amplifying the essentials. This chapter focuses on relational databases, but many of the same principles are applicable to other types of data stores such as document-oriented databases or even plain text file storages.

10.1 Prerequisites for testing the database

As you might recall from chapter 8, managed dependencies should be included *as-is* in integration tests. That makes working with those dependencies more laborious than unmanaged ones because using a mock is out of the question. But even before you start writing tests, you must take preparatory steps to enable integration testing. In this section, you'll see these prerequisites:

- Keeping the database in the source control system
- Using a separate database instance for every developer
- Applying the migration-based approach to database delivery

Like almost everything in testing, though, practices that facilitate testing also improve the health of your database in general. You'll get value out of those practices even if you don't write integration tests.

10.1.1 Keeping the database in the source control system

The first step on the way to testing the database is treating the database schema as regular code. Just as with regular code, a database schema is best stored in a source control system such as Git.

I've worked on projects where programmers maintained a dedicated database instance, which served as a reference point (a *model database*). During development, all schema changes accumulated in that instance. Upon production deployments, the team compared the production and model databases, used a special tool to generate upgrade scripts, and ran those scripts in production (figure 10.1).

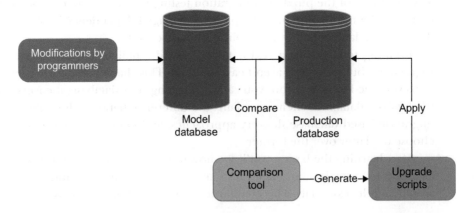

Figure 10.1 Having a dedicated instance as a model database is an anti-pattern. The database schema is best stored in a source control system.

Using a model database is a horrible way to maintain database schema. That's because there's

- *No change history*—You can't trace the database schema back to some point in the past, which might be important when reproducing bugs in production.
- *No single source of truth*—The model database becomes a competing source of truth about the state of development. Maintaining two such sources (Git and the model database) creates an additional burden.

On the other hand, keeping all the database schema updates in the source control system helps you to maintain a single source of truth and also to track database changes along with the changes of regular code. No modifications to the database structure should be made outside of the source control.

10.1.2 *Reference data is part of the database schema*

When it comes to the database schema, the usual suspects are tables, views, indexes, stored procedures, and anything else that forms a blueprint of how the database is constructed. The schema itself is represented in the form of SQL scripts. You should be able to use those scripts to create a fully functional, up-to-date database instance of your own at any time during development. However, there's another part of the database that belongs to the database schema but is rarely viewed as such: reference data.

> **DEFINITION** *Reference data* is data that must be prepopulated in order for the application to operate properly.

Take the CRM system from the earlier chapters, for example. Its users can be either of type `Customer` or type `Employee`. Let's say that you want to create a table with all user types and introduce a foreign key constraint from `User` to that table. Such a constraint would provide an additional guarantee that the application won't ever assign a user a nonexistent type. In this scenario, the content of the `UserType` table would be reference data because the application relies on its existence in order to persist users in the database.

> **TIP** There's a simple way to differentiate reference data from regular data. If your application can modify the data, it's regular data; if not, it's reference data.

Because reference data is essential for your application, you should keep it in the source control system along with tables, views, and other parts of the database schema, in the form of SQL `INSERT` statements.

Note that although reference data is normally stored separately from regular data, the two can sometimes coexist in the same table. To make this work, you need to introduce a flag differentiating data that can be modified (regular data) from data that can't be modified (reference data) and forbid your application from changing the latter.

10.1.3 *Separate instance for every developer*

It's difficult enough to run tests against a real database. It becomes even more difficult if you have to share that database with other developers. The use of a shared database hinders the development process because

- Tests run by different developers interfere with each other.
- Non-backward-compatible changes can block the work of other developers.

Keep a separate database instance for every developer, preferably on that developer's own machine in order to maximize test execution speed.

10.1.4 *State-based vs. migration-based database delivery*

There are two major approaches to database delivery: *state-based* and *migration-based*. The migration-based approach is more difficult to implement and maintain initially, but it works much better than the state-based approach in the long run.

THE STATE-BASED APPROACH

The state-based approach to database delivery is similar to what I described in figure 10.1. You also have a model database that you maintain throughout development. During deployments, a comparison tool generates scripts for the production database to bring it up to date with the model database. The difference is that with the state-based approach, you don't actually have a physical model database as a source of truth. Instead, you have SQL scripts that you can use to create that database. The scripts are stored in the source control.

In the state-based approach, the comparison tool does all the hard lifting. Whatever the state of the production database, the tool does everything needed to get it in sync with the model database: delete unnecessary tables, create new ones, rename columns, and so on.

THE MIGRATION-BASED APPROACH

On the other hand, the migration-based approach emphasizes the use of explicit migrations that transition the database from one version to another (figure 10.2). With this approach, you don't use tools to automatically synchronize the production and development databases; you come up with upgrade scripts yourself. However, a database comparison tool can still be useful when detecting undocumented changes in the production database schema.

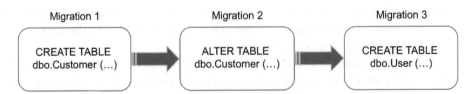

Figure 10.2   The migration-based approach to database delivery emphasizes the use of explicit migrations that transition the database from one version to another.

In the migration-based approach, migrations and not the database state become the artifacts you store in the source control. Migrations are usually represented with plain SQL scripts (popular tools include Flyway [https://flywaydb.org] and Liquibase [https://liquibase.org]), but they can also be written using a DSL-like language that gets translated into SQL. The following example shows a C# class that represents a database migration with the help of the FluentMigrator library (https://github.com/fluentmigrator/fluentmigrator):

```
[Migration(1)]                                        ◁─┐  Migration
public class CreateUserTable : Migration                 │  number
{
    public override void Up()           ◁─┐  Forward
    {                                       │  migration
        Create.Table("Users");
    }

    public override void Down()        ◁─┐  Backward migration (helpful
    {                                      │  when downgrading to an
        Delete.Table("Users");             │  earlier database version to
    }                                      │  reproduce a bug)
}
```

PREFER THE MIGRATION-BASED APPROACH OVER THE STATE-BASED ONE
The difference between the state-based and migration-based approaches to database delivery comes down to (as their names imply) *state* versus *migrations* (see figure 10.3):

- The state-based approach makes the state explicit (by virtue of storing that state in the source control) and lets the comparison tool implicitly control the migrations.
- The migration-based approach makes the migrations explicit but leaves the state implicit. It's impossible to view the database state directly; you have to assemble it from the migrations.

	State of the database	Migration mechanism
State-based approach	✓ Explicit	✗ Implicit
Migration-based approach	✗ Implicit	✓ Explicit

Figure 10.3 The state-based approach makes the state explicit and migrations implicit; the migration-based approach makes the opposite choice.

Such a distinction leads to different sets of trade-offs. The explicitness of the database state makes it easier to handle merge conflicts, while explicit migrations help to tackle data motion.

> **DEFINITION**   *Data motion* is the process of changing the shape of existing data so that it conforms to the new database schema.

Although the alleviation of merge conflicts and the ease of data motion might look like equally important benefits, in the vast majority of projects, *data motion is much more important than merge conflicts*. Unless you haven't yet released your application to production, you always have data that you can't simply discard.

For example, when splitting a Name column into FirstName and LastName, you not only have to drop the Name column and create the new FirstName and LastName columns, but you also have to write a script to split all existing names into two pieces. There is no easy way to implement this change using the state-driven approach; comparison tools are awful when it comes to managing data. The reason is that while the database schema itself is objective, meaning there is only one way to interpret it, data is context-dependent. No tool can make reliable assumptions about data when generating upgrade scripts. You have to apply domain-specific rules in order to implement proper transformations.

As a result, the state-based approach is impractical in the vast majority of projects. You can use it temporarily, though, while the project still has not been released to production. After all, test data isn't that important, and you can re-create it every time you change the database. But once you release the first version, you will have to switch to the migration-based approach in order to handle data motion properly.

> **TIP**   Apply every modification to the database schema (including reference data) through migrations. Don't modify migrations once they are committed to the source control. If a migration is incorrect, create a new migration instead of fixing the old one. Make exceptions to this rule only when the incorrect migration can lead to data loss.

10.2   *Database transaction management*

Database transaction management is a topic that's important for both production and test code. Proper transaction management in production code helps you avoid data inconsistencies. In tests, it helps you verify integration with the database in a close-to-production setting.

In this section, I'll first show how to handle transactions in the production code (the controller) and then demonstrate how to use them in integration tests. I'll continue using the same CRM project you saw in the earlier chapters as an example.

10.2.1 *Managing database transactions in production code*

Our sample CRM project uses the Database class to work with User and Company. Database creates a separate SQL connection on each method call. Every such connection implicitly opens an independent transaction behind the scenes, as the following listing shows.

Listing 10.1 Class that enables access to the database

```
public class Database
{
    private readonly string _connectionString;

    public Database(string connectionString)
    {
        _connectionString = connectionString;
    }

    public void SaveUser(User user)
    {
        bool isNewUser = user.UserId == 0;

        using (var connection =
            new SqlConnection(_connectionString))
        {
            /* Insert or update the user depending on isNewUser */
        }
    }

    public void SaveCompany(Company company)
    {
        using (var connection =
            new SqlConnection(_connectionString))
        {
            /* Update only; there's only one company */
        }
    }
}
```

Opens a database transaction (annotation pointing to the two `using (var connection = new SqlConnection(_connectionString))` statements)

As a result, the user controller creates a total of four database transactions during a single business operation, as shown in the following listing.

Listing 10.2 User controller

```
public string ChangeEmail(int userId, string newEmail)
{
    object[] userData = _database.GetUserById(userId);
    User user = UserFactory.Create(userData);

    string error = user.CanChangeEmail();
    if (error != null)
        return error;
```

Opens a new database transaction (annotation pointing to the `_database.GetUserById(userId)` / `UserFactory.Create(userData)` lines)

```
object[] companyData = _database.GetCompany();
Company company = CompanyFactory.Create(companyData);

user.ChangeEmail(newEmail, company);

_database.SaveCompany(company);
_database.SaveUser(user);
_eventDispatcher.Dispatch(user.DomainEvents);

return "OK";
}
```

Opens a new database transaction

It's fine to open multiple transactions during read-only operations: for example, when returning user information to the external client. But if the business operation involves data mutation, all updates taking place during that operation should be atomic in order to avoid inconsistencies. For example, the controller can successfully persist the company but then fail when saving the user due to a database connectivity issue. As a result, the company's NumberOfEmployees can become inconsistent with the total number of Employee users in the database.

> **DEFINITION**   *Atomic updates* are executed in an all-or-nothing manner. Each update in the set of atomic updates must either be complete in its entirety or have no effect whatsoever.

SEPARATING DATABASE CONNECTIONS FROM DATABASE TRANSACTIONS

To avoid potential inconsistencies, you need to introduce a separation between two types of decisions:

- What data to update
- Whether to keep the updates or roll them back

Such a separation is important because the controller can't make these decisions simultaneously. It only knows whether the updates can be kept when all the steps in the business operation have succeeded. And it can only take those steps by accessing the database and trying to make the updates. You can implement the separation between these responsibilities by splitting the Database class into repositories and a transaction:

- *Repositories* are classes that enable access to and modification of the data in the database. There will be two repositories in our sample project: one for User and the other for Company.
- A *transaction* is a class that either commits or rolls back data updates in full. This will be a custom class relying on the underlying database's transactions to provide atomicity of data modification.

Not only do repositories and transactions have different responsibilities, but they also have different lifespans. A transaction lives during the whole business operation and is disposed of at the very end of it. A repository, on the other hand, is short-lived. You can dispose of a repository as soon as the call to the database is completed. As a result, repositories always work on top of the current transaction. When connecting to the database, a repository enlists itself into the transaction so that any data modifications made during that connection can later be rolled back by the transaction.

Figure 10.4 shows how the communication between the controller and the database looks in listing 10.2. Each database call is wrapped into its own transaction; updates are not atomic.

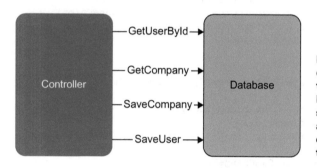

Figure 10.4 **Wrapping each database call into a separate transaction introduces a risk of inconsistencies due to hardware or software failures. For example, the application can update the number of employees in the company but not the employees themselves.**

Figure 10.5 shows the application after the introduction of explicit transactions. The transaction mediates interactions between the controller and the database. All four database calls are still there, but now data modifications are either committed or rolled back in full.

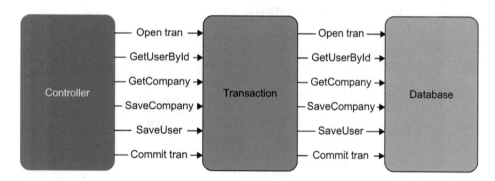

Figure 10.5 **The transaction mediates interactions between the controller and the database and thus enables atomic data modification.**

The following listing shows the controller after introducing a transaction and repositories.

Listing 10.3 User controller, repositories, and a transaction

```
public class UserController
{
    private readonly Transaction _transaction;
    private readonly UserRepository _userRepository;
```

```
        private readonly CompanyRepository _companyRepository;
        private readonly EventDispatcher _eventDispatcher;

        public UserController(
            Transaction transaction,          ◁─┐ Accepts a
            MessageBus messageBus,               │ transaction
            IDomainLogger domainLogger)
        {
            _transaction = transaction;
            _userRepository = new UserRepository(transaction);
            _companyRepository = new CompanyRepository(transaction);
            _eventDispatcher = new EventDispatcher(
                messageBus, domainLogger);
        }

        public string ChangeEmail(int userId, string newEmail)
        {
            object[] userData = _userRepository
                .GetUserById(userId);
            User user = UserFactory.Create(userData);

            string error = user.CanChangeEmail();
            if (error != null)
                return error;

            object[] companyData = _companyRepository
                .GetCompany();
            Company company = CompanyFactory.Create(companyData);

            user.ChangeEmail(newEmail, company);

            _companyRepository.SaveCompany(company);
            _userRepository.SaveUser(user);
            _eventDispatcher.Dispatch(user.DomainEvents);

            _transaction.Commit();            ◁─┐ Commits the
            return "OK";                         │ transaction
        }                                        │ on success
    }

    public class UserRepository
    {
        private readonly Transaction _transaction;

        public UserRepository(Transaction transaction)     ◁─┐ Injects a
        {                                                     │ transaction into
            _transaction = transaction;                       │ a repository
        }

        /* ... */
    }

    public class Transaction : IDisposable
    {
```

Uses the repositories instead of the Database class

```
    public void Commit() { /* ... */ }
    public void Dispose() { /* ... */ }
}
```

The internals of the `Transaction` class aren't important, but if you're curious, I'm using .NET's standard `TransactionScope` behind the scenes. The important part about `Transaction` is that it contains two methods:

- `Commit()` *marks the transaction as successful.* This is only called when the business operation itself has succeeded and all data modifications are ready to be persisted.

- `Dispose()` *ends the transaction.* This is called indiscriminately at the end of the business operation. If `Commit()` was previously invoked, `Dispose()` persists all data updates; otherwise, it rolls them back.

Such a combination of `Commit()` and `Dispose()` guarantees that the database is altered only during *happy paths* (the successful execution of the business scenario). That's why `Commit()` resides at the very end of the `ChangeEmail()` method. In the event of any error, be it a validation error or an unhandled exception, the execution flow returns early and thereby prevents the transaction from being committed.

`Commit()` is invoked by the controller because this method call requires decision-making. There's no decision-making involved in calling `Dispose()`, though, so you can delegate that method call to a class from the infrastructure layer. The same class that instantiates the controller and provides it with the necessary dependencies should also dispose of the transaction once the controller is done working.

Notice how `UserRepository` requires `Transaction` as a constructor parameter. This explicitly shows that repositories always work on top of transactions; a repository can't call the database on its own.

UPGRADING THE TRANSACTION TO A UNIT OF WORK

The introduction of repositories and a transaction is a good way to avoid potential data inconsistencies, but there's an even better approach. You can upgrade the `Transaction` class to a unit of work.

> **DEFINITION** A *unit of work* maintains a list of objects affected by a business operation. Once the operation is completed, the unit of work figures out all updates that need to be done to alter the database and executes those updates as a single unit (hence the pattern name).

The main advantage of a unit of work over a plain transaction is the deferral of updates. Unlike a transaction, a unit of work executes all updates at the end of the business operation, thus minimizing the duration of the underlying database transaction and reducing data congestion (see figure 10.6). Often, this pattern also helps to reduce the number of database calls.

> **NOTE** Database transactions also implement the unit-of-work pattern.

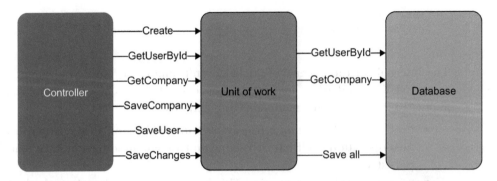

Figure 10.6   A unit of work executes all updates at the end of the business operation. The updates are still wrapped in a database transaction, but that transaction lives for a shorter period of time, thus reducing data congestion.

Maintaining a list of modified objects and then figuring out what SQL script to generate can look like a lot of work. In reality, though, you don't need to do that work yourself. Most object-relational mapping (ORM) libraries implement the unit-of-work pattern for you. In .NET, for example, you can use NHibernate or Entity Framework, both of which provide classes that do all the hard lifting (those classes are `ISession` and `DbContext`, respectively). The following listing shows how `UserController` looks in combination with Entity Framework.

Listing 10.4   User controller with Entity Framework

```
public class UserController
{
    private readonly CrmContext _context;
    private readonly UserRepository _userRepository;
    private readonly CompanyRepository _companyRepository;
    private readonly EventDispatcher _eventDispatcher;

    public UserController(
        CrmContext context,
        MessageBus messageBus,
        IDomainLogger domainLogger)
    {
        _context = context;
        _userRepository = new UserRepository(
            context);
        _companyRepository = new CompanyRepository(
            context);
        _eventDispatcher = new EventDispatcher(
            messageBus, domainLogger);
    }

    public string ChangeEmail(int userId, string newEmail)
    {
        User user = _userRepository.GetUserById(userId);
```

CrmContext replaces Transaction.

```
        string error = user.CanChangeEmail();
        if (error != null)
            return error;

        Company company = _companyRepository.GetCompany();

        user.ChangeEmail(newEmail, company);

        _companyRepository.SaveCompany(company);
        _userRepository.SaveUser(user);
        _eventDispatcher.Dispatch(user.DomainEvents);

        _context.SaveChanges();        ◁——  CrmContext
        return "OK";                         replaces
    }                                        Transaction.
}
```

CrmContext is a custom class that contains mapping between the domain model and the database (it inherits from Entity Framework's DbContext). The controller in listing 10.4 uses CrmContext instead of Transaction. As a result,

- Both repositories now work on top of CrmContext, just as they worked on top of Transaction in the previous version.
- The controller commits changes to the database via context.SaveChanges() instead of transaction.Commit().

Notice that there's no need for UserFactory and CompanyFactory anymore because Entity Framework now serves as a mapper between the raw database data and domain objects.

Data inconsistencies in non-relational databases

It's easy to avoid data inconsistencies when using a relational database: all major relational databases provide atomic updates that can span as many rows as needed. But how do you achieve the same level of protection with a non-relational database such as MongoDB?

The problem with most non-relational databases is the lack of transactions in the classical sense; atomic updates are guaranteed only within a single document. If a business operation affects multiple documents, it becomes prone to inconsistencies. (In non-relational databases, a *document* is the equivalent of a *row*.)

Non-relational databases approach inconsistencies from a different angle: they require you to design your documents such that no business operation modifies more than one of those documents at a time. This is possible because documents are more flexible than rows in relational databases. A single document can store data of any shape and complexity and thus capture side effects of even the most sophisticated business operations.

> **(continued)**
>
> In domain-driven design, there's a guideline saying that you shouldn't modify more than one aggregate per business operation. This guideline serves the same goal: protecting you from data inconsistencies. The guideline is only applicable to systems that work with document databases, though, where each document corresponds to one aggregate.

10.2.2 Managing database transactions in integration tests

When it comes to managing database transactions in integration tests, adhere to the following guideline: *don't reuse database transactions or units of work between sections of the test.* The following listing shows an example of reusing `CrmContext` in the integration test after switching that test to Entity Framework.

Listing 10.5   Integration test reusing `CrmContext`

```csharp
[Fact]
public void Changing_email_from_corporate_to_non_corporate()
{
    using (var context =
        new CrmContext(ConnectionString))          Creates a
    {                                                context
        // Arrange
        var userRepository =
            new UserRepository(context);
        var companyRepository =
            new CompanyRepository(context);
        var user = new User(0, "user@mycorp.com",        Uses the context
            UserType.Employee, false);                    in the arrange
        userRepository.SaveUser(user);                    section ...
        var company = new Company("mycorp.com", 1);
        companyRepository.SaveCompany(company);
        context.SaveChanges();

        var busSpy = new BusSpy();
        var messageBus = new MessageBus(busSpy);
        var loggerMock = new Mock<IDomainLogger>();
        var sut = new UserController(
            context,                              ... in act ...
            messageBus,
            loggerMock.Object);

        // Act
        string result = sut.ChangeEmail(user.UserId, "new@gmail.com");

        // Assert
        Assert.Equal("OK", result);

        User userFromDb = userRepository
            .GetUserById(user.UserId);            ... and in assert
```

```
        Assert.Equal("new@gmail.com", userFromDb.Email);
        Assert.Equal(UserType.Customer, userFromDb.Type);

        Company companyFromDb = companyRepository      │ ... and in assert
            .GetCompany();                             │
        Assert.Equal(0, companyFromDb.NumberOfEmployees);

        busSpy.ShouldSendNumberOfMessages(1)
            .WithEmailChangedMessage(user.UserId, "new@gmail.com");
        loggerMock.Verify(
            x => x.UserTypeHasChanged(
                user.UserId, UserType.Employee, UserType.Customer),
            Times.Once);
    }
}
```

This test uses the same instance of CrmContext in all three sections: arrange, act, and assert. This is a problem because such reuse of the unit of work creates an environment that doesn't match what the controller experiences in production. In production, each business operation has an exclusive instance of CrmContext. That instance is created right before the controller method invocation and is disposed of immediately after.

To avoid the risk of inconsistent behavior, integration tests should replicate the production environment as closely as possible, which means the act section must not share CrmContext with anyone else. The arrange and assert sections must get their own instances of CrmContext too, because, as you might remember from chapter 8, it's important to check the state of the database independently of the data used as input parameters. And although the assert section does query the user and the company independently of the arrange section, these sections still share the same database context. That context can (and many ORMs do) cache the requested data for performance improvements.

> **TIP** Use at least three transactions or units of work in an integration test: one per each arrange, act, and assert section.

10.3 Test data life cycle

The shared database raises the problem of isolating integration tests from each other. To solve this problem, you need to

- Execute integration tests sequentially.
- Remove leftover data between test runs.

Overall, your tests shouldn't depend on the state of the database. Your tests should bring that state to the required condition on their own.

10.3.1 Parallel vs. sequential test execution

Parallel execution of integration tests involves significant effort. You have to ensure that all test data is unique so no database constraints are violated and tests don't accidentally pick up input data after each other. Cleaning up leftover data also becomes trickier. It's more practical to run integration tests sequentially rather than spend time trying to squeeze additional performance out of them.

Most unit testing frameworks allow you to define separate test collections and selectively disable parallelization in them. Create two such collections (for unit and integration tests), and then disable test parallelization in the collection with the integration tests.

As an alternative, you could parallelize tests using containers. For example, you could put the model database on a Docker image and instantiate a new container from that image for each integration test. In practice, though, this approach creates too much of an additional maintenance burden. With Docker, you not only have to keep track of the database itself, but you also need to

- Maintain Docker images
- Make sure each test gets its own container instance
- Batch integration tests (because you most likely won't be able to create all container instances at once)
- Dispose of used-up containers

I don't recommend using containers unless you absolutely need to minimize your integration tests' execution time. Again, it's more practical to have just one database instance per developer. You *can* run that single instance in Docker, though. I advocate against premature parallelization, not the use of Docker per se.

10.3.2   *Clearing data between test runs*

There are four options to clean up leftover data between test runs:

- *Restoring a database backup before each test*—This approach addresses the problem of data cleanup but is much slower than the other three options. Even with containers, the removal of a container instance and creation of a new one usually takes several seconds, which quickly adds to the total test suite execution time.
- *Cleaning up data at the end of a test*—This method is fast but susceptible to skipping the cleanup phase. If the build server crashes in the middle of the test, or you shut down the test in the debugger, the input data remains in the database and affects further test runs.
- *Wrapping each test in a database transaction and never committing it*—In this case, all changes made by the test and the SUT are rolled back automatically. This approach solves the problem of skipping the cleanup phase but poses another issue: the introduction of an overarching transaction can lead to inconsistent behavior between the production and test environments. It's the same problem as with reusing a unit of work: the additional transaction creates a setup that's different than that in production.
- *Cleaning up data at the beginning of a test*—This is the best option. It works fast, doesn't result in inconsistent behavior, and isn't prone to accidentally skipping the cleanup phase.

TIP There's no need for a separate teardown phase; implement that phase as part of the arrange section.

The data removal itself must be done in a particular order, to honor the database's foreign key constraints. I sometimes see people use sophisticated algorithms to figure out relationships between tables and automatically generate the deletion script or even disable all integrity constraints and re-enable them afterward. This is unnecessary. Write the SQL script manually: it's simpler and gives you more granular control over the deletion process.

Introduce a base class for all integration tests, and put the deletion script there. With such a base class, you will have the script run automatically at the start of each test, as shown in the following listing.

Listing 10.6   Base class for integration tests

```
public abstract class IntegrationTests
{
    private const string ConnectionString = "...";

    protected IntegrationTests()
    {
        ClearDatabase();
    }

    private void ClearDatabase()
    {
        string query =
            "DELETE FROM dbo.[User];" +          Deletion
            "DELETE FROM dbo.Company;";          script

        using (var connection = new SqlConnection(ConnectionString))
        {
            var command = new SqlCommand(query, connection)
            {
                CommandType = CommandType.Text
            };

            connection.Open();
            command.ExecuteNonQuery();
        }
    }
}
```

TIP The deletion script must remove all regular data but none of the reference data. Reference data, along with the rest of the database schema, should be controlled solely by migrations.

10.3.3   *Avoid in-memory databases*

Another way to isolate integration tests from each other is by replacing the database with an in-memory analog, such as SQLite. In-memory databases can seem beneficial because they

- Don't require removal of test data
- Work faster
- Can be instantiated for each test run

Because in-memory databases aren't shared dependencies, integration tests in effect become unit tests (assuming the database is the only managed dependency in the project), similar to the approach with containers described in section 10.3.1.

In spite of all these benefits, I don't recommend using in-memory databases because they aren't consistent functionality-wise with regular databases. This is, once again, the problem of a mismatch between production and test environments. Your tests can easily run into false positives or (worse!) false negatives due to the differences between the regular and in-memory databases. You'll never gain good protection with such tests and will have to do a lot of regression testing manually anyway.

> **TIP**   Use the same database management system (DBMS) in tests as in production. It's usually fine for the version or edition to differ, but the vendor must remain the same.

10.4   *Reusing code in test sections*

Integration tests can quickly grow too large and thus lose ground on the maintainability metric. It's important to keep integration tests as short as possible but without coupling them to each other or affecting readability. Even the shortest tests shouldn't depend on one another. They also should preserve the full context of the test scenario and shouldn't require you to examine different parts of the test class to understand what's going on.

The best way to shorten integration is by extracting technical, non-business-related bits into private methods or helper classes. As a side bonus, you'll get to reuse those bits. In this section, I'll show how to shorten all three sections of the test: arrange, act, and assert.

10.4.1   *Reusing code in arrange sections*

The following listing shows how our integration test looks after providing a separate database context (unit of work) for each of its sections.

> **Listing 10.7   Integration test with three database contexts**

```
[Fact]
public void Changing_email_from_corporate_to_non_corporate()
{
    // Arrange
    User user;
```

```
using (var context = new CrmContext(ConnectionString))
{
    var userRepository = new UserRepository(context);
    var companyRepository = new CompanyRepository(context);
    user = new User(0, "user@mycorp.com",
        UserType.Employee, false);
    userRepository.SaveUser(user);
    var company = new Company("mycorp.com", 1);
    companyRepository.SaveCompany(company);

    context.SaveChanges();
}

var busSpy = new BusSpy();
var messageBus = new MessageBus(busSpy);
var loggerMock = new Mock<IDomainLogger>();

string result;
using (var context = new CrmContext(ConnectionString))
{
    var sut = new UserController(
        context, messageBus, loggerMock.Object);

    // Act
    result = sut.ChangeEmail(user.UserId, "new@gmail.com");
}

// Assert
Assert.Equal("OK", result);

using (var context = new CrmContext(ConnectionString))
{
    var userRepository = new UserRepository(context);
    var companyRepository = new CompanyRepository(context);

    User userFromDb = userRepository.GetUserById(user.UserId);
    Assert.Equal("new@gmail.com", userFromDb.Email);
    Assert.Equal(UserType.Customer, userFromDb.Type);

    Company companyFromDb = companyRepository.GetCompany();
    Assert.Equal(0, companyFromDb.NumberOfEmployees);

    busSpy.ShouldSendNumberOfMessages(1)
        .WithEmailChangedMessage(user.UserId, "new@gmail.com");
    loggerMock.Verify(
        x => x.UserTypeHasChanged(
            user.UserId, UserType.Employee, UserType.Customer),
        Times.Once);
}
}
```

As you might remember from chapter 3, the best way to reuse code between the tests' arrange sections is to introduce private factory methods. For example, the following listing creates a user.

Listing 10.8   A separate method that creates a user

```
private User CreateUser(
    string email, UserType type, bool isEmailConfirmed)
{
    using (var context = new CrmContext(ConnectionString))
    {
        var user = new User(0, email, type, isEmailConfirmed);
        var repository = new UserRepository(context);
        repository.SaveUser(user);

        context.SaveChanges();

        return user;
    }
}
```

You can also define default values for the method's arguments, as shown next.

Listing 10.9   Adding default values to the factory

```
private User CreateUser(
    string email = "user@mycorp.com",
    UserType type = UserType.Employee,
    bool isEmailConfirmed = false)
{
    /* ... */
}
```

With default values, you can specify arguments selectively and thus shorten the test even further. The selective use of arguments also emphasizes which of those arguments are relevant to the test scenario.

Listing 10.10   Using the factory method

```
User user = CreateUser(
    email: "user@mycorp.com",
    type: UserType.Employee);
```

Object Mother vs. Test Data Builder

The pattern shown in listings 10.9 and 10.10 is called the *Object Mother*. The *Object Mother* is a class or method that helps create *test fixtures* (objects the test runs against).

There's another pattern that helps achieve the same goal of reusing code in arrange sections: *Test Data Builder*. It works similarly to Object Mother but exposes a fluent interface instead of plain methods. Here's a Test Data Builder usage example:

```
User user = new UserBuilder()
    .WithEmail("user@mycorp.com")
    .WithType(UserType.Employee)
    .Build();
```

Test Data Builder slightly improves test readability but requires too much boilerplate. For that reason, I recommend sticking to the Object Mother (at least in C#, where you have optional arguments as a language feature).

WHERE TO PUT FACTORY METHODS

When you start distilling the tests' essentials and move the technicalities out to factory methods, you face the question of where to put those methods. Should they reside in the same class as the tests? The base `IntegrationTests` class? Or in a separate helper class?

Start simple. Place the factory methods in the same class by default. Move them into separate helper classes only when code duplication becomes a significant issue. Don't put the factory methods in the base class; reserve that class for code that has to run in every test, such as data cleanup.

10.4.2 Reusing code in act sections

Every act section in integration tests involves the creation of a database transaction or a unit of work. This is how the act section currently looks in listing 10.7:

```
string result;
using (var context = new CrmContext(ConnectionString))
{
    var sut = new UserController(
        context, messageBus, loggerMock.Object);

    // Act
    result = sut.ChangeEmail(user.UserId, "new@gmail.com");
}
```

This section can also be reduced. You can introduce a method accepting a delegate with the information of what controller function needs to be invoked. The method will then decorate the controller invocation with the creation of a database context, as shown in the following listing.

Listing 10.11 Decorator method

```
private string Execute(
    Func<UserController, string> func,      ◁─┐ Delegate defines
    MessageBus messageBus,                      a controller
    IDomainLogger logger)                       function.
{
    using (var context = new CrmContext(ConnectionString))
    {
        var controller = new UserController(
```

```
        context, messageBus, logger);
    return func(controller);
    }
}
```

With this decorator method, you can boil down the test's act section to just a couple of lines:

```
string result = Execute(
    x => x.ChangeEmail(user.UserId, "new@gmail.com"),
    messageBus, loggerMock.Object);
```

10.4.3 *Reusing code in assert sections*

Finally, the assert section can be shortened, too. The easiest way to do that is to introduce helper methods similar to `CreateUser` and `CreateCompany`, as shown in the following listing.

Listing 10.12   Data assertions after extracting the querying logic

```
User userFromDb = QueryUser(user.UserId);              ◁┐
Assert.Equal("new@gmail.com", userFromDb.Email);        │   New helper
Assert.Equal(UserType.Customer, userFromDb.Type);       │   methods
                                                        │
Company companyFromDb = QueryCompany();                ◁┘
Assert.Equal(0, companyFromDb.NumberOfEmployees);
```

You can take a step further and create a fluent interface for these data assertions, similar to what you saw in chapter 9 with `BusSpy`. In C#, a fluent interface on top of existing domain classes can be implemented using extension methods, as shown in the following listing.

Listing 10.13   Fluent interface for data assertions

```
public static class UserExtensions
{
    public static User ShouldExist(this User user)
    {
        Assert.NotNull(user);
        return user;
    }

    public static User WithEmail(this User user, string email)
    {
        Assert.Equal(email, user.Email);
        return user;
    }
}
```

With this fluent interface, the assertions become much easier to read:

```
User userFromDb = QueryUser(user.UserId);
userFromDb
    .ShouldExist()
```

```
        .WithEmail("new@gmail.com")
        .WithType(UserType.Customer);

Company companyFromDb = QueryCompany();
companyFromDb
    .ShouldExist()
    .WithNumberOfEmployees(0);
```

10.4.4 *Does the test create too many database transactions?*

After all the simplifications made earlier, the integration test has become more readable and, therefore, more maintainable. There's one drawback, though: the test now uses a total of five database transactions (units of work), where before it used only three, as shown in the following listing.

> **Listing 10.14 Integration test after moving all technicalities out of it**

```
public class UserControllerTests : IntegrationTests
{
    [Fact]
    public void Changing_email_from_corporate_to_non_corporate()
    {
        // Arrange
 ┌─▷ User user = CreateUser(
 │          email: "user@mycorp.com",
 │          type: UserType.Employee);
 ├─▷ CreateCompany("mycorp.com", 1);
 │
 │      var busSpy = new BusSpy();
 │      var messageBus = new MessageBus(busSpy);
 │      var loggerMock = new Mock<IDomainLogger>();
 │
 │      // Act
 ├─▷ string result = Execute(
 │          x => x.ChangeEmail(user.UserId, "new@gmail.com"),
 │          messageBus, loggerMock.Object);
 │
 │      // Assert
 │      Assert.Equal("OK", result);
 │
 ├─▷ User userFromDb = QueryUser(user.UserId);
 │      userFromDb
 │          .ShouldExist()
 │          .WithEmail("new@gmail.com")
 │          .WithType(UserType.Customer);
 │
 └─▷ Company companyFromDb = QueryCompany();
        companyFromDb
            .ShouldExist()
            .WithNumberOfEmployees(0);

        busSpy.ShouldSendNumberOfMessages(1)
            .WithEmailChangedMessage(user.UserId, "new@gmail.com");
        loggerMock.Verify(
```

Instantiates a new database context behind the scenes

```
        x => x.UserTypeHasChanged(
            user.UserId, UserType.Employee, UserType.Customer),
        Times.Once);
    }
}
```

Is the increased number of database transactions a problem? And, if so, what can you do about it? The additional database contexts are a problem to some degree because they make the test slower, but there's not much that can be done about it. It's another example of a trade-off between different aspects of a valuable test: this time between fast feedback and maintainability. It's worth it to make that trade-off and exchange performance for maintainability in this particular case. The performance degradation shouldn't be that significant, especially when the database is located on the developer's machine. At the same time, the gains in maintainability are quite substantial.

10.5   *Common database testing questions*

In this last section of the chapter, I'd like to answer common questions related to database testing, as well as briefly reiterate some important points made in chapters 8 and 9.

10.5.1   *Should you test reads?*

Throughout the last several chapters, we've worked with a sample scenario of changing a user email. This scenario is an example of a *write* operation (an operation that leaves a side effect in the database and other out-of-process dependencies). Most applications contain both write and read operations. An example of a *read* operation would be returning the user information to the external client. Should you test both writes and reads?

It's crucial to thoroughly test writes, because the stakes are high. Mistakes in write operations often lead to data corruption, which can affect not only your database but also external applications. Tests that cover writes are highly valuable due to the protection they provide against such mistakes.

This is not the case for reads: a bug in a read operation usually doesn't have consequences that are as detrimental. Therefore, the threshold for testing reads should be higher than that for writes. Test only the most complex or important read operations; disregard the rest.

Note that there's also no need for a domain model in reads. One of the main goals of domain modeling is encapsulation. And, as you might remember from chapters 5 and 6, encapsulation is about preserving data consistency in light of any changes. The lack of data changes makes encapsulation of reads pointless. In fact, you don't need a fully fledged ORM such as NHibernate or Entity Framework in reads, either. You are better off using plain SQL, which is superior to an ORM performance-wise, thanks to bypassing unnecessary layers of abstraction (figure 10.7).

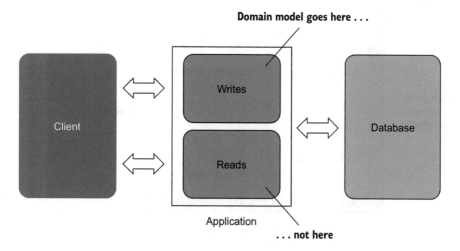

Figure 10.7 There's no need for a domain model in reads. And because the cost of a mistake in reads is lower than it is in writes, there's also not as much need for integration testing.

Because there are hardly any abstraction layers in reads (the domain model is one such layer), unit tests aren't of any use there. If you decide to test your reads, do so using integration tests on a real database.

10.5.2 *Should you test repositories?*

Repositories provide a useful abstraction on top of the database. Here's a usage example from our sample CRM project:

```
User user = _userRepository.GetUserById(userId);
_userRepository.SaveUser(user);
```

Should you test repositories independently of other integration tests? It might seem beneficial to test how repositories map domain objects to the database. After all, there's significant room for a mistake in this functionality. Still, such tests are a net loss to your test suite due to high maintenance costs and inferior protection against regressions. Let's discuss these two drawbacks in more detail.

HIGH MAINTENANCE COSTS

Repositories fall into the controllers quadrant on the types-of-code diagram from chapter 7 (figure 10.8). They exhibit little complexity and communicate with an out-of-process dependency: the database. The presence of that out-of-process dependency is what inflates the tests' maintenance costs.

When it comes to maintenance costs, testing repositories carries the same burden as regular integration tests. But does such testing provide an equal amount of benefits in return? Unfortunately, it doesn't.

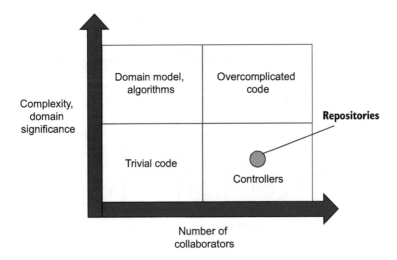

Figure 10.8   Repositories exhibit little complexity and communicate with the out-of-process dependency, thus falling into the controllers quadrant on the types-of-code diagram.

INFERIOR PROTECTION AGAINST REGRESSIONS

Repositories don't carry that much complexity, and a lot of the gains in protection against regressions overlap with the gains provided by regular integration tests. Thus, tests on repositories don't add significant enough value.

The best course of action in testing a repository is to extract the little complexity it has into a self-contained algorithm and test that algorithm exclusively. That's what UserFactory and CompanyFactory were for in earlier chapters. These two classes performed all the mappings without taking on any collaborators, out-of-process or otherwise. The repositories (the Database class) only contained simple SQL queries.

Unfortunately, such a separation between data mapping (formerly performed by the factories) and interactions with the database (formerly performed by Database) is impossible when using an ORM. You can't test your ORM mappings without calling the database, at least not without compromising resistance to refactoring. Therefore, adhere to the following guideline: *don't test repositories directly, only as part of the overarching integration test suite.*

Don't test EventDispatcher separately, either (this class converts domain events into calls to unmanaged dependencies). There are too few gains in protection against regressions in exchange for the too-high costs required to maintain the complicated mock machinery.

10.6   *Conclusion*

Well-crafted tests against the database provide bulletproof protection from bugs. In my experience, they are one of the most effective tools, without which it's impossible to gain full confidence in your software. Such tests help enormously when you refactor the database, switch the ORM, or change the database vendor.

In fact, our sample project transitioned to the Entity Framework ORM earlier in this chapter, and I only needed to modify a couple of lines of code in the integration test to make sure the transition was successful. Integration tests working directly with managed dependencies are the most efficient way to protect against bugs resulting from large-scale refactorings.

Summary

- Store database schema in a source control system, along with your source code. *Database schema* consists of tables, views, indexes, stored procedures, and anything else that forms a blueprint of how the database is constructed.
- Reference data is also part of the database schema. It is data that must be prepopulated in order for the application to operate properly. To differentiate between reference and regular data, look at whether your application can modify that data. If so, it's regular data; otherwise, it's reference data.
- Have a separate database instance for every developer. Better yet, host that instance on the developer's own machine for maximum test execution speed.
- The *state-based* approach to database delivery makes the state explicit and lets a comparison tool implicitly control migrations. The *migration-based* approach emphasizes the use of explicit migrations that transition the database from one state to another. The explicitness of the database state makes it easier to handle *merge conflicts*, while explicit migrations help tackle *data motion*.
- Prefer the migration-based approach over state-based, because handling data motion is much more important than merge conflicts. Apply every modification to the database schema (including reference data) through migrations.
- Business operations must update data atomically. To achieve atomicity, rely on the underlying database's transaction mechanism.
- Use the unit of work pattern when possible. A unit of work relies on the underlying database's transactions; it also defers all updates to the end of the business operation, thus improving performance.
- Don't reuse database transactions or units of work between sections of the test. Each arrange, act, and assert section should have its own transaction or unit of work.
- Execute integration tests sequentially. Parallel execution involves significant effort and usually is not worth it.
- Clean up leftover data at the start of a test. This approach works fast, doesn't result in inconsistent behavior, and isn't prone to accidentally skipping the cleanup phase. With this approach, you don't have to introduce a separate teardown phase, either.

- Avoid in-memory databases such as SQLite. You'll never gain good protection if your tests run against a database from a different vendor. Use the same database management system in tests as in production.
- Shorten tests by extracting non-essential parts into private methods or helper classes:
  - For the arrange section, choose Object Mother over Test Data Builder.
  - For act, create decorator methods.
  - For assert, introduce a fluent interface.
- The threshold for testing reads should be higher than that for writes. Test only the most complex or important read operations; disregard the rest.
- Don't test repositories directly, but only as part of the overarching integration test suite. Tests on repositories introduce too high maintenance costs for too few additional gains in protection against regressions.

Part 4

Unit testing anti-patterns

This final part of the book covers common unit testing anti-patterns. You've most likely encountered some of them in the past. Still, it's interesting to look at this topic using the four attributes of a good unit test defined in chapter 4. You can use those attributes to analyze any unit testing concepts or patterns; anti-patterns aren't an exception.

Unit testing anti-patterns

This chapter is an aggregation of lesser related topics (mostly anti-patterns) that didn't fit in earlier in the book and are better served on their own. An *anti-pattern* is a common solution to a recurring problem that looks appropriate on the surface but leads to problems further down the road.

You will learn how to work with time in tests, how to identify and avoid such anti-patterns as unit testing of private methods, code pollution, mocking concrete classes, and more. Most of these topics follow from the first principles described in part 2. Still, they are well worth spelling out explicitly. You've probably heard of at least some of these anti-patterns in the past, but this chapter will help you connect the dots, so to speak, and see the foundations they are based on.

11.1 Unit testing private methods

When it comes to unit testing, one of the most commonly asked questions is how to test a private method. The short answer is that you shouldn't do so at all, but there's quite a bit of nuance to this topic.

11.1.1 Private methods and test fragility

Exposing methods that you would otherwise keep private just to enable unit testing violates one of the foundational principles we discussed in chapter 5: testing observable behavior only. Exposing private methods leads to coupling tests to implementation details and, ultimately, damaging your tests' resistance to refactoring—the most important metric of the four. (All four metrics, once again, are protection against regressions, resistance to refactoring, fast feedback, and maintainability.) Instead of testing private methods directly, test them indirectly, as part of the overarching observable behavior.

11.1.2 Private methods and insufficient coverage

Sometimes, the private method is too complex, and testing it as part of the observable behavior doesn't provide sufficient coverage. Assuming the observable behavior already has reasonable test coverage, there can be two issues at play:

- *This is dead code.* If the uncovered code isn't being used, this is likely some extraneous code left after a refactoring. It's best to delete this code.
- *There's a missing abstraction.* If the private method is too complex (and thus is hard to test via the class's public API), it's an indication of a missing abstraction that should be extracted into a separate class.

Let's illustrate the second issue with an example.

Listing 11.1 A class with a complex private method

```
public class Order
{
    private Customer _customer;
    private List<Product> _products;              The complex private
                                                  method is used by a
    public string GenerateDescription()           much simpler public
    {                                                          method.
        return $"Customer name: {_customer.Name}, " +
            $"total number of products: {_products.Count}, " +
            $"total price: {GetPrice()}";          ⟵
    }
                                          Complex private
    private decimal GetPrice()    ⟵       method
    {
        decimal basePrice = /* Calculate based on _products */;
        decimal discounts = /* Calculate based on _customer */;
        decimal taxes = /* Calculate based on _products */;
```

```
            return basePrice - discounts + taxes;
        }
    }
```

The GenerateDescription() method is quite simple: it returns a generic description of the order. But it uses the private GetPrice() method, which is much more complex: it contains important business logic and needs to be thoroughly tested. That logic is a *missing abstraction*. Instead of exposing the GetPrice method, make this abstraction explicit by extracting it into a separate class, as shown in the next listing.

Listing 11.2 Extracting the complex private method

```
public class Order
{
    private Customer _customer;
    private List<Product> _products;

    public string GenerateDescription()
    {
        var calc = new PriceCalculator();

        return $"Customer name: {_customer.Name}, " +
            $"total number of products: {_products.Count}, " +
            $"total price: {calc.Calculate(_customer, _products)}";
    }
}

public class PriceCalculator
{
    public decimal Calculate(Customer customer, List<Product> products)
    {
        decimal basePrice = /* Calculate based on products */;
        decimal discounts = /* Calculate based on customer */;
        decimal taxes = /* Calculate based on products */;
        return basePrice - discounts + taxes;
    }
}
```

Now you can test PriceCalculator independently of Order. You can also use the output-based (functional) style of unit testing, because PriceCalculator doesn't have any hidden inputs or outputs. See chapter 6 for more information about styles of unit testing.

11.1.3 *When testing private methods is acceptable*

There are exceptions to the rule of never testing private methods. To understand those exceptions, we need to revisit the relationship between the code's publicity and purpose from chapter 5. Table 11.1 sums up that relationship (you already saw this table in chapter 5; I'm copying it here for convenience).

Table 11.1   The relationship between the code's publicity and purpose

	Observable behavior	Implementation detail
Public	Good	Bad
Private	N/A	Good

As you might remember from chapter 5, making the observable behavior public and implementation details private results in a well-designed API. On the other hand, leaking implementation details damages the code's encapsulation. The intersection of observable behavior and private methods is marked N/A in the table because for a method to become part of observable behavior, it has to be used by the client code, which is impossible if that method is private.

Note that testing private methods isn't bad in and of itself. It's only bad because those private methods are a proxy for implementation details. Testing implementation details is what ultimately leads to test brittleness. Having that said, there are rare cases where a method is both private and part of observable behavior (and thus the N/A marking in table 11.1 isn't entirely correct).

Let's take a system that manages credit inquiries as an example. New inquiries are bulk-loaded directly into the database once a day. Administrators then review those inquiries one by one and decide whether to approve them. Here's how the Inquiry class might look in that system.

Listing 11.3   A class with a private constructor

```
public class Inquiry
{
    public bool IsApproved { get; private set; }
    public DateTime? TimeApproved { get; private set; }

    private Inquiry(                              Private
        bool isApproved, DateTime? timeApproved)  constructor
    {
        if (isApproved && !timeApproved.HasValue)
            throw new Exception();

        IsApproved = isApproved;
        TimeApproved = timeApproved;
    }

    public void Approve(DateTime now)
    {
        if (IsApproved)
            return;

        IsApproved = true;
        TimeApproved = now;
    }
}
```

The private constructor is private because the class is restored from the database by an object-relational mapping (ORM) library. That ORM doesn't need a public constructor; it may well work with a private one. At the same time, our system doesn't need a constructor, either, because it's not responsible for the creation of those inquiries.

How do you test the `Inquiry` class given that you can't instantiate its objects? On the one hand, the approval logic is clearly important and thus should be unit tested. But on the other, making the constructor public would violate the rule of not exposing private methods.

`Inquiry`'s constructor is an example of a method that is both private and part of the observable behavior. This constructor fulfills the contract with the ORM, and the fact that it's private doesn't make that contract less important: the ORM wouldn't be able to restore inquiries from the database without it.

And so, making `Inquiry`'s constructor public won't lead to test brittleness in this particular case. In fact, it will arguably bring the class's API closer to being well-designed. Just make sure the constructor contains all the preconditions required to maintain its encapsulation. In listing 11.3, such a precondition is the requirement to have the approval time in all approved inquiries.

Alternatively, if you prefer to keep the class's public API surface as small as possible, you can instantiate `Inquiry` via reflection in tests. Although this looks like a hack, you are just following the ORM, which also uses reflection behind the scenes.

11.2 Exposing private state

Another common anti-pattern is exposing private state for the sole purpose of unit testing. The guideline here is the same as with private methods: don't expose state that you would otherwise keep private—test observable behavior only. Let's take a look at the following listing.

Listing 11.4 A class with private state

```
public class Customer
{
    private CustomerStatus _status =        Private
        CustomerStatus.Regular;             state

    public void Promote()
    {
        _status = CustomerStatus.Preferred;
    }

    public decimal GetDiscount()
    {
        return _status == CustomerStatus.Preferred ? 0.05m : 0m;
    }
}

public enum CustomerStatus
{
```

```
    Regular,
    Preferred
}
```

This example shows a `Customer` class. Each customer is created in the `Regular` status and then can be promoted to `Preferred`, at which point they get a 5% discount on everything.

How would you test the `Promote()` method? This method's side effect is a change of the `_status` field, but the field itself is private and thus not available in tests. A tempting solution would be to make this field public. After all, isn't the change of status the ultimate goal of calling `Promote()`?

That would be an anti-pattern, however. Remember, *your tests should interact with the system under test (SUT) exactly the same way as the production code and shouldn't have any special privileges.* In listing 11.4, the `_status` field is hidden from the production code and thus is not part of the SUT's observable behavior. Exposing that field would result in coupling tests to implementation details. How to test `Promote()`, then?

What you should do, instead, is look at how the production code uses this class. In this particular example, the production code doesn't care about the customer's status; otherwise, that field would be public. The only information the production code does care about is the discount the customer gets after the promotion. And so that's what you need to verify in tests. You need to check that

- A newly created customer has no discount.
- Once the customer is promoted, the discount becomes 5%.

Later, if the production code starts using the customer status field, you'd be able to couple to that field in tests too, because it would officially become part of the SUT's observable behavior.

NOTE   Widening the public API surface for the sake of testability is a bad practice.

11.3   *Leaking domain knowledge to tests*

Leaking domain knowledge to tests is another quite common anti-pattern. It usually takes place in tests that cover complex algorithms. Let's take the following (admittedly, not that complex) calculation algorithm as an example:

```
public static class Calculator
{
    public static int Add(int value1, int value2)
    {
        return value1 + value2;
    }
}
```

This listing shows an *incorrect* way to test it.

Listing 11.5   Leaking algorithm implementation

```
public class CalculatorTests
{
    [Fact]
    public void Adding_two_numbers()
    {
        int value1 = 1;
        int value2 = 3;
        int expected = value1 + value2;      <────  The leakage

        int actual = Calculator.Add(value1, value2);

        Assert.Equal(expected, actual);
    }
}
```

You could also parameterize the test to throw in a couple more test cases at almost no additional cost.

Listing 11.6   A parameterized version of the same test

```
public class CalculatorTests
{
    [Theory]
    [InlineData(1, 3)]
    [InlineData(11, 33)]
    [InlineData(100, 500)]
    public void Adding_two_numbers(int value1, int value2)
    {
        int expected = value1 + value2;      <────  The leakage

        int actual = Calculator.Add(value1, value2);

        Assert.Equal(expected, actual);
    }
}
```

Listings 11.5 and 11.6 look fine at first, but they are, in fact, examples of the anti-pattern: these tests duplicate the algorithm implementation from the production code. Of course, it might not seem like a big deal. After all, it's just one line. But that's only because the example is rather simplified. I've seen tests that covered complex algorithms and did nothing but reimplement those algorithms in the arrange part. They were basically a copy-paste from the production code.

These tests are another example of coupling to implementation details. They score almost zero on the metric of resistance to refactoring and are worthless as a result. Such tests don't have a chance of differentiating legitimate failures from false positives. Should a change in the algorithm make those tests fail, the team would most likely just copy the new version of that algorithm to the test without even trying to identify the root cause (which is understandable, because the tests were a mere duplication of the algorithm in the first place).

How to test the algorithm properly, then? *Don't imply any specific implementation when writing tests.* Instead of duplicating the algorithm, hard-code its results into the test, as shown in the following listing.

Listing 11.7   Test with no domain knowledge

```
public class CalculatorTests
{
    [Theory]
    [InlineData(1, 3, 4)]
    [InlineData(11, 33, 44)]
    [InlineData(100, 500, 600)]
    public void Adding_two_numbers(int value1, int value2, int expected)
    {
        int actual = Calculator.Add(value1, value2);
        Assert.Equal(expected, actual);
    }
}
```

It can seem counterintuitive at first, but hardcoding the expected result is a good practice when it comes to unit testing. The important part with the hardcoded values is to precalculate them using something other than the SUT, ideally with the help of a domain expert. Of course, that's only if the algorithm is complex enough (we are all experts at summing up two numbers). Alternatively, if you refactor a legacy application, you can have the legacy code produce those results and then use them as expected values in tests.

11.4   Code pollution

The next anti-pattern is code pollution.

> **DEFINITION**   *Code pollution* is adding production code that's only needed for testing.

Code pollution often takes the form of various types of switches. Let's take a logger as an example.

Listing 11.8   Logger with a Boolean switch

```
public class Logger
{
    private readonly bool _isTestEnvironment;

    public Logger(bool isTestEnvironment)        ◁──── The switch
    {
        _isTestEnvironment = isTestEnvironment;
    }
```

```
    public void Log(string text)
    {
        if (_isTestEnvironment)          ◁──── The switch
            return;

        /* Log the text */
    }
}

public class Controller
{
    public void SomeMethod(Logger logger)
    {
        logger.Log("SomeMethod is called");
    }
}
```

In this example, Logger has a constructor parameter that indicates whether the class runs in production. If so, the logger records the message into the file; otherwise, it does nothing. With such a Boolean switch, you can disable the logger during test runs, as shown in the following listing.

Listing 11.9   A test using the Boolean switch

```
[Fact]
public void Some_test()
{
    var logger = new Logger(true);      ◁─┐  Sets the parameter to
    var sut = new Controller();           │  true to indicate the
                                          │  test environment
    sut.SomeMethod(logger);

    /* assert */
}
```

The problem with code pollution is that it mixes up test and production code and thereby increases the maintenance costs of the latter. To avoid this anti-pattern, keep the test code out of the production code base.

In the example with Logger, introduce an ILogger interface and create two implementations of it: a real one for production and a fake one for testing purposes. After that, re-target Controller to accept the interface instead of the concrete class, as shown in the following listing.

Listing 11.10   A version without the switch

```
public interface ILogger
{
    void Log(string text);
}
```

```
public class Logger : ILogger
{
    public void Log(string text)
    {
        /* Log the text */
    }
}
```
Belongs in the production code

```
public class FakeLogger : ILogger
{
    public void Log(string text)
    {
        /* Do nothing */
    }
}
```
Belongs in the test code

```
public class Controller
{
    public void SomeMethod(ILogger logger)
    {
        logger.Log("SomeMethod is called");
    }
}
```

Such a separation helps keep the production logger simple because it no longer has to account for different environments. Note that ILogger itself is arguably a form of code pollution: it resides in the production code base but is only needed for testing. So how is the new implementation better?

The kind of pollution ILogger introduces is less damaging and easier to deal with. Unlike the initial Logger implementation, with the new version, you can't accidentally invoke a code path that isn't intended for production use. You can't have bugs in interfaces, either, because they are just contracts with no code in them. In contrast to Boolean switches, interfaces don't introduce additional surface area for potential bugs.

11.5 *Mocking concrete classes*

So far, this book has shown mocking examples using interfaces, but there's an alternative approach: you can mock concrete classes instead and thus preserve part of the original classes' functionality, which can be useful at times. This alternative has a significant drawback, though: it violates the Single Responsibility principle. The next listing illustrates this idea.

Listing 11.11 A class that calculates statistics

```
public class StatisticsCalculator
{
    public (double totalWeight, double totalCost) Calculate(
        int customerId)
    {
        List<DeliveryRecord> records = GetDeliveries(customerId);
```

```
        double totalWeight = records.Sum(x => x.Weight);
        double totalCost = records.Sum(x => x.Cost);

        return (totalWeight, totalCost);
    }

    public List<DeliveryRecord> GetDeliveries(int customerId)
    {
        /* Call an out-of-process dependency
        to get the list of deliveries */
    }
}
```

StatisticsCalculator gathers and calculates customer statistics: the weight and cost of all deliveries sent to a particular customer. The class does the calculation based on the list of deliveries retrieved from an external service (the GetDeliveries method). Let's also say there's a controller that uses StatisticsCalculator, as shown in the following listing.

Listing 11.12   A controller using StatisticsCalculator

```
public class CustomerController
{
    private readonly StatisticsCalculator _calculator;

    public CustomerController(StatisticsCalculator calculator)
    {
        _calculator = calculator;
    }

    public string GetStatistics(int customerId)
    {
        (double totalWeight, double totalCost) = _calculator
            .Calculate(customerId);

        return
            $"Total weight delivered: {totalWeight}. " +
            $"Total cost: {totalCost}";
    }
}
```

How would you test this controller? You can't supply it with a real Statistics-Calculator instance, because that instance refers to an unmanaged out-of-process dependency. The unmanaged dependency has to be substituted with a stub. At the same time, you don't want to replace StatisticsCalculator entirely, either. This class contains important calculation functionality, which needs to be left intact.

One way to overcome this dilemma is to mock the StatisticsCalculator class and override only the GetDeliveries() method, which can be done by making that method virtual, as shown in the following listing.

Listing 11.13 Test that mocks the concrete class

```
[Fact]
public void Customer_with_no_deliveries()
{
    // Arrange
    var stub = new Mock<StatisticsCalculator> { CallBase = true };
    stub.Setup(x => x.GetDeliveries(1))
        .Returns(new List<DeliveryRecord>());
    var sut = new CustomerController(stub.Object);

    // Act
    string result = sut.GetStatistics(1);

    // Assert
    Assert.Equal("Total weight delivered: 0. Total cost: 0", result);
}
```

GetDeliveries() must be made virtual.

The `CallBase = true` setting tells the mock to preserve the base class's behavior unless it's explicitly overridden. With this approach, you can substitute only a part of the class while keeping the rest as-is. As I mentioned earlier, this is an anti-pattern.

NOTE The necessity to mock a concrete class in order to preserve part of its functionality is a result of violating the Single Responsibility principle.

`StatisticsCalculator` combines two unrelated responsibilities: communicating with the unmanaged dependency and calculating statistics. Look at listing 11.11 again. The `Calculate()` method is where the domain logic lies. `GetDeliveries()` just gathers the inputs for that logic. Instead of mocking `StatisticsCalculator`, split this class in two, as the following listing shows.

Listing 11.14 Splitting `StatisticsCalculator` into two classes

```
public class DeliveryGateway : IDeliveryGateway
{
    public List<DeliveryRecord> GetDeliveries(int customerId)
    {
        /* Call an out-of-process dependency
        to get the list of deliveries */
    }
}

public class StatisticsCalculator
{
    public (double totalWeight, double totalCost) Calculate(
        List<DeliveryRecord> records)
    {
        double totalWeight = records.Sum(x => x.Weight);
        double totalCost = records.Sum(x => x.Cost);

        return (totalWeight, totalCost);
    }
}
```

The next listing shows the controller after the refactoring.

Listing 11.15   Controller after the refactoring

```
public class CustomerController
{
    private readonly StatisticsCalculator _calculator;
    private readonly IDeliveryGateway _gateway;

    public CustomerController(
        StatisticsCalculator calculator,       Two separate
        IDeliveryGateway gateway)              dependencies
    {
        _calculator = calculator;
        _gateway = gateway;
    }

    public string GetStatistics(int customerId)
    {
        var records = _gateway.GetDeliveries(customerId);
        (double totalWeight, double totalCost) = _calculator
            .Calculate(records);

        return
            $"Total weight delivered: {totalWeight}. " +
            $"Total cost: {totalCost}";
    }
}
```

The responsibility of communicating with the unmanaged dependency has transitioned to `DeliveryGateway`. Notice how this gateway is backed by an interface, which you can now use for mocking instead of the concrete class. The code in listing 11.15 is an example of the Humble Object design pattern in action. Refer to chapter 7 to learn more about this pattern.

11.6   Working with time

Many application features require access to the current date and time. Testing functionality that depends on time can result in false positives, though: the time during the act phase might not be the same as in the assert. There are three options for stabilizing this dependency. One of these options is an anti-pattern; and of the other two, one is preferable to the other.

11.6.1   Time as an ambient context

The first option is to use the *ambient context* pattern. You already saw this pattern in chapter 8 in the section about testing loggers. In the context of time, the ambient context would be a custom class that you'd use in code instead of the framework's built-in `DateTime.Now`, as shown in the next listing.

Listing 11.16   Current date and time as an ambient context

```
public static class DateTimeServer
{
    private static Func<DateTime> _func;
    public static DateTime Now => _func();

    public static void Init(Func<DateTime> func)
    {
        _func = func;
    }
}

DateTimeServer.Init(() => DateTime.Now);              ◄────┐   Initialization code
                                                            │   for production

DateTimeServer.Init(() => new DateTime(2020, 1, 1));  ◄────┐   Initialization code
                                                            │   for unit tests
```

Just as with the logger functionality, using an ambient context for time is also an anti-pattern. The ambient context *pollutes* the production code and makes testing more difficult. Also, the static field introduces a dependency shared between tests, thus transitioning those tests into the sphere of integration testing.

11.6.2   *Time as an explicit dependency*

A better approach is to inject the time dependency explicitly (instead of referring to it via a static method in an ambient context), either as a service or as a plain value, as shown in the following listing.

Listing 11.17   Current date and time as an explicit dependency

```
public interface IDateTimeServer
{
    DateTime Now { get; }
}

public class DateTimeServer : IDateTimeServer
{
    public DateTime Now => DateTime.Now;
}

public class InquiryController
{
    private readonly IDateTimeServer _dateTimeServer;

    public InquiryController(
        IDateTimeServer dateTimeServer)       ◄────┐   Injects time as
    {                                               │   a service
        _dateTimeServer = dateTimeServer;
    }

    public void ApproveInquiry(int id)
    {
        Inquiry inquiry = GetById(id);
```

```
        inquiry.Approve(_dateTimeServer.Now);      ◁──┐  Injects time as
        SaveInquiry(inquiry);                          │  a plain value
    }
}
```

Of these two options, prefer injecting the time as a value rather than as a service. It's easier to work with plain values in production code, and it's also easier to stub those values in tests.

Most likely, you won't be able to always inject the time as a plain value, because dependency injection frameworks don't play well with value objects. A good compromise is to inject the time as a service at the start of a business operation and then pass it as a value in the remainder of that operation. You can see this approach in listing 11.17: the controller accepts `DateTimeServer` (the service) but then passes a `DateTime` value to the `Inquiry` domain class.

11.7 Conclusion

In this chapter, we looked at some of the most prominent real-world unit testing use cases and analyzed them using the four attributes of a good test. I understand that it may be overwhelming to start applying all the ideas and guidelines from this book at once. Also, your situation might not be as clear-cut. I publish reviews of other people's code and answer questions (related to unit testing and code design in general) on my blog at https://enterprisecraftsmanship.com. You can also submit your own question at https://enterprisecraftsmanship.com/about. You might also be interested in taking my online course, where I show how to build an application from the ground up, applying all the principles described in this book in practice, at https://unittesting-course.com.

You can always catch me on twitter at @vkhorikov, or contact me directly through https://enterprisecraftsmanship.com/about. I look forward to hearing from you!

Summary

- Exposing private methods to enable unit testing leads to coupling tests to implementation and, ultimately, damaging the tests' resistance to refactoring. Instead of testing private methods directly, test them indirectly as part of the overarching observable behavior.
- If the private method is too complex to be tested as part of the public API that uses it, that's an indication of a missing abstraction. Extract this abstraction into a separate class instead of making the private method public.
- In rare cases, private methods do belong to the class's observable behavior. Such methods usually implement a non-public contract between the class and an ORM or a factory.
- Don't expose state that you would otherwise keep private for the sole purpose of unit testing. Your tests should interact with the system under test exactly the same way as the production code; they shouldn't have any special privileges.

- Don't imply any specific implementation when writing tests. Verify the production code from a black-box perspective; avoid leaking domain knowledge to tests (see chapter 4 for more details about black-box and white-box testing).
- *Code pollution* is adding production code that's only needed for testing. It's an anti-pattern because it mixes up test and production code and increases the maintenance costs of the latter.
- The necessity to mock a concrete class in order to preserve part of its functionality is a result of violating the Single Responsibility principle. Separate that class into two classes: one with the domain logic, and the other one communicating with the out-of-process dependency.
- Representing the current time as an ambient context pollutes the production code and makes testing more difficult. Inject time as an explicit dependency—either as a service or as a plain value. Prefer the plain value whenever possible.

index